UNVEILING
MERCY

The Lord your God is in your midst, a mighty one who will save; he will rejoice over you with gladness; he will quiet you by his love; he will exult over you with loud singing.

–Zephaniah 3:17

Thank you for all you do in service to our Lord. May God richly bless you in the coming year!

Merry Christmas

from the
Missionary Care Team &
Westwood Community Church

December 2020

UNVEILING MERCY

MERCY

365
DAILY
DEVOTIONS

BASED ON INSIGHTS FROM
OLD TESTAMENT HEBREW

CHAD BIRD

Unveiling Mercy

© 2020 New Reformation Publications

Published by:
1517 Publishing
PO Box 54032
Irvine, CA 92619-4032

Publisher's Cataloging-In-Publication Data
(Prepared by The Donohue Group, Inc.)

Names: Bird, Chad, author.
Title: Unveiling mercy : 365 daily devotionals based on insights from Old Testament Hebrew
    / by Chad Bird.
Description: Irvine, CA : 1517 Publishing, [2020]
Identifiers: ISBN 9781948969390 (jacketed hardcover) | ISBN 9781948969406 (paperback)
    | ISBN 9781948969413 (ebook)
Subjects: LCSH: Bible. Old Testament—Devotional use. | Bible. Old Testament—Devotional
    literature. | Bible. Old Testament—Terminology. | Hebrew language—Terms and phrases.
    | Christianity—Prayers and devotions. | Devotional exercises.
Classification: LCC BS1151.55 .B57 2020 (print) | LCC BS1151.55 (ebook) | DDC
    242.5—dc23

Printed in the United States of America

Cover art by Brenton Clarke Little

CONTENTS

CONTENTS

INTRODUCTION

Late one Sunday afternoon, in the spring of the year, three Jews walked side by side on the seven-mile road that wound from Jerusalem to Emmaus. The stories of their Hebrew forefathers, which had echoed even in their infant ears, were embedded in them as deeply as the marrow of their bones. Abraham clasping the uplifted knife. Doorways in Egypt daubed bloodred. The God-soaked psalms. Daniel sleeping alongside docile lions. The nouns and verbs of their people's past populated their hearts and minds. The Scriptures of Israel—these they knew by heart.

Yet on this day, one of the three Jews began to pick up narrative pearls from all these scrolls and to string them together. Genesis to Isaiah. Nahum to Numbers. Joshua to Jeremiah. Pearl kissed pearl, prophecy slid beside psalm. One after the other, he strung these into a flowing and fantastic necklace of redemption. How wide their eyes must have been. Their mouths agape in mute astonishment. They were hearing stories they knew . . . but did not know.

Sacred texts sparked as they struck one another, prophetic flint to Torah steel. Fires of epiphany erupted. Dark corners of their minds were illumined in the flames. Scales slid off their eyes. God was unveiling his merciful plan of redemption before them. Later, as they recounted to one another what the experience had been like, only one image would suffice: "Did not our hearts burn within us while he talked to us on the road, while he opened to us the Scriptures?" (Luke 24:32).

Almost three decades ago, when I was a young man in seminary, I began to experience that same kind of holy fire, sparking, flaming, burning within my heart. The fire fell in a room where Hebrew Bibles lay open and a man of God, full of wisdom, began to string together the same kinds of pearls that Jesus had done for his disciples so long ago. I finally heard, as with ears tuned to a new frequency, that all the music of Scripture, like a vast orchestra, blends its many sounds into a messianic harmony, the crescendo of which is Christ incarnate.

And so, with heart aflame, I began my thirty-year pilgrimage into the hills, valleys, and wilderness of the Hebrew language.

Since those early days, I have studied Hebrew to prepare for classes and sermons while serving as a pastor in Christ's flock. In the same seminary lecture halls where I fell in love with the Old Testament and its Christ-centered narratives, I was privileged to return as a professor, to teach Hebrew, to kindle fires in other hearts, and to bid them join me in the exploration of this ancient and exciting language. For several years, I sat at the feet of rabbis and scholars at Hebrew Union College—reading vast swaths of the Scriptures and wading into the wild and playful waters of early rabbinic commentaries. Every day was a gift. Every day I not only learned more but, more importantly, desired to learn more.

One might say then that *Unveiling Mercy* has been written over the course of three decades. I am its author, but encircling my desk were many others—some alive, some dead for centuries—who have bequeathed to me their wisdom. My early teachers. My fellow believers. My rabbinic professors. My students. All of them, in one way or another, have added more fuel to the Hebrew fire that still burns hot within me.

One of the rabbinic scholars with whom I studied liked to say that reading the Bible in translation is like "kissing the bride through the veil." Each of these 365 devotions is crafted so as to lift that veil ever so slightly, to let us touch skin to skin, as it were, with the original language. You do not need to know anything about Hebrew to profit from these meditations. They are not written to teach you the language of Abraham, Moses, and Isaiah, but to give you a taste of their insights, to expose you to their eloquence, to laugh with them at their winking wordplays, to un-English their idioms, and—most importantly—to trace their trajectories all the way into the preaching of the Messiah and the writings of his evangelists and apostles.

A Jewish sage named Ben Bag-Bag, possibly a contemporary of Jesus, once said of the Torah, "Turn it, and turn it, for everything is in it." So we will. We will take the Torah in hand, turn it, shake it, turn it over, shake it again, and keep shaking it to see, over the course of this year, what jewels of wisdom plummet from its pages. So we will do with every book of the Old Testament, for all of them have at least one devotion based on them. We will by no means have exhausted all there is to learn, needless to say, but we will have a sizable collection of jewels that will enrich our understanding of God's unveiling mercy. These bejeweled words will be, as Abraham Joshua Heschel called them, "hyphens between heaven and earth."

Let me explain, briefly, a few items that will arise as you proceed day by day.

1. I make occasional reference to the Greek translation of the Old Testament called the Septuagint. Because the authors of the New Testament were heavily influenced by this translation, its renderings of the Hebrew into Greek are vital background for bridging the gap between the two testaments.

2. The order of the books in the Old Testament is not the same in Hebrew as in English Bibles. To accommodate most readers, I have followed the order of the latter. The devotions are arranged canonically, that is, we will begin in January with Genesis and work our way, book by book, all the way to Malachi in December.

3. The covenant name of God is often written in other resources just with the consonants YHWH. Though there is some disagreement as to how this was originally written with vowels, most scholars think it was pronounced as Yahweh. I will use that spelling. As in most English Bibles, when "Lord" appears in all caps, the Hebrew is Yahweh.

4. All biblical quotations, unless otherwise noted, are from the English Standard Version (ESV).

5. Though I have used multiple resources, most of the definitions are from *The Hebrew and Aramaic Lexicon of the Old Testament* (HALOT).

6. When possible, for the prayers that conclude each devotion, I have used verses from the psalms, many of which employ the same Hebrew word discussed that day.

A note to my readers who know Hebrew: because this devotional is for everyone, I have endeavored to keep the transliterations as simple and streamlined as possible. That will mean, for instance, that when I insert a Hebrew word into a translated verse, the transliteration will usually be the simple lexical form of the word. On occasion, I "Englishize" a Hebrew word by adding an *s* to a verb, for instance, just for rhetorical purposes. Moreover, you will see that the Hebrew words at the head of every day are only in their consonantal form, usually only the trilateral root, without vowels, dagesh, and so on.

May our good and gracious Father, through his Son and in his Holy Spirit, richly bless your meditations as you read, mark, learn, and inwardly digest his Word.

An Alphabetic Parable ב

IN THE BEGINNING . . .

GENESIS 1:1

The opening letter of the Bible, a *bet* (*b*) in *b'reshit* ("in the beginning"), resembles a square closed on all sides except one. Since Hebrew is read from right to left, the open side ushers us into the rest of the sacred writings. The rabbis saw the shape of the letter as a kind of alphabetic parable. It's closed on the right, top, and bottom to indicate that what came before creation is not our concern; neither should we go poking our noses into what's above us or below us.

On what would our Father have us focus? On what follows the open side of the *bet*. It's the portal through which we journey into the rest of the Scriptures, which "are able to make [us] wise for salvation through faith in Christ Jesus" (2 Tim. 3:15). "The secret things belong to the LORD our God" (Deut. 29:29). That's his concern. Ours? "The things that are revealed belong to us" (v. 29). His revealed Word. His promises. His gospel. As the psalmist says, "I do not occupy myself with things too great and too marvelous for me" (131:1). Instead, let us occupy ourselves wholly with Christ, "in whom are hidden all the treasures of wisdom and knowledge" (Col. 2:3). In the Messiah and his words, the Father is unveiling mercy, revealing everything he wants us to know.

O Lord, "open my eyes, that I may behold wondrous things out of your law" (Ps. 119:18).

The Beginning Word of God בְּרֵאשִׁית

IN THE BEGINNING, GOD CREATED THE
HEAVENS AND THE EARTH.

GENESIS 1:1

The opening three words of the Bible, "In the beginning," are one word in Hebrew, *b'reshit*. Already in the word, *reshit* ("beginning"), God winks at the Word by whom all things came into being. An ancient Jewish paraphrase, called a Targum, read, "In Wisdom, God created." Why Wisdom? Because in Proverbs, Wisdom says, "The LORD possessed me at the beginning [*reshit*] of his work [of creation]" (8:22). Wisdom is saying, "I am the Beginning, by whom God created all things."

The Messiah is this Wisdom of God, the Beginning by whom God the Father formed all things. "In the beginning was the Word," John writes, nodding toward Genesis (1:1). Later, in Revelation, Jesus identifies himself as "the Beginning [Greek: *arche*] of God's creation" (3:14). He is the Beginning not because he is made—he is eternal with the Father and Spirit—but because "by him all things were created . . . all things were created through him and for him" (Col. 1:16).

Jesus the Beginning restarts the world in love. "If anyone is in Christ, he is a new creation" (2 Cor. 5:17). We receive a regenesis from this divine *Reshit*. Dead but now alive. Darkened but now enlightened by Christ, the "light of the world" (John 8:12). In him by whom all things came to be, all the good gifts of God come to us.

Beginning God, begin and complete in us the fullness of life in Christ.

Tohu Vavohu תהו ובהו

THE EARTH WAS WITHOUT FORM AND VOID, AND
DARKNESS WAS OVER THE FACE OF THE DEEP.

GENESIS 1:2

When God starts something, it often looks as if nothing will come of it. Before he says, "Let there be light," the earth is *tohu* ("wasteland") and *vohu* ("emptiness"). Nothing here to make the angels cheer. Darkness blankets this water-soaked chaos. So far, things don't look good. Not yet anyway. The good, and the very good, will come as soon as the Father opens his mouth to speak the rest of creation into being by his Word and Spirit.

When Jeremiah warns the idol-worshipping Israelites that God's about to stomp their land into oblivion, he reaches back to Genesis to hammer home his point. He says the earth has become *tohu vavohu* yet again (4:23). Isaiah too, depicting the effects of humanity's rebellion, says "the line of confusion [*tohu*]" and "the plumb line of emptiness [*vohu*]" are stretched over the land (34:11). Sin undermines creation by rebelling against the very Word that spoke creation into existence. Instead of light and life, there broods darkness and death.

The Word thus becomes flesh, of creation, to redeem creation. Into a *tohu vavohu* world, Jesus comes to reform and refashion a new creation. "He has done all things well," the crowds say (Mark 7:37). Indeed, he has, this Creator who makes all things new (Rev. 21:5).

Put a new song in our mouths, O God, that we may glory in your creative love.

The Hovering Spirit of God רוח אלהים

THE SPIRIT OF GOD WAS HOVERING
OVER THE FACE OF THE WATERS.

GENESIS 1:2

God doesn't work remotely from his creation. He's right in the thick of things, even when—maybe *especially* when—they're dark, formless, void, and waterlogged. The *Ruach Elohim*, God's Spirit, isn't soaring high in the ether, peering down on a world far below. No, he's hovering and fluttering on the face of the waters, unafraid of getting wet.

Ruach can mean spirit, wind, or breath. All three fit what the Holy Spirit does. Like the wind, he blows where he wishes (John 3:8), sometimes over wet creations and sometimes down into valleys of dry bones (Ezek. 37:1). This Spirit who made us is the vivifying "breath of the Almighty" (Job 33:4). He is also the absolving exhalation of Jesus, blown on his disciples that they might re-create sinners by the power of absolution (John 20:22).

This Spirit, who hovered over creation's waters, alighted on Jesus at the Jordan (Matt. 3:16). Once more, he's in the thick of the things of creation, working with the Word to put us in communion with the Father. He sticks close to water, repeating his opening act at every baptism, uniting us to the "one baptism" of Jesus (Eph. 4:5) so that in him we might be people fully alive.

O Lord, "cast me not away from your presence, and take not your Holy Spirit from me" (Ps. 51:11).

Let There Be Light! יהי אור

THEN GOD SAID, "LET THERE BE LIGHT,"
AND THERE WAS LIGHT.

GENESIS 1:3

The first two spoken words of God, *y'hi or*, are both simple and sublime. They are not complicated in grammar or meaning. *Y'hi* is a form of the verb "to be"; *or* is the word for "light." Yet their simplicity masks sublimity. Light is voiced into being. Not stumbled upon by chance or constructed by careful engineering, but "worded" into being. Light shines forth from the face of God—specifically, his mouth.

This light is a more profound light than the sun, moon, and stars, which will be created on day four. It chains the darkness, erects a barrier between night and day. It says to darkness, "Here you shall go, and no further." To flourish in this light is to escape darkness and thrive before the radiant face of the God.

As such, this verse proclaims the Gospel according to Genesis, for it points us to the "Light of Light," Jesus Christ. "For God, who said, 'Let light shine out of darkness,' has shone in our hearts to give the light of the knowledge of the glory of God in the face of Jesus Christ" (2 Cor. 4:6). He shatters the cosmic midnight in our hearts. From Christ's face bursts forth rays of the glorious, life-giving light of God that transfigures us into his image (Matt. 17:2).

"Lift up the light of your face upon us, O LORD!" (Ps. 4:6).

Day and Night יום לילה

GOD CALLED THE LIGHT DAY, AND THE DARKNESS
HE CALLED NIGHT. AND THERE WAS EVENING
AND THERE WAS MORNING, THE FIRST DAY.

GENESIS 1:5

Parents name their children on the day of their birth. So also, when God brought forth the mountains, the earth, and the world (Ps. 90:2), he started naming things left and right. The first two to be christened were *Yom* ("Day") and *Laylah* ("Night"). These two halves of the day were like twin brothers, with *Laylah* being the firstborn (darkness preceding light) and *Yom* the second-born. Yet, as with other biblical twins, it was the second-born, the younger *Yom*, whom God chose as his special instrument.

"We are not of the night or of the darkness," Paul says (1 Thess. 5:5). It was during *Laylah*'s half of the day when Judas betrayed Jesus and Peter denied him, when thieves come, when people get drunk. We are children of light, children of *Yom*, "so then let us not sleep, as others do, but let us keep awake and be sober" (5:6). "The night is far gone; the day is at hand. So then let us cast off the works of darkness and put on the armor of light" (Rom. 13:12), for we await the arrival of the New Jerusalem, where the "gates will never be shut by day—and there will be no night there" (Rev. 21:25).

"Be gracious to me, O LORD, for to you do I cry all the day" (Ps. 86:3).

Good, Yes, Very Good טוב

AND GOD SAW EVERYTHING THAT HE HAD
MADE, AND BEHOLD, IT WAS VERY GOOD.

GENESIS 1:31

The word *tov* can mean good, pleasant, desirable, usable, or beautiful. It is a word of affirmation, a kind of divine grin that spreads over the face of our creating God. But first the Lord uses his eyes. He didn't ruminate in his heart on the goodness of creation; he "saw" (*ra'ah*). Later, Hagar will even name him *El Roi*, the God who sees (Gen. 16:13). He assumes nothing. He makes sure. Before he says it's *tov* or *tov me'od* (*me'od* means "very"), he opens his eyes to inspect his handiwork.

Later, when his good world had gone bad, God looked "down from heaven on the children of man" and saw that "there is none who does good [*tov*], not even one" (Ps. 14:2–3). So, in mercy, he became that one who does the good. Even the crowds saw it, proclaiming of Jesus, "He has done all things well" (Mark 7:37). If you want something done right, do it yourself. So God did. He did things right for us. And now, in Christ, he sees us not only as *tov* but as *tov me'od*. When he sees us, a smile erupts on his face, and we know that we "shall see the goodness of the LORD in the land of the living" (Ps. 27:13).

Good and gracious Father, "you are my Lord; I have no good apart from you" (Ps. 16:2).

God's First and Last Sabbath שבת

AND ON THE SEVENTH DAY GOD FINISHED HIS WORK
THAT HE HAD DONE, AND HE RESTED ON THE SEVENTH
DAY FROM ALL HIS WORK THAT HE HAD DONE. SO GOD
BLESSED THE SEVENTH DAY AND MADE IT HOLY.

GENESIS 2:2-3

The first part of creation that is called holy is not land or a person but time. Indeed, time beats at the heart of creation's story. We hear of the times called day and night. The celestial bodies are "for signs and for seasons, and for days and years" (1:14). Like a dance, creation has rhythm and movement, guided by the music of time. And the refrain of this music is *Shabbat* ("Sabbath"). The verb *shabbat* means to rest, cease, or celebrate. Israel's weekly *Shabbat* celebrated God's love in creation (Exod. 20:11) and redemption (Deut. 5:15). They were both very good—complete, perfect—so Israel could rest in the Lord of creative redemption and redemptive creation.

When God's Son came to us, he beckoned, "Come to me . . . and I will give you rest" (Matt. 11:28). In other words, "I will be your *Shabbat*." Having completed his work of re-creation and redemption while nailed to the wood of his creation, he said, "It is finished" (John 19:30). He then rested in his *Shabbat* tomb and stepped forth alive again so we can rest forever in his unending grace.

Bring us, O Lord, through your Son, into the Sabbath rest for the people of God (Heb. 4:9).

The Earth Man אדם

THEN THE LORD GOD FORMED THE MAN OF
DUST FROM THE GROUND AND BREATHED
INTO HIS NOSTRILS THE BREATH OF LIFE, AND
THE MAN BECAME A LIVING CREATURE.

GENESIS 2:7

Our father, Adam, is named after the *adamah* ("earth or arable ground") from which he was formed. His name also becomes the word for all people. This is important. Hebrew speaks not of a generic "humanity" but *adam* (*adamkind*, if you will). In that one specific man we began. This was his genesis—and ours. God, the divine potter, got his hands dirty as he formed and shaped us like clay (Isa. 64:8). By the breath of the Almighty, this first man rose from the earth.

"The first man was from the earth, a man of dust; the second man is from heaven" (1 Cor. 15:47). This "second man" from heaven came down to earth as a second Adam to begin a new humanity. As Adam's "one trespass led to condemnation for all men, so one act of righteousness leads to justification and life for all men" (Rom. 5:18). In this one specific man we begin anew. Like the first Adam rose to life from the *adamah*, the second Adam rose to life again from the *adamah* of the grave, "for as in Adam all die, so also in Christ shall all be made alive" (1 Cor. 15:22).

Raise us, O LORD, from the dust, that we might sit with Christ in the heavenly places.

The Garden in Eden גַּן עֵדֶן

AND THE LORD GOD PLANTED A GARDEN
IN EDEN, IN THE EAST, AND THERE HE PUT
THE MAN WHOM HE HAD FORMED.

GENESIS 2:8

God is multivocational at creation. He is the world's maker, a soon-to-be matchmaker, Adam's surgeon, Eve's builder, and now Eden's gardener. Notice that Eden is not the garden, though we usually equate the two. The garden is in the broader region named Eden, which is located somewhere "in the east." A *gan* is a walled garden, a protected place, where flowers and fruits and vegetables grow. The Greek translation rendered *gan* as *paradeisos*—thus our word "Paradise."

In God's masterful shaping of events, after paradise is lost, it is regained when God takes up the vocation of gardening again. The same Lord who queried Adam, "Where are you?" (Gen. 3:9), asked Mary Magdalene, "Woman, why are you weeping? Whom are you seeking?" (John 20:15). She supposed this man to be a gardener—and, oh, how right she was. The same Lord who planted a garden in Eden had now planted life in the soil above his vacated tomb. He'd come to cultivate the life of the Spirit within us, to cause us to bear abundant fruit, to feed us from the new tree of life, and—on our last day—to say to each of us, "Today you will be with me in paradise" (Luke 23:43).

Plant your grace within our hearts, O Lord, that we might find all our delight in you.

Ish and Ishsha אִישׁ אִשָּׁה

THEN THE MAN SAID, "THIS AT LAST IS BONE OF MY
BONES AND FLESH OF MY FLESH; SHE SHALL BE CALLED
WOMAN, BECAUSE SHE WAS TAKEN OUT OF MAN."

GENESIS 2:23

Man's first recorded exclamation was over a woman. This seems very fitting.
She was, quite literally, bone of his bones, having been "built" (*banah*) from
his rib (v. 22). When the Father escorted his daughter down the aisle of
Eden to be wedded to Adam in this garden paradise, the man instantly recognized a creature who mirrored himself. Having come from him, formed
from his very own body, he gave her a name that came from his. He was an
ish ("man") so he called her *ishshah* ("woman").

A curious incident happened ages later, long after Eden had vanished. Another
ish, a man, was dying. God caused a "deep sleep" to fall on him, the sleep
of death itself. From his side, pierced with a spear, blood and water gushed
forth (John 19:34). From the side of this man, God built a new *ishshah*—
baptized with water and given the blood of Christ to drink. She is called
Christian because she was taken out of Christ. She is his bride, one unmis-
takably like himself, for she is bone of his bones and flesh of his flesh, united
as a head to a body.

Praise to you, O Christ, for making us your own, by cleansing us with the
washing of water with the Word.

Naked and Crafty עָרוּם

AND THE MAN AND HIS WIFE WERE BOTH NAKED
AND WERE NOT ASHAMED. NOW THE SERPENT
WAS MORE CRAFTY THAN ANY OTHER BEAST OF
THE FIELD THAT THE LORD GOD HAD MADE.

GENESIS 2:25–3:1

Hebrew can be a playful language, coupling similar-sounding words, like *tohu vavohu* (Gen. 1:2) or *adam* and *adamah* (2:7). Here we encounter another one: the man and woman were *arummim* ("naked") and the serpent was *arum* ("crafty, clever, cunning"). Eliphaz uses this same word when he speaks of "the tongue of the *arumim* [crafty]" (Job 15:5). We might try to replicate the Genesis wordplay with "nude" and "shrewd," but, alas, it's no match for the cleverness of the Hebrew author.

Nor were this naked pair any match for their devilishly clever foe. Their nudity was emblematic of innocence and a pristine existence—the very gifts of God this smooth-talking serpent was about to attack with his own crafty tongue. The psalmist probably has this in mind when he says of violent men: "they make their tongue sharp as a serpent's, and under their lips is the venom of asps" (140:3). Against both lying serpents and lying men, however, hangs the Truth, Wisdom himself, the second Adam, stripped naked atop the cross. He is bruised and battered from head to toe. Only his tongue is unfettered and unwounded—that he might intercede for us all.

Lord Jesus, wisdom from on high, clothe us with your righteousness.

Take and Eat אכל

SO WHEN THE WOMAN SAW THAT THE TREE WAS
GOOD FOR FOOD, AND THAT IT WAS A DELIGHT
TO THE EYES, AND THAT THE TREE WAS TO BE
DESIRED TO MAKE ONE WISE, SHE TOOK OF ITS
FRUIT AND ATE, AND SHE ALSO GAVE SOME TO HER
HUSBAND WHO WAS WITH HER, AND HE ATE.

GENESIS 3:6

To eat is to *akal*. When we *akal*, we acknowledge that all life comes from outside us as a gift. We don't grow vegetables in our hearts or raise cattle in our stomachs. What we eat to live has its origin in the external world. To eat is to acknowledge that we are not self-sufficient. We need God. "The eyes of all look to you, [O Lord,] and you give them their food in due season" (Ps. 145:15). Eve's eyes, however, along with Adam's, were not looking to the Lord. They saw "a delight to the eyes" and played as if they were no longer creatures but aspiring divinities themselves.

Rather than ditching the food approach, however, God used good eating to reverse the effects of this bad eating. He bid the Israelites eat the Passover lamb. He fed them manna and quail. And, finally, to humanity who'd taken and eaten what they should not, he said, "Take, eat; this is my body" (Matt. 26:26). To eat the Messiah is to live forever (John 6:54).

O Lord, "open your hand and satisfy the desires of every living thing" (Ps. 145:16 NIV).

The Seed of Promise זֶרַע

"I WILL PUT ENMITY BETWEEN YOU AND THE
WOMAN, AND BETWEEN YOUR OFFSPRING
AND HER OFFSPRING; HE SHALL BRUISE YOUR
HEAD, AND YOU SHALL BRUISE HIS HEEL."

GENESIS 3:15

The Hebrew word for seed or offspring is *zera*. It can refer to the seed of a plant, the semen of a man, or the descendant(s) of people. It sounds strange to our ears, but *zera* is at the heart of the Old Testament's way of Gospel preaching. We first hear this "Seed Gospel" in Genesis 3:15. Eve's *zera* and the serpent's *zera* will be locked in a long and fierce war. Good and evil will never sign a peace treaty. Their warfare will wage until finally both a head and a heel are "bruised."

Israel's entire history chronicles this coming seed. Each genealogy keeps track of its unfolding. It gradually narrows from Eve's seed, to Abraham's, to Judah's, to David's: "I will raise up your *zera* after you," God says to David, and "establish his kingdom" (2 Sam. 7:12). This regal seed of David has a peculiar throne, however. It is a cross. And on it, his heel crushes the head of the serpent even as the fangs of the serpent strike his heel. By death, this seed destroys death. And by him we are made the seed, the offspring, the children of our heavenly Father.

O Seed of David, our King, deliver us from evil and bring us into your kingdom of life.

The Mother of All Living חוה

THE MAN CALLED HIS WIFE'S NAME EVE, BECAUSE SHE WAS THE MOTHER OF ALL LIVING.

GENESIS 3:20

Eve's name is *Chavvah* in Hebrew, Zoe in Greek. Her name reflects the word for life, *chai* (think of the common Jewish toast, *l'chaim!* "to life!"). In a dark and dismal chapter, this is a welcome ray of light. In fact, one might say it's a name of faith, for *Chavvah* hasn't even had a baby yet. God has promised she will, however, so Adam's name-bestowing and her name-bearing are confessions of faith in the God who always sticks to his word. Just as the Lord will, in the next verse, clothe them with better garments, so Adam wraps a new name around his wife.

Chavvah is the mother of all living in more than one sense. Yes, her womb is the origin of all humanity; all people trace their lineage back to her. In a more profound way, however, she is the mother of life itself, for it will be her seed who crushes death and resurrects life for all (Gen. 3:15). Indeed, the Messiah is "the resurrection and the life" (John 11:25). "In him was life, and the life was the light of men" (1:4). His biological mother was Mary, but his primal mother was *Chavvah*, the mother of the seed who is the life of God himself.

Christ Jesus, "with you is the fountain of life; in your light do we see light" (Ps. 36:9).

A Kick in the Pants גרש

THEREFORE THE LORD GOD SENT [ADAM] OUT FROM THE
GARDEN OF EDEN TO WORK THE GROUND FROM WHICH
HE WAS TAKEN. HE DROVE OUT THE MAN.

GENESIS 3:23-24A

The Hebrew verb for "drive out" is *garash*. You don't smile and politely ask someone to leave when you *garash* them. You kick 'em in the pants. You shove them out, push them away, as Sarah told Abraham to do to Hagar (Gen. 21:10), Pharaoh did to Israel (Exod. 11:1), and the Lord did to the Canaanites (23:28-30). When Solomon "expelled" Abiathar from being a priest, he *garash* him (1 Kings 2:27). It's a kind of violent expulsion, like a bar's bouncer tossing an unruly customer into the street.

How surprising, then, that when Mark wrote about the temptation of Jesus, he chose a Greek word that's the counterpart to *garash*. He said, "The Spirit immediately drove [Jesus] out into the wilderness" (1:12). Indeed, the Greek verb that Mark chose, *ekballo*, is used to translate *garash* in the Greek version of Genesis 3:24. Why? It's Mark's subtle way of telling us that Jesus is Adam #2. He's come to relive Adam's expulsion, to be driven east of the Jordan. There he will be tempted but resist, succeed where Adam #1 failed, and finally return us to the good graces of the Father, who will never drive us away.

Drive out from us, Holy Spirit, all that is contrary to you, and bring us to the Father.

Riding Angels כרוב

AT THE EAST OF THE GARDEN OF EDEN [GOD] PLACED
THE CHERUBIM AND A FLAMING SWORD THAT TURNED
EVERY WAY TO GUARD THE WAY TO THE TREE OF LIFE.

GENESIS 3:24

Angels are dangerous. There is nothing cute or sweet or precious about them. When they show up, people cower in fear—and rightly so. Cherub (singular) or cherubim (plural) is *k'ruv* and *k'ruvim* in Hebrew. (The *im* in Hebrew is a plural ending, like our English *s*.)

These *k'ruvim* are warriors, unsheathed swords of fire in their hands, to ensure Adam and Eve don't tiptoe back into the garden. Later, two golden *k'ruvim* will stretch out their wings atop the ark of the covenant, acting as God's throne (Exod. 25:18-20). Sometimes these angels are pictured with multiple wings and four faces, bearing an ambulatory throne (Ezek. 1, 10). In one unforgettable image, God "rode upon a cherub and flew" (Ps. 18:10).

K'ruvim are soldiers in the unseen army that infiltrates our world. They are a kind of spiritual Special Forces that defend us from diabolical angels that went to the dark side eons ago. But now, rather than guarding us from the tree of life, they provide a military escort for us as we march to the tree of the cross and receive from Christ the fruit of life.

Heavenly Father, let your holy angel be with us, that the evil foe may have no power over us (Luther).

The First Two Humans קנה

NOW ADAM KNEW EVE HIS WIFE, AND SHE
CONCEIVED AND BORE CAIN, SAYING, "I HAVE
GOTTEN A MAN WITH THE HELP OF THE LORD."

GENESIS 4:1

Cain and Abel were the first two human beings—at least, in the ordinary sense. Being crafted from dirt and a rib makes Adam and Eve a little hard to identify with. But Cain and Abel were conceived during a roll in the hay. Both had birthdays. We get them. Most likely, they were twins since there is no "and she conceived again" between the report of their two births. Cain's name in Hebrew is *Qayin*, which is derived from the verb *qanah*. It can mean get, buy, create, or beget, depending on the context. Thus Eve's nativity announcement, "I have *qanah* a man."

Martin Luther argued that Eve thought she had given birth to the seed whom God had promised earlier (3:15). He read the Hebrew as "I have gotten the man of the LORD." It's a possible but improbable translation. That being said, had Eve thought Cain was the promised seed, she was woefully wrong. Cain, a murderer, would have scored a big, fat *F* in messiahship. No, Eve would have to wait, as did generations after her. But one day another "Eve" named Mary would *qanah* another son, a man who truly was "a Savior, who is Christ the Lord" (Luke 2:11).

Conceive faith in us, dear Father, which receives from you all that Christ has won for us.

The Voice of Blood דם

AND THE LORD SAID, "WHAT HAVE YOU DONE?
THE VOICE OF YOUR BROTHER'S BLOOD IS
CRYING TO ME FROM THE GROUND."

GENESIS 4:10

The word for blood, *dam*, is in the plural here. Cain shed "bloods." The plural is almost always used in situations of bloodguilt or bloodshed. Early Jewish commentators, who found significance in every miniscule detail, argued that "bloods" was written instead of "blood" because Cain murdered not just one man but also all his potential descendants. This led to the rabbinic saying that he who destroys one life has destroyed the whole world. We recognize the truth of this, for there is never one victim of a murder—countless others are "killed" emotionally or psychologically by this heinous crime.

We learn from Cain's story three vital truths: blood has a voice, it uses that voice to cry to God, and that bloody voice is heard. Now if God heard Abel's blood, just think of how much louder the blood of Christ rings in his ears! For his blood "speaks a better word than the blood of Abel" (Heb. 12:24). His death, far from destroying a whole world, saved it, for through him God reconciled "to himself all things, whether on earth or in heaven, making peace by the blood of his cross" (Col. 1:20).

May your blood, O Christ, which through the eternal Spirit you offered without blemish to God, cleanse our conscience from dead works to serve the living God (Heb. 9:14).

Call on the Name of Yahweh קרא

TO SETH ALSO A SON WAS BORN, AND HE CALLED HIS NAME ENOSH. AT THAT TIME PEOPLE BEGAN TO CALL UPON THE NAME OF THE LORD.

GENESIS 4:26

There's a sly contrast suggested by two names in this verse, one human, one divine. The name Enosh, which is another word for "man," is derived from a Hebrew root (*anash*), meaning "weak" or "sickly." It's the same root that Jeremiah uses to describe the heart that is deceitful and "sick/incurable" (*anush*) above all things (17:9). So Enosh isn't exactly a strong, herculean name. If anything, it encapsulates humanity's condition in a fractured world. That's all the more reason, then, to *qara* ("call") on the name of the LORD—the strong, healthy, and dependable name of God.

The verb *qara* can be used both to invoke ("call upon") and to proclaim ("call out"). In our crumbling lives, we invoke him, knowing that "the name of the LORD is a strong tower; the righteous man runs into it and is safe" (Prov. 18:10). In our sin-sick world, we proclaim his healing name (Acts 3:16). And we rely on Jesus, who bears the name above all names—Yahweh—with every knee bowing, every tongue confessing, that he is Lord, to the glory of God the Father (Phil. 2:9-11).

"Not to us, O LORD, not to us, but to your name give glory, for the sake of your steadfast love and your faithfulness!" (Ps. 115:1).

A Bad Frame of Mind יצר

THE LORD SAW THAT THE WICKEDNESS OF
MAN WAS GREAT IN THE EARTH, AND THAT
EVERY INTENTION OF THE THOUGHTS OF HIS
HEART WAS ONLY EVIL CONTINUALLY.

GENESIS 6:5

In six chapters, we've gone from people being "very good" to "every intention of the thoughts of his heart [being] only evil continually." Things fell apart precipitously. The word for "intention" is *yetzer*. Because *yetzer* is also connected with forming and framing, we can think of it as a "frame of mind," a holistic outlook on life. And in this case, it's all bad. Rabbis spoke of people having a *yetzer ha-tov* ("propensity to good") and *yetzer ha-ra* ("propensity to evil"). God "knows our *yetzer* ['frame']; he remembers that we are dust" (Ps. 103:14). And in Noah's day, this "human dust" was about to get very, very muddy.

One thing we can always count on: with every disaster, the Lord also creates a way of redemption. Every burning house has an open door. And this story's "open door" is in the side of an ark. In it the God who "formed [*yatzar*] the man of dust from the ground" (Gen. 2:7) saved a family by which to re-form humanity. And, finally, he rescued us all through the Redeemer whom he "formed [*yatzar*] . . . from the womb to be his servant" (Isa. 49:5).

O Lord, you who saw the days formed for us when as yet there was none of them, create in us clean hearts (Pss. 139:16; 51:10).

The Major and Minor Arks תבה

"MAKE YOURSELF AN ARK OF GOPHER WOOD.
MAKE ROOMS IN THE ARK, AND COVER
IT INSIDE AND OUT WITH PITCH."

GENESIS 6:14

An ark is a *tevah*—a chest-shaped or box-shaped boat. (The "ark" in "ark of the covenant" is a different Hebrew word.)

There are only two arks in the Bible: one big enough to hold a tiny world; the other just big enough to hold a tiny baby. Noah built his *tevah* and the mother of Moses built one for him (Exod. 2:3). Both were waterproofed with pitch. The mini-*tevah* for Moses is usually translated as "basket," though the King James Version (KJV) chose "ark"—and wisely so, because we were meant to hitch these two boats together in our minds.

Noah and Moses floated above waters in which many others drowned. Both were kept safe. Both brought forth a new people for God after a massive destruction. And both are connected with baptism: Noah saved his family, typifying baptism (1 Pet. 3:20–21), and Israel was "baptized into Moses" at the Red Sea (1 Cor. 10:2). From ancient times, the church too has been pictured, architecturally, as a boat or ark. "Pulpit," for instance, also means "front of a ship." Baptized into the body of Christ, we are saved, protected, and become part of God's people in the ark of the church.

Heavenly Father, keep us high and dry in the holy ark of your church, safe from the floods that rage around us.

God's Remembering Actions זכר

BUT GOD REMEMBERED NOAH AND ALL THE BEASTS
AND ALL THE LIVESTOCK THAT WERE WITH HIM
IN THE ARK. AND GOD MADE A WIND BLOW OVER
THE EARTH, AND THE WATERS SUBSIDED.

GENESIS 8:1

In Hebrew, to *zakar* ("remember") isn't so much a cerebral activity as it is a hand and mouth action. It's akin to remembering someone's birthday by the very act of throwing them a party. Such a Hebrew party would constitute the remembrance. Similarly, to remember a name isn't just to recall someone's name but to speak it—or, in God's case, to praise it. "I will cause your name to be remembered [*zakar*]," the psalmist says, meaning, the "nations will praise you forever and ever" (45:17). Remembering *was* praising. So when the Lord remembered Noah and the animals, it wasn't as if God slapped his forehead and exclaimed, "Good grief—I forgot all about the ship!" No, he remembered them in the very act of making the wind blow over the earth. Sending the wind *was* the act of remembrance.

When God remembers us, he acts to save and bless us. Likewise, when he does not remember our sins (Isa. 43:25), he doesn't act to punish us for them. Christ is the Father's remembrance incarnate. He is the tangible, verifiable, embodied gift of God's redemptive remembering.

"Remember not the sins of my youth or my transgressions; according to your steadfast love remember me, for the sake of your goodness, O LORD!" (Ps. 25:7).

The Prophetic and Feathered Jonah יונה

AND THE DOVE CAME BACK TO [NOAH] IN THE
EVENING, AND BEHOLD, IN HER MOUTH WAS A
FRESHLY PLUCKED OLIVE LEAF. SO NOAH KNEW THAT
THE WATERS HAD SUBSIDED FROM THE EARTH.

GENESIS 8:11

The Hebrew *y* is usually written as an English *j*. Thus Jonah is *Yonah*. His name means "dove," though this pigheaded prophet exhibited a decidedly more hawkish personality. Part of his story has him aboard a ship, ravaged by a raging sea. In that way, he is connected with another ship and another sea. Noah released two birds from his ship: a raven and a dove (*yonah*). One preached bad news, as it were: the waters were not dried up. But the dove preached good news, sporting an olive leaf in her beak when she returned. Finally, the floodwaters had subsided.

Biblical stories, read side by side, often produce fascinating results. Like the bird *yonah*, the prophet *Yonah* will bring peace, but the bird does it with an olive branch while the prophet does it by being cast into the sea itself! Both bird and man, however, unite as smaller parts of a larger story: the story of a Savior who compared his three days in the tomb to Jonah's three days in the fish, and on whom the dove of the Spirit would land at the Jordan to mark him as God's chosen peace for us all.

Holy Spirit, preacher of peace, proclaim and establish peace in our turbulent hearts.

The Axis of Heaven and Earth מזבח

THEN NOAH BUILT AN ALTAR TO THE LORD AND
TOOK SOME OF EVERY CLEAN ANIMAL AND
SOME OF EVERY CLEAN BIRD AND OFFERED
BURNT OFFERINGS ON THE ALTAR.

GENESIS 8:20

Mizbeach is a noun formed from the verb *zavach*, to sacrifice. So a *mizbeach* ("altar") is simply "the place for sacrificing." Its simple meaning, however, hides a profound importance. The altar is where God and humanity clasp hands. It is the axis of heaven and earth. Every altar is a minimountain where sinners climb up, the Lord steps down, and there is a rendezvous of mercy. In the aftermath of the flood, Noah built this altar in a purged world, eager for a fresh start.

But more was needed than this fresh start. Noah built his altar, as would Abraham, Isaac, Jacob, Moses, David, and many others. Each altar provided temporary relief, not lasting atonement. God and humanity would clasp hands, but they needed a permanent embrace. The lasting embrace finally happened on a very different kind of altar, built not by Jews but Romans, erected outside the temple, at the place of the skull. Here, he who was both God and man stepped up to be the sacrifice, to swallow the flood, to become the sweet-smelling aroma that wafted to heaven. The *mizbeach* of the cross of Jesus became the everlasting rendezvous of mercy.

Heavenly Father, meet us in mercy at the altar of your Son.

God's Retired Weapon קשת

"I HAVE SET MY BOW IN THE CLOUD, AND IT SHALL
BE A SIGN OF THE COVENANT BETWEEN ME AND THE
EARTH. WHEN I BRING CLOUDS OVER THE EARTH AND
THE BOW IS SEEN IN THE CLOUDS, I WILL REMEMBER
MY COVENANT THAT IS BETWEEN ME AND YOU
AND EVERY LIVING CREATURE OF ALL FLESH."

GENESIS 9:13-15

Though often translated "rainbow," the word *qeshet* ordinarily refers to a "bow," the weapon. Notice two things: one, this *qeshet* is not in the hands of the heavenly archer, who shot the arrows of the flood on the earth. It hangs from the clouds. The Lord has retired his weapon. Second, it faces not downward, at us, but upward, at God. We are unthreatened by it. God transformed a weapon of war into an emblem of peace.

But it gets even better. Later, when God appears to Ezekiel, looking like a man, this likeness of the glory of the Lord is "like the appearance of the *qeshet* that is in the cloud on the day of rain" (Ezek. 1:28). This man-like glory is the Father's Son, whom John sees in heaven, "and around the throne was a rainbow" (Rev. 4:3). The two ends of the bow, joining Genesis to Revelation, point us to Christ, for "he himself is our peace" (Eph. 2:14).

"In peace I will both lie down and sleep; for you alone, O Lord, make me dwell in safety" (Ps. 4:8).

The Fruit of the Vine יַיִן

NOAH BEGAN TO BE A MAN OF THE SOIL, AND HE
PLANTED A VINEYARD. HE DRANK OF THE WINE AND
BECAME DRUNK AND LAY UNCOVERED IN HIS TENT.

GENESIS 9:20-21

The early stories about *yayin* ("wine") do not bode well for its future positive use. Noah gets three sheets to the wind and sprawls naked in his tent. Lot's daughters get their dad drunk on wine, then have sex with him (19:30–38). Not a good first impression of the fruit of the vine. But its reputation brightens in other narratives. The priest-king Melchizedek, who is a foreshadowing of Jesus, brings out bread and *yayin* to Abraham (14:18). When Jacob blesses Judah, he says that tribe will be so rich in wine that they can use it to wash garments (49:11). And the end-time feast of the Messiah will feature "well-aged wine" (Isa. 25:6).

On the night of his final Passover with his disciples, Jesus lifted up a cup of wine and said, "Drink of it, all of you, for this is my blood of the covenant, which is poured out for many for the forgiveness of sins" (Matt. 26:27–28). *Yayin*, called the "blood of grapes" in Jacob's blessing of his Judah (Gen. 49:11), is the drink of choice by the Messiah from Judah as he gives us his covenant blood to drink, that we might receive (what some church fathers called) the "sober intoxication of the Spirit."

Quench our thirst, O Lord, with the wine of your mercy.

Building Blocks of Language לבנה

AND THEY SAID TO ONE ANOTHER, "COME, LET US
MAKE BRICKS, AND BURN THEM THOROUGHLY . . .
COME, LET US BUILD OURSELVES A CITY AND
A TOWER WITH ITS TOP IN THE HEAVENS."

GENESIS 11:3-4

The Tower of Babel story is riddled with Hebrew inside jokes. The most obvious is they're poking fun at the "great and glorious" city of Babel (Hebrew: *Bavel*), later called Babylon. It's called *Bavel* because the Lord *balal* ("confused") their language (v. 9). Also, God humorously had to come down (v. 5) to inspect this city, although its tower is supposedly "in the heavens" (v. 4). And, finally, the Lord chose to "confuse their language" (v. 7). The consonants in this form of the verb for "confuse," n-b-l, is a scrambling of the three consonants, l-b-n, in the word for brick. Because God n-b-l ("confused") their language, they could no longer use their l-b-n ("brick"). We might say that God destroyed the building blocks of their speech.

All this humor at Babylon's expense is well earned. In the Bible, she is the symbol of evil, a world turned against God. Babylon, Israel's ancient enemy, is called the "mother of prostitutes and of earth's abominations" (Rev. 17:5). In the end, however, she is "Fallen, fallen!" (18:2), but the victorious Christ has built for us the New Jerusalem, "coming down out of heaven, prepared as a bride adorned for her husband" (21:2).

Praise to you, O Christ, for building us Zion, the New Jerusalem, as our everlasting home with you.

God's Marching Orders הלך

NOW THE LORD SAID TO ABRAM, "GO FROM YOUR COUNTRY AND YOUR KINDRED AND YOUR FATHER'S HOUSE TO THE LAND THAT I WILL SHOW YOU."

GENESIS 12:1

God's first utterance to Abram was not "build" or "serve" or even "believe." It was *lek-l'ka! Lek* is an imperative form of *halak*, which means "walk or go"; *l'ka* is literally "for yourself." The KJV renders it "Get thee out." We might say, "Get going!"

Abram could kiss sedentary life goodbye. He was a man on the move, walking "by faith . . . not knowing where he was going" (Heb. 11:8). His life, therefore, becomes like a parable. He lives as a stranger in a foreign land, banking on the unseen promise of God. "He was looking forward to the city that has foundations, whose designer and builder is God" (11:10).

Abraham walked by faith, which is "the conviction of things not seen" (Heb. 11:1), yet he also rejoiced that he would see the day of Christ; indeed, he "saw it and was glad" (John 8:56). Before Abraham heard God say, "Go!"— before Abraham even was—Jesus says, "I am" (8:58). The Son showed up at Abraham's tent (Gen. 18:1-15), appeared in a vision (Gen. 15), and visited him in the form of a heavenly messenger (Gen. 22:11). The same God who commanded *Lek!* was also close at hand. The "I am" has always been our Emmanuel.

Lord Jesus, lead us, with Abraham, to the everlasting city, whose builder is God.

The Unfruitful Earth רֶעָב

NOW THERE WAS A FAMINE IN THE LAND. SO
ABRAM WENT DOWN TO EGYPT TO SOJOURN THERE,
FOR THE FAMINE WAS SEVERE IN THE LAND.

GENESIS 12:10

The word *ra'av*, translated here as "famine," is the general word for "hunger." God wasn't joking when he told Adam "cursed is the ground because of you; in pain you shall eat of it all the days of your life" (Gen. 3:17). He who ate the forbidden fruit would henceforth fight thorn and thistle, drought and fire, insects and floods, to bend the soil to his agricultural will. Yet the Lord knows how to transform a curse into a blessing, for famines also loom large in his plans of mercy. By a *ra'av* he brings Abram into Egypt to enrich him; Jacob into Egypt to reunite him with Joseph; Naomi into Moab to welcome Ruth into her family; and Israel to repentance under Elijah.

Jesus refers to the famine in the days of Elijah as exemplary of his people's stubborn refusal to hear God's Word, as well as his divine mercy to the Gentiles (Luke 4:24–26). To both Jew and Gentile, Christ says, "I am the bread of life; whoever comes to me shall not hunger, and whoever believes in me shall never thirst" (John 6:35). During our most severe famines of body and soul, Christ alone is our salvation.

Heavenly Father, who satisfies the longing soul, and fills the hungry soul with good things, satisfy and fill us with your Son.

When God Punches נגע

BUT THE LORD AFFLICTED PHARAOH
AND HIS HOUSE WITH GREAT PLAGUES
BECAUSE OF SARAI, ABRAM'S WIFE.

GENESIS 12:17

The verb *naga* can mean "touch, strike, or plague." The first two occurrences involve women. Eve, one-upping God's command, said to the serpent that she and Adam couldn't even *naga* the fruit (Gen. 3:3). And when Pharaoh absconds with Sarai, God *naga* the king. Clearly, being "touched" in this second way is like heaven's fist pummeling your face. Hebrew likes to use the same root word for nouns and verbs, so God "plagued [*naga*] Pharaoh with great plagues." Bruised and battered on the boxing mat of Egypt, the king got the message, loud and clear.

Of course, all this plaguing in Genesis 12 foreshadows the future clobbering of a far more muleheaded Pharaoh in Exodus. Only after a tenfold *naga* from God did he finally unlock Israel's shackles. That worked for Israel, but all humanity was under a far worse imprisonment: "Before faith came, we were held captive under the law, imprisoned until the coming faith would be revealed" (Gal. 3:23). Our liberty came when the Messiah was pierced for our transgressions, crushed for our iniquities, chastised for us (Isa. 53:5). We "esteemed him stricken [*naga*], smitten by God, and afflicted" (v. 4). Christ was plagued for us. Now we are forever free in him, for "with his wounds we are healed" (v. 5).

Christ crucified, hear our prayer, heal our wounds, and free us for life abundant in you.

Claimed by Feet רגל

[THE LORD TOLD ABRAM,] "ARISE, WALK
THROUGH THE LENGTH AND BREADTH OF
THE LAND, FOR I WILL GIVE IT TO YOU."

GENESIS 13:17

God told Abram to use his eyes and feet. First, look "northward and southward and eastward and westward" he said (13:14). Then he told him to get to walking. Later, he told Israel, "Every place on which the sole of your foot treads shall be yours" (Deut. 11:24). The sole of Israel's *regel* ("foot") wrote their signature on the soil. This reflects the ancient practice, common in those cultures, of kings and others assuming or reaffirming ownership of land by walking the length and breadth of their property. Similarly, when Boaz redeemed land for Naomi, the other man handed over his sandal, relinquishing any right to the soil (Ruth 4:7–8).

Jesus didn't settle down in one spot when preaching and healing. His was a peripatetic ministry. Like the patriarch, he walked the length and breadth of Israel. God had come down to his people, become a man, and stamped his name on earth's soil with his own *regel*. But he wasn't just claiming Israel; he was owning "all nations" (Matt. 28:19). Still today, when his ambassadors set their feet in a location and preach the kingdom of God, how beautiful are those feet (Isa. 52:7), for they bring the good news that the Lord of grace reigns supreme.

Lord Jesus, stand in our midst with your nail-scarred feet to claim our lives as your own.

The Priest-King
of Salem מלכי־צדק

AND MELCHIZEDEK KING OF SALEM BROUGHT OUT
BREAD AND WINE. (HE WAS PRIEST OF GOD MOST
HIGH.) AND HE BLESSED HIM AND SAID, "BLESSED BE
ABRAM BY GOD MOST HIGH, POSSESSOR OF HEAVEN
AND EARTH; AND BLESSED BE GOD MOST HIGH, WHO
HAS DELIVERED YOUR ENEMIES INTO YOUR HAND!"
AND ABRAM GAVE HIM A TENTH OF EVERYTHING.

GENESIS 14:18-20

The book of Hebrews unpacks Melchizedek's name into two words: *malki* ("king of") and *tzedeq* ("righteousness"). His city's name, Salem (a shortened form of "Jerusalem"), is related to the word *shalom* ("peace"). Thus Hebrews says, "[Melchizedek] is first, by translation of his name, king of righteousness, and then he is also king of Salem, that is, king of peace" (7:2). He's also the first priest mentioned in the Bible, long before Aaron and his sons. It's no wonder that David, speaking of the Messiah, sings that "the LORD has sworn and will not change his mind, 'You are a priest forever after the order of Melchizedek'" (Ps. 110:4).

This ancient priest-king resembles the Son of God (Heb. 7:3), who is our peace, our righteousness, our king, and our priest. He doesn't get his office by descent from Aaron, but "by the power of an indestructible life" (7:16). As Melchizedek once blessed Abram, so Christ blesses us, Abraham's sons and daughters, and bids us feast on bread and wine from his altar of life.

Jesus, our Priest and King, rule over us by mercy and intercede for us in love.

The Visible
Word of God דבר

AND BEHOLD, THE WORD OF THE LORD CAME TO
[ABRAM]: "THIS MAN SHALL NOT BE YOUR HEIR; YOUR
VERY OWN SON SHALL BE YOUR HEIR." AND HE BROUGHT
HIM OUTSIDE AND SAID, "LOOK TOWARD HEAVEN, AND
NUMBER THE STARS, IF YOU ARE ABLE TO NUMBER THEM."
THEN HE SAID TO HIM, "SO SHALL YOUR OFFSPRING BE."

GENESIS 15:4-5

Sometimes God's Word is for the ears *and the eyes*. The word *davar*, usually translated as "word," can also mean "thing or matter." When the Lord's *davar* came to Abram, he "brought him outside." Spoken words don't usher people out-of-doors. Similarly, when the *davar* spoke to Jeremiah, he also "put out his hand and touched [Jeremiah's] mouth" (1:4-9). This divine *davar* is thus more than a voice dropping from the sky; it is the seeable, touchable manifestation of God on earth.

This visible *davar* of the Old Testament is the same *davar* who was in the beginning, who was with God, who is God, and who became flesh and dwelled among us (John 1:1, 14). John says we have seen him with our eyes, we have looked on him, and our hands have touched him (1 John 1:1). He was there all along with his people before his incarnation. And now, everlastingly both divine and human, he is with us, "the only Son from the Father, full of grace and truth" (John 1:14).

Christ Jesus, the Word made flesh, may we all receive from you grace upon grace.

The Amen of Faith אָמֵן

AND [ABRAM] BELIEVED THE LORD, AND HE
COUNTED IT TO HIM AS RIGHTEOUSNESS.

GENESIS 15:6

The verb "believe" is *aman*, the same root from which we get Amen, the Hebrew word found in virtually every language. To *aman* is to say Amen. It is the quintessential word of faith. Abram stood firm, trusted, was certain that God would indeed give him offspring like the innumerable stars in the heavens (Gen. 15:5). He didn't understand how. He was an octogenarian, after all, and Sarai ten years his junior. Paul, rather bluntly, said Abram was so old he was "as good as dead" and his wife's womb was dead (Rom. 4:19). Nevertheless, he was "fully convinced that God was able to do what he had promised" (v. 21). In other words, despite all appearances to the contrary, Abram said Amen to God's seemingly foolish and impossible word.

So do we. If from a man "as good as dead" and a woman's "dead" womb God could bring forth the promised son, Isaac, then that same God could and did bring forth his own dead Son from tomb of death in his glorious resurrection. To Easter we say Amen. We stand firm in the promise of God. And that faith is counted to us as righteousness. Not because we've done anything, but because God in Christ has done it all for us.

Lord Jesus, our Amen, the faithful and true witness, give us faith to trust you in all things (Rev. 3:14).

The Eyes-Wide-Open God אל ראי

SO [HAGAR] CALLED THE NAME OF THE LORD WHO SPOKE
TO HER, "YOU ARE A GOD OF SEEING," FOR SHE SAID,
"TRULY HERE I HAVE SEEN HIM WHO LOOKS AFTER ME."

GENESIS 16:13

The only person in the Old Testament to name God is a pregnant Egyptian woman, on the run, in the wilderness, with nowhere to go. Hagar was the victim of Abram and Sarai's faltering faith. Frustrated with the slowness of God to give them a promised son, they took matters into their own hands—and Hagar into Abram's bed. According to the custom of those days, the child of Sarai's servant, Hagar, would legally belong to Sarai. But the plan backfired. Hagar got uppity, Sarai became angry and mistreated her servant, and into the desert Hagar fled.

When the Lord's messenger found her, he told her to return to her mistress, that she would be the mother of a multitude, and—most importantly—that the "LORD has listened to [her] affliction" (Gen. 16:11). In response, she named the Lord *El Roi*, "a God of seeing." The word *Roi* is from the verb *ra'ah*, to see. She who felt unseen was truly seen by God. He looked after her. He sees us too with eyes of compassion and mercy. He is not blind to our suffering, for we are the "apple of his eye" (Deut. 32:10).

Look on us, El Roi, with eyes that see us as your beloved children.

The Name-Changing God אברהם שׂרה

GENESIS 17:5, 15-16

God changes the name of Abram ("exalted father") to Abraham ("father of a multitude"), and the name of Sarai ("princess") to Sarah (a variant of "princess"). In Hebrew, the changes are slight: Abraham's name is one letter longer, and Sarah's new name substitutes an *h* for a *y*. But the significance of the changes are not slight. A name is a one-word summation of the totality of a person. A new name is a new creation of sorts. It says, "You were this but now you are that." When God changes people's names, he endows them with a new identity.

Hiding in Abraham's and Sarah's new names is the story of God gradually unwrapping the gift who will be named Jesus. The "multitude" that comes from Abraham will narrow down to a single promised seed, planted inside a virgin by the Spirit. And the "kings" that come from Sarah will lead to a single king, the Son of David, who will reign in hidden glory from the throne of the cross.

Thanks be to you, heavenly Father, for writing your own name upon us (Rev. 3:12).

A Covenant in the Flesh מול

"THIS IS MY COVENANT, WHICH YOU SHALL KEEP,
BETWEEN ME AND YOU AND YOUR OFFSPRING AFTER
YOU: EVERY MALE AMONG YOU SHALL BE CIRCUMCISED."

GENESIS 17:10

The verb *mul* means "to remove the foreskin." Many ancient cultures practiced circumcision, probably as a puberty ritual. But God took this existing practice and transformed it. To us, it might seem a strange place on the body for a "sign of the covenant," but it's quite fitting. God's covenant with Abraham is centered on the *zera* ("seed"), which means both descendant and semen. So the Lord selected the very organ from which this seed passes from man to woman as the sign-bearing body part. The *removal* of the foreskin was an indelible, lifelong sign that God would *give* seed to Abraham and Israel, children of the covenant.

When Jesus, the messianic seed, finally arrived, he himself was circumcised (Luke 2:21). The lawgiver kept his own law. In him, we too are circumcised (male and female), but "with a circumcision made without hands, by putting off the flesh, by the circumcision of Christ" (Col. 2:11). How? Paul goes on: "having been buried with [Christ] in baptism" (v. 12). We, "dead in [our] trespasses and the uncircumcision of [our] flesh, God made alive together with [Christ]" (v. 13). Our baptism into Christ is the indelible, lifelong gift by which we belong to him.

O Lord, circumcise our hearts and minds to hear your Word and to receive your life in Christ.

The Divine Comedian צחק

THE LORD SAID, "I WILL SURELY RETURN TO YOU
ABOUT THIS TIME NEXT YEAR, AND SARAH YOUR WIFE
SHALL HAVE A SON." AND SARAH WAS LISTENING AT
THE TENT DOOR BEHIND HIM . . . SO SARAH LAUGHED
TO HERSELF, SAYING, "AFTER I AM WORN OUT, AND
MY LORD IS OLD, SHALL I HAVE PLEASURE?"

GENESIS 18:10, 12

How could Sarah not laugh? God was being quite the comedian. At almost ninety years old, Sarah was as likely to get pregnant as a virgin was to conceive. So she *tzachaq*—she "laughed." But of course God had the last laugh. Or, rather, his divine laughter was infectious, for when her son was born, Sarah said, "God has made laughter for me; everyone who hears will *tzachaq* over me" (21:6). All involved were cracking up, doubling over with delight at how insanely wonderful it all was. So what else would they name their son but *Yitzchaq*? Isaac is Laughter.

Christianity might have the reputation, in some circles, of being morose and ultraserious, but it is the faith of joy, delight, and—yes—laughter. The seeming impossibility of a ninety-year-old conceiving was followed finally by a virgin conceiving. We shake our heads and smile in wonder. God is up to something. Like a comedian waiting to deliver the punch line, God will eventually deliver the unexpected resurrection. All creation gasps with the happiness of irrepressible joy.

O Lord Jesus, fill our mouths with laughter and our tongues with shouts of joy (Ps. 126:2).

Fire and Brimstone גפרית

THEN THE LORD RAINED UPON SODOM AND GOMORRAH
SULFUR AND FIRE FROM THE LORD OUT OF HEAVEN.

GENESIS 19:24 (KJV)

Because of Sodom and Gomorrah, the material *gofrit*, "brimstone" or "sulfur," is forever synonymous with cataclysmic demolition. The destruction of these cities was an uncreation, like a preview of the end of the world. Before, the vicinity was "like the garden of the LORD" (13:10). After, "the smoke of the land went up like the smoke of a furnace" (19:28). When describing God's coming wrath, Isaiah takes a page from Genesis, saying Edom's soil shall be turned into *gofrit* (34:9). The prophets smelled in *gofrit*, as it were, the aroma of sin's ultimate undoing.

"History doesn't repeat itself, but it does rhyme," Mark Twain said. When Revelation describes hell as the "lake of fire and brimstone" (20:10 KJV), it sees the final punishment "rhyming" with Sodom's punishment. Indeed, Jesus says, "On the day when Lot went out from Sodom, fire and sulfur rained from heaven and destroyed them all—so will it be on the day when the Son of Man is revealed" (Luke 17:29-30). Yet just as the Lord rescued Lot from Sodom, he "knows how to rescue the godly from trials" (2 Pet. 2:7-9). On the day Christ is revealed, he will deliver us and bring us into his kingdom of peace.

Lord Jesus, call us out of darkness into your marvelous light of freedom and peace.

Mt. Moriah יהוה יראה

SO ABRAHAM CALLED THE NAME OF THAT PLACE, "THE
LORD WILL PROVIDE"; AS IT IS SAID TO THIS DAY, "ON
THE MOUNT OF THE LORD IT SHALL BE PROVIDED."

GENESIS 22:14

God told Abraham to sacrifice Isaac "in the land of Moriah" (Gen. 22:2). When God spared Isaac, Abraham named Moriah *Yahweh Yireh* ("the LORD will provide"). Why? Abraham is playing off the name Moriah, which is connected to the verb *ra'ah* ("to see"). *Yireh* is also from the verb *ra'ah*. *Yahweh Yireh* thus has to do with the Lord seeing or being seen. Moriah is the place where the Lord will "see to it" that a sacrifice is provided.

On this mountain in Jerusalem, where Abraham built an altar, David built an altar to stop a plague from God, then Solomon built the temple with its altar (2 Chron. 3:1). Throughout the generations, on Moriah the Lord "saw to it" that sacrifices were provided.

When Jesus "set his face to go to Jerusalem" (Luke 9:51), he was in synch with Moriah's tradition. By divine necessity, his death had to take place near Moriah. He is the promised seed of Abraham, the one who stops the plague of sin, who is the true temple and true sacrifice appointed. In Jesus, God "sees to it" that all our salvation is provided for.

See to it, heavenly Father, that we are in your Son, and he in us, that we receive from him all you desire us to have.

A Heel of a Man יעקב

AFTERWARD [ESAU'S] BROTHER CAME OUT
WITH HIS HAND HOLDING ESAU'S HEEL,
SO HIS NAME WAS CALLED JACOB.

GENESIS 25:26

Isaac's two sons were named Hairy and Heel. We know them as Esau and Jacob. The name Esau is (remotely) related to the word *se'ar* ("hairy"). Jacob's name in Hebrew, *Ya'aqov*, is a play off the word *'aqev* ("heel"), which is connected to the verb *'aqav* ("to betray, hamper, hinder"). Jacob was born holding his brother's heel, trying, as it were, to pull him back into the womb so as to be the firstborn. His nativity prophesied his life's goal—to outdo and outmaneuver his brother. Jacob's ambition was to be #1, even if that meant lies, betrayal, and identity theft. Esau was correct when, riffing off his brother's name, he lamented, "Is he not rightly named Jacob? For he has cheated ['jacobed'] me these two times" (27:36).

This heel of a man embodies our worst instincts. Rather than doing "nothing from selfish ambition or conceit, but in humility" counting others more significant than ourselves (Phil. 2:3), we want to be first. Masters, not servants. For such as Jacob, and ourselves, the Messiah's own heel was struck by the serpent (Gen. 3:15). In grace, the Firstborn of God even dresses us in his own clothing of righteousness, that we might receive the blessed inheritance of the Father.

Clothe us sinners, O Lord, in robes of righteousness, that we might be part of the church of the Firstborn.

God's Place Name מָקוֹם

JACOB LEFT BEERSHEBA AND WENT TOWARD HARAN. AND HE CAME TO A CERTAIN PLACE AND STAYED THERE THAT NIGHT, BECAUSE THE SUN HAD SET. TAKING ONE OF THE STONES OF THE PLACE, HE PUT IT UNDER HIS HEAD AND LAY DOWN IN THAT PLACE TO SLEEP.

GENESIS 28:10-11

Although he didn't know it at the time, Jacob was beginning a twenty-year exile. He says he left with only his staff in his hand (Gen. 32:10), but he left with something much more important: the promise of God in his pocket. That promise came to him not at a random place, but a very "certain place." In Hebrew, "place" is *maqom*, but this is *hamaqom* ("the place"). A special place, indeed. The Lord operates with geographical specificity. This *maqom* Jacob will name Bethel ("House of God"), for here God welcomed Jacob into his home and bound himself to live and dwell with him over the next two decades, and beyond.

Later Jewish tradition, reflecting on Genesis 28, sometimes called God *Maqom* or *Hamaqom*. He is The Place, the ever-present, all-encompassing one. He is also the God who comes to us in specified places: Bethel, the temple, and finally the flesh-and-blood man who "is the radiance of his glory" and "the exact imprint of his nature" (Heb. 1:3). Jesus is *Hamaqom* of God, the human temple in which all divine glory dwells.

"O Lord, we love the habitation of your house and the place where your glory dwells" (Ps. 26:8).

The Lord at the Ladder's Bottom סלם

[JACOB] HAD A DREAM; A STAIRWAY WAS SET ON THE GROUND AND ITS TOP REACHED TO THE SKY, AND ANGELS OF GOD WERE GOING UP AND DOWN IT. AND THE LORD WAS STANDING BESIDE HIM.

GENESIS 28:12-13A (NJPS)

The flight of steps joining earth to sky was a *sullam* ("ladder" or "stairway"). On it God's messengers moved in both directions, but the Lord moved only down. He descended to Jacob; Jacob did not mount the ladder to climb to him. Although many translations render the prepositional phase *alav* as "above it" or "at the top" (God in heaven above Jacob), the Hebrew could be translated "beside him" (God on earth with Jacob). The Lord descends to us, comes and speaks with us. He is a boots-on-the-ground kind of Lord, especially when, like Jacob, we are on the run, in the dark, in need of consolation.

The same God who stood beside Jacob stood on the earth as a man in Jesus. He is our Emmanuel—God with us and beside us. He even identified himself with Jacob's *sullam*: "Truly, truly, I say to you, you will see heaven opened, and the angels of God ascending and descending on the Son of Man" (John 1:51). Our "*sullam* to heaven" is our Savior, who comes down to us to bring us all the blessings of his Father.

O come to us, Emmanuel, to be our help, our consolation, at the bottom of life's ladder.

The Unloved Wife שׂנֵא

SO JACOB WENT IN TO RACHEL ALSO, AND HE LOVED RACHEL
MORE THAN LEAH, AND SERVED LABAN FOR ANOTHER
SEVEN YEARS. WHEN THE LORD SAW THAT LEAH WAS
HATED, HE OPENED HER WOMB, BUT RACHEL WAS BARREN.

GENESIS 29:30-31

Jacob, the trickster, had himself been tricked by Laban. Now he had two sister wives, in a sort of marriage love triangle. But as the short story writer O. Henry once quipped, such triangles "are always isosceles—never equilateral." And Leah's corner of that triangle was small indeed. We're told both that Jacob "loved Rachel more than Leah" (which implies he loved her some) and also that God saw "that Leah was hated" (which suggests Jacob didn't love her at all). The verb *sane* ("hate") probably carries the connotation here of "unloved" or "unchosen." Whether she was "hated" or "loved less," however, probably made little difference to Leah. All she felt was frozen out of a marriage she never asked for in the first place.

When commenting on this passage, Martin Luther notes that God especially cares for those who are despised and thrown away, as Leah was. God gathers such people. To him they are precious and holy. Come unto me, Jesus might say, all you who are unloved, unwanted, thrown away like garbage, for I will treasure you. He welcomes all of us into his beloved family.

Fill us with your love, heavenly Father, that we may know and love you, through Christ.

The Rise of Leah's Fourth Son יהודה

AND [LEAH] CONCEIVED AGAIN AND BORE A
SON, AND SAID, "THIS TIME I WILL PRAISE THE
LORD." THEREFORE SHE CALLED HIS NAME
JUDAH. THEN SHE CEASED BEARING.

GENESIS 29:35

When Leah's fourth son was born, she chose a more positive name for him than her prior three sons. She named him *Yehudah* ("Judah"), from the verb *yadah*, "to praise." Our first impressions of Judah, however, are not exactly praiseworthy. He was the unfraternal mastermind behind selling Joseph into slavery (Gen. 37:26–27). Later, thinking his disguised daughter-in-law, Tamar, was a prostitute, he had sex with her (38:12–30). But by the end of the Joseph story, Judah has undergone a change. He assumes responsibility and leadership. He becomes the humble spokesman for his brothers. And by the time Jacob blesses his sons, our friend whose name means Praise is told "your brothers shall *yadah* [praise] you" (49:8). What's more, Jacob prophesies that Judah shall rule over his brothers (49:8–12).

This prophecy was true in more than one sense. David, from Judah's tribe, did indeed rule over Israel. But David was a king, not the King of kings. That kingliest King, the Messiah, would himself be born in the tribe of Judah. He himself is our praise, our Hallelujah to the Father, for his is the kingdom and the power and the glory forever and ever.

King Jesus, Lion of the tribe of Judah, reign over us that we might serve you in freedom.

The Ineptitude
of Idols תרפים

NOW RACHEL HAD TAKEN THE HOUSEHOLD GODS
AND PUT THEM IN THE CAMEL'S SADDLE AND SAT
ON THEM. LABAN FELT ALL ABOUT THE TENT, BUT
DID NOT FIND THEM. AND SHE SAID TO HER FATHER,
"LET NOT MY LORD BE ANGRY THAT I CANNOT RISE
BEFORE YOU, FOR THE WAY OF WOMEN IS UPON ME."

GENESIS 31:34-35

The Bible does not wink at pseudogods or their images. They are merci-lessly mocked and condemned. Genesis 31 is a vivid (and darkly humorous) example. This variety, called *t'rafim* ("household gods"), are probably small humanoid figurines. The comedy of the situation is evident: not only are Rachel's glutes on these gods, but she is menstruating, which made her rit-ually unclean. These *t'rafim* are such failures at godhood that they (1) can't keep themselves from being stolen, (2) can't do anything about being sat on, and (3) are themselves made unclean. Three strikes, *t'rafim*; you're out of the god game.

The Old Testament (OT) and New Testament (NT) unmask faux deities as the disguises of demons. In Israel's idolatry, "they sacrificed to demons that were no gods" (Deut. 32:17). Paul says, "What pagans sacrifice they offer to demons" (1 Cor. 10:20). Christ has triumphed over all these in his res-urrection, stomping the powers of hell. In the Messiah we are liberated to worship him and the Father in the Spirit of truth.

Gracious Father, destroy in us all attachments to false gods and give us hearts devoted exclusively to you.

Israel the God-Fighter שׂרה

AND JACOB WAS LEFT ALONE. AND A MAN WRESTLED
WITH HIM UNTIL THE BREAKING OF THE DAY . . .
THEN HE SAID, "YOUR NAME SHALL NO LONGER BE
CALLED JACOB, BUT ISRAEL, FOR YOU HAVE STRIVEN
WITH GOD AND WITH MEN, AND HAVE PREVAILED."

GENESIS 32:24, 28

Jacob's opponent is called "a man" (Gen. 32:24), "God" (Hosea 12:3), and "the angel" (12:4). In short, this is a wrestling match between Jacob and God who appears as a messenger in human form. That the Lord would grapple with a man in the mud is, of course, astonishing. What is truly jaw dropping, however, is that the Almighty would lose the fight. But that is what he himself says when he renames the patriarch. Jacob has *sarah* ("striven" or "contended") with both God and men and has overcome. He therefore gets the new name *Yisra'el*: from *yisra* (a verbal form of *sarah*) and *El* ("God"). Jacob is now Israel, the God-Fighter.

Isn't it just like our Lord, however, to lose? Jacob's nocturnal battle with this God in human form is a preview of the entirety of Jesus' ministry. When he arrived in our darkened world, he faced a lifetime of fierce, deadly opposition. Humanity wrestled with him until finally he was pinned atop the cross. There he lost everything for us, that in him we might gain everything the Father wants to give us.

Christ, may we too count everything loss for the surpassing greatness of knowing you as our Lord.

The Coat of Many Colors כתנת פסים

NOW ISRAEL LOVED JOSEPH MORE THAN ANY OTHER
OF HIS SONS, BECAUSE HE WAS THE SON OF HIS OLD
AGE. AND HE MADE HIM A ROBE OF MANY COLORS.
BUT WHEN HIS BROTHERS SAW THAT THEIR FATHER
LOVED HIM MORE THAN ALL HIS BROTHERS, THEY HATED
HIM AND COULD NOT SPEAK PEACEFULLY TO HIM.

GENESIS 37:3-4

How best to translate *k'tonet passim* is long-standing question. A *k'tonet* is a long robe. *Passim* is less clear. It may be connected to *pas* ("the palm of the hand or sole of the foot"). If so, it's a long-sleeved tunic reaching down to the feet. Most translations take their cue from the Greek, which rendered it "a multicolored frock." Thus the KJV's "coat of many colors." Although *what it was* is debated, *what it did* is indisputable: this article of clothing unrobed the naked hostility of fraternal hatred.

Joseph's story is a wardrobe narrative: his brothers tore this robe off (37:23), Potiphar's wife unrobed him as he fled from her (39:12), he donned new clothes when he left prison (41:14), and Pharaoh finally "clothed him in garments of fine linen" (41:42). God finally got the right clothes on him: the garments of one who would save his people. And therein is foreshadowed the greater Joseph, our Savior and Lord, robed in splendor and majesty, who wraps us in garments of white (Rev. 7:9).

Robe us in righteousness, our God and King, that we may reflect the glory of your name.

From Sister-in-Law to Wife יבם

BUT ONAN KNEW THAT THE OFFSPRING WOULD NOT BE
HIS. SO WHENEVER HE WENT IN TO HIS BROTHER'S WIFE
[TAMAR] HE WOULD WASTE THE SEMEN ON THE GROUND,
SO AS NOT TO GIVE OFFSPRING TO HIS BROTHER.

GENESIS 38:9

This story may be unpopular in Sunday school, but it's important. Here is our first encounter with "levirate marriage." Levirate is from the Latin *levir* ("brother's wife"). In Hebrew, the verb is *yavam* ("to consummate a marriage with a brother-in-law"), related to *y'vamah* ("brother's widow"). The law is this: if a brother dies without leaving offspring, his surviving brother marries the widow (Deut. 25:5–10). Their child will carry on the name and inheritance of the deceased brother. This is why Onan "wasted his semen." He didn't want to impregnate Tamar and thus "give offspring to his brother." He wanted all the inheritance to himself.

With this law in mind, the Sadducees challenged Jesus with the story of the widow who married seven brothers in a row, each one dying, none leaving offspring (Matt. 22:23–33). "Whose wife will she be in the resurrection?" they demand to know. Silly Sadducees. They knew neither the Scriptures nor the power of God. Wedding rings won't adorn resurrected fingers. Marriages and baby-making will be over in the New Jerusalem, for we will be the children of God and members of the bride of Jesus Christ.

Holy Spirit, grant us love for our brothers and sisters and a firm hope in the resurrection of the body.

Seventy שׁבעים

ALL THE PERSONS OF THE HOUSE OF JACOB
WHO CAME INTO EGYPT WERE SEVENTY.

GENESIS 46:27

The Bible's numerical symbolism begins already in Genesis 1 with seven days and continues all the way to Revelation with the number "666." The Hebrew number seventy, *shiv'im*, is part of this symbolic world.

Seventy is the number of large-scale completeness, a great and full totality. Add up all the families of the world listed in the genealogy of Genesis 10 and it comes to seventy. When Jacob and his family journeyed to Egypt, they were seventy in all (Gen. 46:27). Israel was represented by seventy elders (Exod. 24:9). Even in nonbiblical literature, such as Ugaritic, there are seventy members of the divine pantheon.

Jesus' choice to send out seventy disciples ahead of him to announce the kingdom was no accident (Luke 10:1 NASB). These spokesmen went with his full authority to proclaim a kingdom that recognized no geographical, racial, or cultural boundaries. Jews and Gentiles were included. Male and female. Everyone. The entire world was the compass of the redeeming work of Christ. All the persons of the house of humanity who came into the Egypt of sin and death and the devil were rescued by the Passover death and resurrection of the Son of God.

O Creator and Redeemer of the world, come quickly to save us from all our adversaries.

Be Fruitful and Multiply פרו ורבו

BUT THE PEOPLE OF ISRAEL WERE FRUITFUL AND INCREASED GREATLY; THEY MULTIPLIED AND GREW EXCEEDINGLY STRONG, SO THAT THE LAND WAS FILLED WITH THEM.

EXODUS 1:7

We associate the phrase *p'ru ur'vu* ("be fruitful and multiply") with God's creative blessing to Adam and Eve (Gen. 1:28). That Israel was "fruitful" and "multiplied" in Egypt ought to cause us to sit up and take notice. When God chose the people of Israel, he made them a corporate replacement for Adam and Eve. Just as the first two people had their sacred garden in Eden, so Israel would have their sacred land. Just as Adam and Eve were to serve and guard the garden (Gen. 2:15), so Israel as a holy priesthood was to serve and guard God's Word, his land, and his house. The Lord was starting over with Israel. And he made that restart clear by blessing them with fruitful marriages and multiplying offspring, even on foreign soil.

All God's promises to Israel find their "Yes" in Jesus Christ (2 Cor. 1:20). The Messiah came to be not only the second Adam but also Israel reduced to one. In him, God fulfills promise after promise, including many offspring, for we who believe in Christ are adopted members of the family of God, born again by the Spirit, by whom we cry, Abba! Father! (Rom. 8:15).

Abba, Father, hear our prayer and make us coheirs with Christ, your Son and our Brother.

The Birth-Helpers מילדת

THEN THE KING OF EGYPT SAID TO THE HEBREW MIDWIVES, ONE OF WHOM WAS NAMED SHIPHRAH AND THE OTHER PUAH, "WHEN YOU SERVE AS MIDWIFE TO THE HEBREW WOMEN AND SEE THEM ON THE BIRTHSTOOL, IF IT IS A SON, YOU SHALL KILL HIM, BUT IF IT IS A DAUGHTER, SHE SHALL LIVE."

EXODUS 1:15-16

The biblical story often turns up its nose at the "big people." In Egypt, the top dog is Pharaoh. Yet he is waved away; no ink is even used to record his name. But these two blue-collar women? Their names are recorded for everlasting posterity. As *m'yalledet* ("birth-helper or midwife"), Shiphrah and Puah were tasked with helping women *yalad* ("give birth"). In this story, however, they did more than that: they feared God, duped the king, and saved countless lives. In response, God "dealt well with the midwives" and "gave them families" (Exod. 1:20-21).

Women figure prominently in Moses' life. These midwives begin his story; his mother and sister save him; Pharaoh's daughter takes him in. Later, his wife, Zipporah, will rescue him from a divine attack (4:24-26). In a world in which women rarely exercised authority, God used these women powerfully in his plan of redeeming the world. All this set the stage for when God would call a teenage virgin, an everyday village girl, to bring forth our Savior into the world.

O Lord, who brings down the mighty from their thrones, uplift the low, the common, the overlooked.

Moses the Water Man משה

WHEN THE CHILD GREW OLDER, SHE BROUGHT
HIM TO PHARAOH'S DAUGHTER, AND HE BECAME
HER SON. SHE NAMED HIM MOSES, "BECAUSE,"
SHE SAID, "I DREW HIM OUT OF THE WATER."

EXODUS 2:10

Moses was a water baby. He had his Noah-like ark, a pitch-covered vessel that saved him from a watery grave. At three months old, his life's work was already foretold by God. He would be a man of water, judgment, and salvation. His name, *Moshe*, is prophetic. It's a play on the verb *masha*, "to draw out." He would grow up to *masha* his people: to draw them out of slavery, to draw them across the Red Sea, to draw water from a rock. In great irony, the daughter of Pharaoh gave her adopted son a name that foreshadowed when he would send Pharaoh himself into a watery grave.

We usually associate Moses with the law, but he's also a man of grace, saving his people through water. In that way his life is a blueprint for the Messiah, a prophet like him (Deut. 18:15). God also rescued Jesus from a tyrant, Herod, when he was a child (Matt. 2:16–18). Then, when he was lifted up on the cross, he drew all people to himself (John 12:32) in his crucifixion baptism (Mark 10:38) by which he destroyed all the powers of evil.

Send from on high, O Lord, and take us; draw us out of many waters (Ps. 18:16).

Drinking from a Beer באר

MOSES FLED FROM PHARAOH AND STAYED IN THE
LAND OF MIDIAN. AND HE SAT DOWN BY A WELL.
NOW THE PRIEST OF MIDIAN HAD SEVEN DAUGHTERS,
AND THEY CAME AND DREW WATER AND FILLED
THE TROUGHS TO WATER THEIR FATHER'S FLOCK.

EXODUS 2:15-16

The Bible is full of beer stories—*b'er*, to be exact. A *b'er* is simply a watering place or well, but what happened at these wells was more than drinking. Abraham's servant found Isaac's future wife, Rebekah, at a well (Gen. 24). Jacob met his bride, Rachel, at a well (Gen. 29). And Moses encountered seven sisters, one of whom would be his wife, Zipporah, at a well (Exod. 2). Judging by the biblical stories, at wells, romance was in the air.

Thus it's not surprising when, at a well in Samaria associated with Jacob, Jesus engages a woman in conversation about marriage (John 4:1-26). She had had five husbands and was living with a sixth man. What she didn't realize at first was that a very different kind of romance was in the air. The Messiah stood at this well to welcome her to be part of his bride, the church. From this divine Husband, the Savior of the world, she would receive living waters. And his Father she would worship in spirit and in truth. His well of mercy and love is deep indeed.

Quench our thirst, O Lord, with living waters that flow from the unfathomable well of your grace.

When God Knows יָדַע

AND GOD HEARD THEIR GROANING, AND GOD
REMEMBERED HIS COVENANT WITH ABRAHAM,
WITH ISAAC, AND WITH JACOB. GOD SAW THE
PEOPLE OF ISRAEL—AND GOD KNEW.

EXODUS 2:24-25

That "God knew" of Israel's sufferings does not mean he acquired fresh information, whereas previously he assumed they were living the Egyptian high life. No, in Hebrew, *yada* ("know") frequently entails an intimate grasp of a subject based on action. Adam, for instance, was obviously acquainted with Eve prior to joining her in bed, but in intercourse he *yada* her (Gen. 4:1). Likewise, the Lord was aware of Abraham's devotion before he nearly sacrificed Isaac, but only then does he say, "Now I *yada* that you fear God" (Gen. 22:12). For God to *yada* Israel's pain meant that when he heard, remembered, and saw them, that was a knowledge that sank, as it were, into his very soul—and prompted him to act on their behalf.

Jesus says, "I am the good shepherd. I know my own and my own know me, just as the Father knows me and I know the Father; and I lay down my life for the sheep" (John 10:14-15). God's knowledge of Israel's suffering, and his sending of Moses to shepherd them to freedom, is a window into what our Good Shepherd has done for us. Us he knows. Us he loves. And for us he lays down his life.

"Make me to know your ways, O LORD; teach me your paths" (Ps. 25:4).

God's Unique Messenger מלאך

AND THE ANGEL OF THE LORD APPEARED TO
[MOSES] IN A FLAME OF FIRE OUT OF THE MIDST
OF A BUSH. HE LOOKED, AND BEHOLD, THE BUSH
WAS BURNING, YET IT WAS NOT CONSUMED.

EXODUS 3:2

The Hebrew *malak*, often translated "angel," simply means "messenger." The prophet Haggai was a human *malak* (1:13). The two messengers sent to Sodom are each an angelic *malak* (Gen. 19:1). This *malak* in the burning bush, however, is unique. In the next few verses, he is called both Yahweh and the God of the patriarchs (vv. 4–6). And yet he is still distinct from the Lord, as his messenger. Later, God will say of him, "My name is in him" (Exod. 23:21): that is, my essence, my identity, is shared by him. Jacob too identifies him with the redeeming God (Gen. 48:15–16).

Who is this *malak* who is distinct from Yahweh yet shares his name, his essence, his power, his Word, his saving actions? He is the Son of God. He did not wait until he became man to visit his people. From the time of Hagar, where he made his first appearance as a *malak* (Gen. 16:7), he is Emmanuel, God with us. He who is the Word made flesh (John 1:14) was, in the Old Testament, the *malak* made visible. Christ has never been—nor ever will be—far from his people.

Visit us, O Christ, as you came to your people of old, with healing in your wings.

Holy Ground קדש

THEN HE SAID, "DO NOT COME NEAR; TAKE YOUR
SANDALS OFF YOUR FEET, FOR THE PLACE ON
WHICH YOU ARE STANDING IS HOLY GROUND."

EXODUS 3:5

Because footwear was universally considered unclean, Moses stands there barefoot, just as later the temple priests would serve unshod. He's on "holy ground." The Bible usually speaks of holiness concretely. Rather than a notion or abstraction, it's a day, a building, a priest, a sacrifice. What makes something holy is God's presence. He is *qadosh*, *qadosh*, *qadosh* ("Holy, holy, holy"; Isa. 6:3), as the seraphim sang, so the ground around him is *qodesh* ("holy"). He alone is intrinsically and essentially holy. We sing of him, "You alone are holy" (Rev. 15:4). Anything else called "holy" borrows holiness from him. Holiness is therefore always a gift, a divine bestowal, never an achievement.

Even a demon knew Jesus was "the Holy One of God" (Mark 1:24). Peter confesses him to be "the Holy One of God" (John 6:69). The church prayed to the Father about "your holy servant, Jesus" (Acts 4:30). All our holiness is from him, as a gift, not a gold star for saintliness. We have been made holy or "sanctified through the offering of the body of Jesus Christ once for all" (Heb. 10:10). Therefore, we enter his holy presence in Christ, our holy priest, with full confidence (v. 19), for he is our "sanctification" (1 Cor. 1:30).

Holy Jesus, draw us near to you and sanctify us with your truth.

I Am Who I Am יהוה

THEN MOSES SAID TO GOD, "IF I COME TO THE
PEOPLE OF ISRAEL AND SAY TO THEM, 'THE GOD OF
YOUR FATHERS HAS SENT ME TO YOU,' AND THEY
ASK ME, 'WHAT IS HIS NAME?' WHAT SHALL I SAY TO
THEM?" GOD SAID TO MOSES, "I AM WHO I AM."

EXODUS 3:13-14

The phrase "I am who I am" can also be translated "I am that I am" or "I will be who I will be." This, however, is not what Yahweh means. Not exactly. "I am" is a first-person verbal form whereas Yahweh is third person, "he is." In other words, God says, "I am who I am," and, by saying his name, we respond, "He is who he is." The name Yahweh is thus our confession, our echo back to God of the name he has given to us. The Greek translators rendered this covenant name of Israel's God as *Kyrios*.

When Jesus says, "Before Abraham was, I am," he is saying, "I am Yahweh, the God who told Moses, 'I am who I am'" (John 8:58). Similarly, when Paul says God gave Jesus "the name that is above every name," he doesn't mean the very common Jewish name "Jesus." No, every tongue will confess that Jesus Christ is *Kyrios*, that he is Yahweh (Phil. 2:9–11). We join Thomas in saying to the Messiah, "My *Kyrios* and my God" (John 20:28).

Jesus Christ, the great I Am, the Lord of lords, be always good and gracious to us, your people.

Sticking It to Enemies מטה

THE LORD SAID TO [MOSES], "WHAT IS THAT IN YOUR HAND?" HE SAID, "A STAFF." AND HE SAID, "THROW IT ON THE GROUND." SO HE THREW IT ON THE GROUND, AND IT BECAME A SERPENT, AND MOSES RAN FROM IT.

EXODUS 4:2-3

Weird weapons line God's arsenal. In Exodus, his weapon of choice is not a sharp sword or flying spear. Rather, it's a *matteh*, a stick. A *matteh* was used for walking, and in Moses' case, also for keeping wayward sheep in line. Sometimes a *matteh* refers to the staff of a tribal leader—thus, by extension, *matteh* can mean "tribe." But at its simplest, it's a piece of wood. What makes the *matteh* of Moses different is that it's also the "staff of God" (Exod. 4:20). By a dry piece of wood, filled with the almighty sap of God's Word, Moses turned the Nile to blood, divided the sea, and destroyed one of the most powerful armies on earth.

The story of salvation is riddled with God's oddball weaponry. From the *matteh* of Moses; to the torches, trumpets, and clay jars of Gideon; to Samson's donkey jawbone; all the way to the strangest weapon of all: two pieces of wood, crisscrossed, blood-splattered, and holding the body of the Word of God himself. By that weapon, all our enemies, including death itself, lay vanquished.

Jesus, King of mercy, who reigns in triumph from the tree, all praise be to you for our salvation.

Sin's Skin Story צָרַעַת

AGAIN, THE LORD SAID TO HIM, "PUT YOUR HAND INSIDE
YOUR CLOAK." AND HE PUT HIS HAND INSIDE HIS CLOAK,
AND WHEN HE TOOK IT OUT, BEHOLD, HIS HAND WAS
LEPROUS LIKE SNOW. THEN GOD SAID, "PUT YOUR HAND
BACK INSIDE YOUR CLOAK." SO HE PUT HIS HAND BACK
INSIDE HIS CLOAK, AND WHEN HE TOOK IT OUT, BEHOLD,
IT WAS RESTORED LIKE THE REST OF HIS FLESH.

EXODUS 4:6-7

Though usually translated "leprosy," the word *tzra'at* is not Hansen's disease. True leprosy is not curable, but biblical *tzra'at* is. Moreover, *tzra'at* not only is found on skin but has effects on clothing and houses (Lev. 13–14). Whatever it was—perhaps "skin disease" is the best translation—its effects were unwelcome. Among the Israelites, those who had it were forced to live alone, unclean, "outside the camp" (Lev. 13:46). A few times, it was divine punishment, such as Miriam, Uzziah, and Gehazi suffered. Mostly, having *tzra'at* simply meant your skin told the tale of sin's impact on the world. It betokened the gradual decay of a body destined for the grave.

Jesus welcomed, cleansed, and even touched those with real leprosy (Matt. 8:3). In so doing, he demonstrated the depths of his mercy in going to those "outside the camp." He came for all, that all might be made clean, whole, and beloved in him, with the promise of resurrection to come.

Jesus, who forgives all our iniquity, who heals all our diseases, have mercy on us.

A Bridegroom of Blood חתן דמים

AT A LODGING PLACE ON THE WAY THE LORD MET HIM AND SOUGHT TO PUT HIM TO DEATH. THEN ZIPPORAH TOOK A FLINT AND CUT OFF HER SON'S FORESKIN AND TOUCHED MOSES' FEET WITH IT AND SAID, "SURELY YOU ARE A BRIDEGROOM OF BLOOD TO ME!" SO HE LET HIM ALONE. IT WAS THEN THAT SHE SAID, "A BRIDEGROOM OF BLOOD," BECAUSE OF THE CIRCUMCISION.

EXODUS 4:24–26

Hardly had Moses begun the trek to Egypt, at God's behest, before God tried to kill him. This might seem bizarre to us—and it is—but Moses had failed the duty of every Israelite father: he hadn't circumcised his son. Zipporah jumps into action and touches the bloody foreskin to the feet of Moses. He was therefore saved by blood. Thus, already married to Zipporah, he becomes not only a husband but *chatan damim*, a "bridegroom of blood." Significantly, the same verb, *naga*, used here for Zipporah "touching" the blood to Moses, is used to describe how the blood of the Passover lamb was to "touch" the lintel and doorposts (12:22).

This nocturnal rescue from divine destruction by blood foreshadows Israel's rescue from the angel of death in Egypt by the blood of the Passover lamb. And it points us to our far greater rescue by a circumcised Son, who becomes the Passover Lamb of God, and the Bridegroom of the church that is saved by blood.

Christ, Bridegroom of the church, protect and cover us with your sacred blood.

Mr. Big House פרעה

AFTERWARD MOSES AND AARON WENT AND SAID
TO PHARAOH, "THUS SAYS THE LORD, THE GOD OF
ISRAEL, 'LET MY PEOPLE GO, THAT THEY MAY HOLD
A FEAST TO ME IN THE WILDERNESS.'" BUT PHARAOH
SAID, "WHO IS THE LORD, THAT I SHOULD OBEY HIS
VOICE AND LET ISRAEL GO? I DO NOT KNOW THE
LORD, AND MOREOVER, I WILL NOT LET ISRAEL GO."

EXODUS 5:1-2

The word *Par'oh* ("Pharaoh") is an Egyptian loanword. It meant "great house." Just as we sometimes equate the White House with the president, so Egyptians used Great House to designate their leader. But he was more than just a leader. In Egyptian theology, *Par'oh* was the incarnation of a god. Thus when Pharaoh scoffs at God and acts like a first-rate, uppity deity, he's thrown down the gauntlet: this will be a theomachy, a God-fight. The Lord of Israel will execute judgment "on all the gods of Egypt" (12:12), including Mr. Big House.

The wars God fought for Israel were against both their human enemies and their false deities. The Lord was stomping out idolatry, unveiling its vanity, and showing Israel and all nations that he alone is God of heaven and earth. On Easter, that revelation was trumpeted to all creation: this resurrected man, God and King, has "disarmed the rulers and authorities" (Col. 2:15) and made his enemies a stool for his feet (Ps. 110:1).

Heavenly Father, in your resurrected Son, deliver us from every evil of body and soul.

Heavy Work and Hard Hearts תכבד העבדה

[PHARAOH SAID,] "LET HEAVIER WORK BE LAID ON THE MEN THAT THEY MAY LABOR AT IT AND PAY NO REGARD TO LYING WORDS."

EXODUS 5:9

Hidden in the phrase *tikbad ha'avodah* ("heavier work") is a masterful suggestion of God's future plan. *Tikbad* is from the root *kavad* ("heavy or hard"), which will also be used to describe the "hard" heart of Pharaoh (8:15). And *ha'avodah*, from the root *avad*, refers not only to "work" but also to the "service" or "worship" that Israel will give to the Lord (12:25). Thus as the story develops, this "heavier work" that the king lays on Israel will give way to his self-destructive hard heart and Israel's worship of their God. Pharaoh's command to make things worse for Israel only makes things much worse for him and his nation. God turns the tables on Pharaoh.

We see something similar when Pilate presented Jesus to the crowd and they cried, "His blood be on us and on our children!" (Matt. 27:25). Hidden in the words they meant for evil was the plan God had for good. The blood of Jesus would indeed be on them—atoning blood, restoring blood, that would remove their hearts of stone and give them hearts of flesh (Ezek. 36:26). Reconciled to him, they would worship as the new and redeemed church, "the Israel of God" (Gal. 6:16).

Create in us clean hearts, O God, and renew right spirits within us, that we may worship you.

Serpents and Crocodiles תנין

THEN THE LORD SAID TO MOSES AND AARON, "WHEN PHARAOH SAYS TO YOU, 'PROVE YOURSELVES BY WORKING A MIRACLE,' THEN YOU SHALL SAY TO AARON, 'TAKE YOUR STAFF AND CAST IT DOWN BEFORE PHARAOH, THAT IT MAY BECOME A SERPENT.'"

EXODUS 7:8-9

In the desert, Moses' staff became a serpent (Exod. 4:3). Imagine his surprise in Egypt when this same staff became a crocodile! Most translations render the reptile in Exodus 4:3 and 7:9 the same, as "serpent," but they are different words in Hebrew. At the burning bush, the staff became a *nachash* ("serpent"), but at the Nile, a *tannin*. In various contexts, a *tannin* is a great sea creature (Gen. 1:21; Ps. 74:13) as well as a monster or dragon (Jer. 51:34). Many scholars think this staff-turned-*tannin* is a Nile crocodile.

The image of the *tannin* as a powerful, dangerous creature associated with water comes up several other times in the Bible. Each time, the *tannin* is emblematic of powerful forces that God—or God through his people—overcomes. The Lord "pierced the *tannin*" (Isa. 51:9) and smashes his head (Ps. 74:13). His people likewise trample the *tannin* underfoot (Ps. 91:13). In other words, God is victorious. None can stand in his way. He who walked on the Sea of Galilee will pierce, smash, and tread on every foe that faces him and his church.

Hear us when we call, O Lord. In trouble, be with us, rescue, and honor us (Ps. 91:15-16).

The Digits of Divinity אצבע

THEN THE MAGICIANS SAID TO PHARAOH,
"THIS IS THE FINGER OF GOD." BUT PHARAOH'S
HEART WAS HARDENED, AND HE WOULD NOT
LISTEN TO THEM, AS THE LORD HAD SAID.

EXODUS 8:19

With their secret arts, Pharaoh's magicians had imitated the staff-become-crocodile (7:11) and water-become-blood (7:22). But when they tried to replicate the third plague, dust-become-gnats, they failed (8:18). Their response: "This is the *etzba Elohim*," the finger of God. The Lord swore to redeem them with "an outstretched arm" (6:6), to stretch out his "hand against Egypt" (7:5), but he also used his fingers. With his *etzba*, he also crafted the heavens (Ps. 8:3) and wrote the law on tablets of stone (Exod. 31:18). With all of who he is, down to his very fingertips, the Lord is creating, teaching, and redeeming.

"If it is by the finger of God that I cast out demons," Jesus said, "then the kingdom of God has come upon you" (Luke 11:20). Christ's ministry was Exodus on replay: he came to liberate us from slavery to evil, to overcome the Pharaoh of hell, to undergo a Passover death. His fingers are the digits of divinity. With those fingers, he crafts the kingdom of freedom into which he brings us in the greater exodus of his gospel. And with them he writes his Word on our hearts in the new covenant (Jer. 31:33).

With your fingers, O Lord, drive evil from us, craft us anew, and write your Word on our hearts.

The Plague War נֶגַע

THE LORD SAID TO MOSES, "YET ONE PLAGUE MORE
I WILL BRING UPON PHARAOH AND UPON EGYPT.
AFTERWARD HE WILL LET YOU GO FROM HERE. WHEN HE
LETS YOU GO, HE WILL DRIVE YOU AWAY COMPLETELY."

EXODUS 11:1

The rabbis used the catchphrase *ma'aseh avot siman l'vanim* ("the actions of the fathers are a sign for the sons") to describe how God's actions in the past, with the patriarchs, established the pattern of Israel's future. So here with the plagues. Long before Moses, while Abram and Sarai were in Egypt, God had "plagued Pharaoh and his house with great plagues because of Sarai Abram's wife" (Gen. 12:17 KJV). Now the Lord repeats that action when his bride, Israel, is under Pharaoh's thumb. The noun *nega* ("plague") is from the verb *naga* ("touch, strike, plague"). When God "touched" Pharaoh, it was like ten consecutive divine fists pulverizing his face until he was KO'd on the mat!

"The LORD is a man of war," Israel will later sing at the Red Sea (Exod. 15:3). He goes on the warpath for his people, his bride, his beloved. And woe betide anyone who stands in his way. Indeed, he will fight to the death, as he did in Christ, and arise a triumphant warrior to lead us out of exile and home again to him.

Arise, O Lord, to fight for us, to trample our enemies, and to lead us into your kingdom.

Israelite Fast Food חפזון

"IN THIS MANNER YOU SHALL EAT IT: WITH YOUR
BELT FASTENED, YOUR SANDALS ON YOUR FEET,
AND YOUR STAFF IN YOUR HAND. AND YOU SHALL
EAT IT IN HASTE. IT IS THE LORD'S PASSOVER."

EXODUS 12:11

The original *Pesach* meal was not to be savored but devoured. Tuck your robes in your belt. Fasten your sandals. Stuff your mouth with one hand while gripping a staff in the other. Clean your plates, Moses says, in *chippazon* ("in haste"). Unleavened bread characterized this *chippazon* food, there being no time for dough to leaven (Deut. 16:3). Why? The Egyptians, fearing for their lives, "were urgent with the people to send them out of the land in haste" (12:33). Fast food for a fast exit from a land that had slowly been killing them. Israel had to get out while the gettin' was good.

How different, Isaiah prophesies, will be the exodus of exoduses, when the Lord's anointed servant brings good news, publishes peace and salvation, and says to Zion, "Your God reigns" (52:7). In the saving, worldwide exodus in Jesus, "you shall not go out in *chippazon* ['in haste']" (v. 12). Why? "The LORD will go before you, and the God of Israel will be your rear guard." There is no need for haste. None can pursue us now. All our foes lay conquered and dead in the tomb he left behind.

Make haste, O God, to deliver us, that we might rest securely and peacefully in your finished work.

Safe Behind the Blood פסח

"THE BLOOD SHALL BE A SIGN FOR YOU, ON THE HOUSES
WHERE YOU ARE. AND WHEN I SEE THE BLOOD, I WILL
PASS OVER YOU, AND NO PLAGUE WILL BEFALL YOU TO
DESTROY YOU, WHEN I STRIKE THE LAND OF EGYPT."

EXODUS 12:13

God sent "the destroyer" (12:23) to kill the Egyptian firstborn. Seeing the blood on the Israelite doors, however, God *pasach* them. In other contexts, *pasach* means to become lame (2 Sam. 4:4) or to limp or dance around an altar (1 Kings 18:26). While usually translated as "pass over," we should probably imagine God leaping over the homes of the Israelites. However we envision it, the verb *pasach* generated the noun *Pesach*, which we usually call Passover. Whatever name we give it, one truth is certain: on that night, God's people were safe behind the blood.

And so are we, "for Christ, our Passover lamb, has been sacrificed" (1 Cor. 5:7). When we are "baptized into his death" (Rom. 6:3), it is sprinkled on our hearts (Heb. 10:22) in a new and better covenant (cf. Exod. 24:8). "The life of the flesh is in the blood" (Lev. 17:11), and that life-giving blood of Jesus is on and in us. We are safe behind the blood of "the Lamb of God, who takes away the sin of the world" (John 1:29).

O Lord, our shield, protect us by your blood, that we may pass from death to life.

Firstborn בכור

THE LORD SAID TO MOSES, "CONSECRATE TO ME
ALL THE FIRSTBORN. WHATEVER IS THE FIRST TO
OPEN THE WOMB AMONG THE PEOPLE OF ISRAEL,
BOTH OF MAN AND OF BEAST, IS MINE."

EXODUS 13:1-2

God flips cultural norms upside down. Although a *b'kor* ("firstborn") was the heir of a double portion and the beginning of a man's strength (Deut. 21:17), the Lord repeatedly handpicked the younger brother. He chose Abel over Cain, Jacob over Esau, Judah over Reuben, Ephraim over Manasseh, David over his brothers. The *b'kor* was still important to him—indeed, it belonged to him—but the Lord prefers to do things backward. The *b'kor* may be the beginning of a man's strength, but God, from the beginning, "chose what is weak in the world to shame the strong" (1 Cor. 1:27).

Christ is, on the one hand, the "firstborn of all creation" (Col. 1:15), "firstborn from the dead" (v. 18), and the founder of "the assembly of the firstborn" (Heb. 12:23). But on the other hand, he is the second-born Adam. As Paul writes, "The first man Adam became a living being; the last Adam became a life-giving spirit" (1 Cor. 15:45). Jesus, this "younger Adam," the head of a new humanity, is the last in the long line of younger brothers. Our Father, through the Messiah's shameful death in mortal weakness, bequeaths to us the inheritance of unending life.

Christ, our Brother, watch over us and keep us as members of your beloved family.

Cloud עָנָן

AND THE LORD WENT BEFORE THEM BY DAY IN A
PILLAR OF CLOUD TO LEAD THEM ALONG THE WAY, AND
BY NIGHT IN A PILLAR OF FIRE TO GIVE THEM LIGHT,
THAT THEY MIGHT TRAVEL BY DAY AND BY NIGHT.

EXODUS 13:21

Almost every time an *anan* ("cloud") is in the Bible, God is visiting the neighborhood. The divine archer hung his retired bow in the clouds (Gen. 9:13). The *anan* on Sinai, which wrapped round the mountain (Exod. 24:15), was also his megaphone to call to Moses (v. 16). The Lord's cloud of glory housed itself within both the tabernacle (Exod. 40:35) and later the temple (1 Kings 8:10–11). He makes clouds the onesie of the newborn sea (Job 38:9). And as Israel traversed the wilderness, the Lord's cloudy pillar guided them by day, and his fiery pillar by night. We associate clouds with shade or rain or funny shapes. But for Israel, clouds were God's mouthpiece, signs, and clothing.

Thus during Jesus' transfiguration, when a cloud appeared, there was no doubt the Father was on the doorstep. "A bright cloud overshadowed them, and a voice from the cloud said, 'This is my beloved Son, with whom I am well pleased; listen to him'" (Matt. 17:5). Jesus ascended into a cloud (Acts 1:9) and he will return "in the clouds" (1 Thess. 4:17), for he is the Father's Word, his promise, and his presence for us.

O Christ, guide us, your church, through the wilderness of this world.

Buried and Born at Sea ים סוף

PHARAOH'S CHARIOTS AND HIS HOST HE CAST INTO THE SEA, AND HIS CHOSEN OFFICERS WERE SUNK IN THE RED SEA.

EXODUS 15:4

The Red Sea is the *yam suf*. A *yam* is a sea, and *suf* is a reed or other water plant. For instance, Moses' mother set his miniark "among the *suf* [reeds]" by the Nile to save him from Pharaoh (Exod. 2:3). Now, eighty years later, God will use this same Moses both to save Israel through the waters and to entomb Pharaoh and his army in the sea of *suf*. Likewise, as Miriam, the sister of Moses, stood by the Nile and spoke to Pharaoh's daughter on her brother's behalf (2:7), she also stands by this body of water and proclaims against Pharaoh, "Sing to the Lord, for he has triumphed gloriously; the horse and his rider he has thrown into the sea" (15:21).

"All were baptized into Moses in the cloud and in the sea," Paul says (1 Cor. 10:2). The *yam suf* was one massive baptismal body bag as well as the liquid womb of life. We are both buried and born at sea. Israel was baptized into Moses there as we "are baptized into Christ Jesus" (Rom. 6:3). The "old Pharaoh" within us drowns; we emerge on the other side of the baptismal *yam suf* alive in the resurrected Jesus.

Drown in us, O Lord, all sinful passions, and raise us up by your forgiving mercy.

Torah and Bitter Waters ירה

WHEN THEY CAME TO MARAH, THEY COULD NOT DRINK
THE WATER OF MARAH BECAUSE IT WAS BITTER;
THEREFORE IT WAS NAMED MARAH. AND THE PEOPLE
GRUMBLED AGAINST MOSES, SAYING, "WHAT SHALL
WE DRINK?" AND HE CRIED TO THE LORD, AND THE
LORD SHOWED HIM A LOG, AND HE THREW IT INTO
THE WATER, AND THE WATER BECAME SWEET.

EXODUS 15:23–25

The *mar* ("bitter") water at Marah elicited the first desert bellyaching. But if the Red Sea taught Israel that the Lord is their Warrior (15:3), then Marah taught them that he is their Teacher and Healer. What did God do? He "showed" Moses a tree. This verb for "show," *yarah*, is also the root of Torah, the "showing" or "teaching" from God. The tree sweetened the waters, and all was well.

But notice: immediately afterward, God tells Israel to "diligently listen to the voice of the LORD your God . . . I am the LORD, your healer" (15:26). The Torah, God's wisdom, is likened elsewhere to the "tree of life" (Prov. 3:18). God's people are diligently to listen to what he *yara* or "*Torah*-ed" them, for his healing word cares for us in this bitter world. Indeed, when the Word himself, Christ as incarnate Torah, hung on the tree of the cross, he became healing for all humanity and bestowed on us the sweetness of life.

Heavenly Father, who forgives all iniquity, who heals all our diseases, forgive and heal us through the crucified Christ.

The What-Is-It Bread מָן

WHEN THE PEOPLE OF ISRAEL SAW IT, THEY SAID TO
ONE ANOTHER, "WHAT IS IT?" FOR THEY DID NOT KNOW
WHAT IT WAS. AND MOSES SAID TO THEM, "IT IS THE
BREAD THAT THE LORD HAS GIVEN YOU TO EAT." . . .
NOW THE HOUSE OF ISRAEL CALLED ITS NAME MANNA.

EXODUS 16:15, 31

The Sinai wilderness is the anti-Eden, a "howling waste" (Deut. 32:10). In this godforsaken land, Israel's grumbling begins anew. The people are so famished that they wish God had just executed them in Egypt (16:3). So the Lord steps in. He transforms badlands into a bread shop. Dew falls, it evaporates, and left behind is a "fine, flake-like thing," spread like icing on the ground (16:14). Unaware of what it is, the people ask, *man hu* ("What is it?"). And that question christens the food: *man hu* is given the name *man* (the longer spelling, manna, is from the Aramaic and Greek translations).

"Your fathers ate the manna in the wilderness," Jesus says, "and they died" (John 6:49). Manna was a fine daily bread, but carbs are not Christ. He is "the bread that comes down from heaven, so that one may eat of it and not die" (6:50). Whoever feeds on the bread of his flesh and drinks his blood has eternal life, and Christ will raise him up on the last day (6:54).

Lord, Holy One of God, to whom shall we go? You have the words, and the bread, of eternal life (John 6:68).

Putting Sin
on the Map נסה

AND HE CALLED THE NAME OF THE PLACE MASSAH
AND MERIBAH, BECAUSE OF THE QUARRELING OF THE
PEOPLE OF ISRAEL, AND BECAUSE THEY TESTED THE
LORD BY SAYING, "IS THE LORD AMONG US OR NOT?"

EXODUS 17:7

Biblical names often tell a story. In the wilderness, those stories are frequently ugly. When God's fire burned up rebels, the place was Taberah ("burning" Num. 11:1-3). When greedy Israelites died during a plague, that place was Kibroth-hattaavah ("graves of greediness" 11:33-34). So here when Israel engaged in a *riv* ("strife or dispute") with God, and *nasah* ("tested") him, the location was forever stamped Meribah (from *riv*) and Massah (from *nasah*). Israel literally put sin on the map.

"Do not harden your hearts, as at Meribah, as on the day at Massah in the wilderness," the psalmist says (95:8). Those hard hearts prompted God to swear, "They shall not enter my rest" (v. 11). Indeed, they did not, but their "bodies fell in the wilderness" due to their unbelief (Heb. 3:17). There remains, however, "a Sabbath rest for the people of God" (4:9), a rest won for us by the Messiah. He, our greater Joshua, leads us into the promised land of the Father's rest, for his saving work mapped out life and hope for us.

Keep us far from testing and striving with you, O Lord, that we may draw near to your throne of grace with confidence to receive rest in your kingdom.

The King's Personal Property סגלה

"NOW THEREFORE, IF YOU WILL INDEED OBEY
MY VOICE AND KEEP MY COVENANT, YOU SHALL
BE MY TREASURED POSSESSION AMONG ALL
PEOPLES, FOR ALL THE EARTH IS MINE."

EXODUS 19:5

When Solomon referred to his vast treasures of silver and gold, he said it was his *s'gullah* (Eccles. 2:8). David likewise called the precious metals he had contributed for the temple's construction his *s'gullah* (1 Chron. 29:3). *S'gullah*, like its parallels in other ancient languages, means personal property. This is what Israel was to God: his "*s'gullah* among all peoples," his "treasured possession" or personal property. "Out of all the peoples who are on the face of the earth," God chose them for his *s'gullah* (Deut. 7:6; 14:2). When the Lord opened his treasure chest, he was looking at the face of Israel.

Jesus Christ "gave himself for us to redeem us from all lawlessness and to purify for himself a people for his own possession who are zealous for good works" (Titus 2:14). In God's Messiah, we are the Israel of God, "a chosen race, a royal priesthood, a holy nation, a people for his own possession, that [we] may proclaim the excellencies of him who called [us] out of darkness into his marvelous light" (1 Pet. 2:9). When Christ opens his treasure chest, he's looking at the face of his bride, the church.

As your treasured people, O Lord, show us your mercy and keep us ever zealous to do good works for our neighbors.

The Ten Words עֲשֶׂרֶת הַדְּבָרִים

SO [MOSES] WAS THERE WITH THE LORD FORTY DAYS
AND FORTY NIGHTS. HE NEITHER ATE BREAD NOR
DRANK WATER. AND HE WROTE ON THE TABLETS THE
WORDS OF THE COVENANT, THE TEN COMMANDMENTS.

EXODUS 34:28

A great irony about the Bible is that the Ten Commandments, arguably the most well-known section, are never called the Ten Commandments in the Bible itself. Where they are numbered at "ten" (Exod. 34:28; Deut. 4:13; 10:4), they are not called ten *mitzvot* (the Hebrew word for "commandments") but *Aseret Had'varim*, "the ten words." However we divide these seventeen verses (20:1-17) into "ten words"—itself a centuries-long disagreement—they summon us to trust in God; to love him with all our heart, soul, and mind; and to love our neighbor as ourselves. And however we divide and number them, this much is beyond doubt: the total number we've kept is a big, fat zero.

Martin Luther famously wrote, "The law says, 'do this,' and it is never done. Grace says, 'believe in this,' and everything is already done." Every spark of shalt or shalt not that enters a sinner's ear kindles a fire of rebellion in his heart. The law is never done. But Christ, who fulfilled the law, graciously proclaims, "It is finished" (John 19:30). We are free, forgiven, and fully alive in Christ Jesus.

Keep us free, O Lord, that we may stand firm and not submit again to a yoke of slavery (Gal. 5:1).

Graven Images פֶּסֶל

"YOU SHALL NOT MAKE FOR YOURSELF A CARVED IMAGE, OR ANY LIKENESS OF ANYTHING THAT IS IN HEAVEN ABOVE, OR THAT IS IN THE EARTH BENEATH, OR THAT IS IN THE WATER UNDER THE EARTH."

EXODUS 20:4

In 63 BC, when the Roman general Pompey captured Jerusalem and entered the temple, he must have been surprised to find no image of God. His surprise would have been shared by any person in the ancient world. All deities had their statues, poles, carvings, or images, which served as a kind of visual rendezvous between the gods and their worshipers.

Not Yahweh. Every "carved image" or *pesel* (from the verb *pasal*, "carve, hew, cut, sculpt") of God was banned on pain of death. Images of angels, oxen, and flowers were in the temple, but not Israel's Lord. Why? Because he had not yet given them his image.

But in Christ, he did. The Messiah "is the image of the invisible God" (Col. 1:15). To see him is to see the Father (John 14:9), "for in him the whole fullness of deity dwells bodily" (Col. 2:9). Hidden in the prohibition against "images of God" is the promise of God giving us his image in his Son, who "is the radiance of the glory of God and the exact imprint of his nature" (Heb. 1:3).

O Christ, the image and glory of the Father, transform us into your image from one degree of glory to another.

Hallowed Not Hollowed שׁוא

"YOU SHALL NOT TAKE THE NAME OF THE LORD
YOUR GOD IN VAIN, FOR THE LORD WILL NOT HOLD
HIM GUILTLESS WHO TAKES HIS NAME IN VAIN."

EXODUS 20:7

To "take [*nasa*] the name" is shorthand for "to take the name of God upon the lips." Thus the psalmist says he will not take (*nasa*) the names of other gods upon his lips (Ps. 16:4). The expression "in vain" is "in *shav*." To be *shav* is to be empty, vain, worthless, unreal—to take God's name upon one's lips emptily, worthlessly, trivially. Since *shav* also refers to idols, using God's name in *shav* entails magic or false prophecy. Basically, God wants his name to be hallowed (treated as holy), not hollowed (treated as empty).

The right use of God's name is integrally connected with God's mission. "As is your name, O God, so is Your praise to the ends of the earth" (Ps. 48:10 NASB). The Lord wants his name "proclaimed in all the earth" (Exod. 9:16). So he protects that name, lest it be belittled or besmirched, and occasion given to the enemies of the Lord to blaspheme his name (cf. 2 Sam. 12:14). He writes his name on baptism (Matt. 28:19). He proclaims his name through preachers (Luke 24:47). And he gives us Jesus the Messiah, who is his embodied and glorified name (John 12:28).

"Our Father in heaven, hallowed be your name . . . on earth as it is in heaven" (Matt. 6:9–10).

God's Favorite Number שֶׁבַע

"SIX DAYS YOU SHALL LABOR, AND DO ALL
YOUR WORK, BUT THE SEVENTH DAY IS A
SABBATH TO THE LORD YOUR GOD."

EXODUS 20:9–10

If God has a favorite number, it's *sheva* ("seven"). The opening sentence of the Bible is seven Hebrew words. He completed his work of creation on the seventh day (Gen. 2:2). This law about the seventh day begins with the seventh letter of the Hebrew alphabet (*zayin*). Seven categories of humans and animals rest on the Sabbath (you, son, daughter, male servant, female servant, livestock, sojourner). Later, God will establish the spring festival of Shavuot ("weeks," a word derived from *sheva*). God's number is seven. We might say that as Father, Son, and Holy Spirit, his number of completeness and totality and perfection is 777.

The number of sinful humanity ("of a man"), however, and of every anti-God power ("of the beast") is 666 (Rev. 13:18). This number is not mystical but pathetic: it's man aping God, the devil straining toward divinity. But we are a falling-short, imperfect 666, and he is a perfect and complete 777. He is God and we are not.

Yet our perfect God also perfectly loves us. He forgives us seventy times seven—and beyond. By joining us to Christ, who rested in the tomb on the seventh day, he brings us into wholeness in his resurrection perfection.

O Lord, "seven times a day I praise You, because of your righteous ordinances" (Ps. 119:164 NASB).

Living Long in the Land ארך

"HONOR YOUR FATHER AND YOUR MOTHER,
THAT YOUR DAYS MAY BE LONG IN THE LAND
THAT THE LORD YOUR GOD IS GIVING YOU."

EXODUS 20:12

The same phrase, "the LORD your God," occurs in the first four "words" or commandments of Exodus 20. Honoring one's parents, therefore, is the bridge between the first and second table of the law. To honor our Father in heaven entails honoring his parental icons on earth. Since the Hebrew verb *kavad* ("honor") literally means "be heavy or weighty," we might say, "Treat your parents with weighty significance" or "Don't make light of your parents." Paul reminds us that this "is the first commandment with a promise" (Eph. 6:2)—namely, that your days will be *arak* ("made long") in the land.

In the OT, the land is the kingdom of God, where the Father reigns over, blesses, and protects his children. For one's days to be *arak* is not simply to shoot for one hundred candles on your cake, but to live a full, blessed, God-soaked life in his kingdom. This long kingdom life was a foretaste of the resurrection, for the Messiah himself, after suffering, will "prolong [*arak*] his days" (Isa. 53:10). Having honored his Father and given himself as an offering for our guilt, he rises to prolong his days in the resurrection kingdom in which we, his brothers and sisters, share.

Heavenly Father, give us grace to love and honor you, along with our earthly parents.

Killing Mosquitoes and Men רצח

"YOU SHALL NOT MURDER."

EXODUS 20:13

Despite its many literary home runs, the KJV struck out in translating this "Thou shalt not kill." Hebrew has a verb for kill, *harag*, but that is not used here. *Harag* is a broad term, used to describe killing people (Gen. 4:8) or animals (Lev. 20:15). The verb used in Exodus 20 is *ratzach*. One frequently hears that *ratzach* refers only to murder, but that is not correct either. It does refer to murder (Ps. 94:6), but it also refers to manslaughter or accidental killings (Num. 35:6). Whatever the situation or motivation, however, to *ratzach* is always to take a human life. One cannot *ratzach* a mosquito. *Ratzach* is also never used for soldiers killing in combat or for when God or his agents exact the death penalty.

To *ratzach* is of ultimate seriousness, because the victim is of ultimate significance. "Whoever sheds the blood of man," God says, "by man shall his blood be shed, for God made man in his own image" (Gen. 9:6). To *ratzach* is to de-image God's image-bearer. This underscores all the more how merciful the Father has been to us in his Son: our shedding of his blood, rather than being the world's end, is the world's new beginning. In the *ratzach* of the Messiah, we are redeemed.

Father, forgive us for all the times we have hurt or harmed our neighbors, and enable us to help and support them in love.

The Great Sin נאף

"YOU SHALL NOT COMMIT ADULTERY."

EXODUS 20:14

When God warned Abimelech not to have sex with Sarah, the king complained that Abraham's lies had almost brought on him and his kingdom "a great sin" (Gen. 20:9). In calling this "a great sin," Abimelech was echoing the name given to adultery in many ancient law codes. In the OT, to *na'af* is not merely to have illicit sexual intercourse, but to engage in intercourse with someone who is not your spouse.

Many references to *na'af*, however, are not about sex but idolatry. In fact, the four other occurrences of "a great sin" refer to Aaron's golden calf (Exod. 32:21, 30–31) and Jeroboam's idolatrous calves (2 Kings 17:21). This accords with the graphic oft-repeated image of Israel "whoring after other gods." This commandment, therefore, and the first commandment, are two sides of the same coin: worship *only* the Lord and have sex *only* with your spouse.

How fitting, therefore, that when Paul depicts the church's connection with the Messiah, he says that the church is Christ's bride. The twofold "great sin"—idolatry and adultery—having been atoned for by Jesus, we both wed and worship our heavenly Groom. "He remains faithful—for he cannot deny himself" (2 Tim. 2:13). Our great sin is no match for his greater redemption.

Our faithful and forgiving Lord, cleanse us of every defilement by sin, that we may lead holy and faithful lives in service to you and others.

Sticky Fingers and Stolen Hearts גנב

"YOU SHALL NOT STEAL."

EXODUS 20:15

There's remarkable overlap between the many nuances of the English verb "steal" and the Hebrew *ganav*. As teenagers "steal [go sneakily] into the house" when they're out past curfew, so men shamefully *ganav* into the city like cowards fleeing a battle (2 Sam. 19:3). We say a man "stole a woman's heart," like Absalom *"ganav* the hearts of the men of Israel" (2 Sam. 15:6). And in both Hebrew and English, kidnapping is theft or *ganav* of a person (Exod. 21:16). The command not to *ganav* is to look on, and treat, what God has bestowed on another person as his gift to them, not our entitlement or potential possession.

It is a great irony that the authorities feared the early Christians would steal the body of Jesus, thus faking the resurrection (Matt. 27:64). This very Messiah had taught that "the thief comes only to steal and kill and destroy. I came that they may have life and have it abundantly" (John 10:10). That abundant life he gives us in his resurrection. And that life bears the fruits of love in our actions. So Paul writes, "Let the thief no longer steal, but rather let him labor, doing honest work with his own hands, so that he may have something to share with anyone in need" (Eph. 4:28).

O Holy Spirit, root out of our hearts the weeds of greed and sow in us the seeds of contentment.

False Witness שֶׁקֶר

"YOU SHALL NOT BEAR FALSE WITNESS
AGAINST YOUR NEIGHBOR."

EXODUS 20:16

In Israel, this law prohibited playing fast and loose with the truth in judicial proceedings. To "bear" is to *anah* ("answer") and *'ed shaqer* is a lying witness. We might paraphrase it: When you testify before the judges concerning your neighbor, don't be a lying witness. Proverbs describes two types of witnesses: "A faithful witness does not lie, but a *'ed shaqer* breathes out lies" (14:5). This exhalation of evil is echoed in the psalms, where false witnesses "breathe out violence" (27:12). Sticks and stones may break my bones, but words break hearts, souls, reputations, livelihoods. No one can tame the tongue, James reminds us, for "it is a restless evil, full of deadly poison" (3:8). The devil's first move was to speak.

When the Truth is embodied in Jesus, lies wage war. His archnemesis is "the father of lies" (John 8:44). "Many bore false witness against him" after the Messiah's arrest, though they couldn't even keep their lies straight (Mark 14:55-59). They breathed out lies, they exhaled violence, until finally the crucified Christ of Truth "breathed his last" (Luke 23:46). But that was only the beginning. Standing alive again, outside his tomb, is "Jesus Christ the faithful witness, the firstborn of the dead, and the ruler of kings on earth" (Rev. 1:5).

"Lead me in your truth and teach me, for you are the God of my salvation; for you I wait all the day long" (Ps. 25:5).

Grasping Not Grounding חמד

"YOU SHALL NOT COVET YOUR NEIGHBOR'S HOUSE; YOU SHALL NOT COVET YOUR NEIGHBOR'S WIFE, OR HIS MALE SERVANT, OR HIS FEMALE SERVANT, OR HIS OX, OR HIS DONKEY, OR ANYTHING THAT IS YOUR NEIGHBOR'S."

EXODUS 20:17

Though we usually call it "the fall," Adam and Eve's sin was grasping, not grounding. Eve stretched out a grasping, coveting hand. She saw that the "tree was to be desired [*chamad*] to make one wise" (3:6). The verb *chamad* is ambiguous: God's laws are to be *chamad* (Ps. 19:10), but you shall not *chamad* anything of your neighbor's (Exod. 20:17). We all know desire can be sweet honey or bitter poison. In this commandment, it's obviously the latter, but the verb *chamad* is a reminder that sins are often misdirected desires. Coveting is directing God-given desire at the wrong object, just as lust is directing God-given sexual desire at the wrong person.

Even the Lord is said to desire, for he *chamad* Zion "for his abode" (Ps. 68:16). But when God sent his Messiah to that abode, "he had no form or majesty that we should look at him, and no beauty that we should desire [*chamad*] him" (Isa. 53:2). He was "as one from whom men hide their faces" (v. 3). But he desires us! And he will have us, for God's greatest desire is to call us his beloved.

O Lord, hear the desire of the afflicted; strengthen their heart; incline your ear (Ps. 10:17).

Full-Bodied Worship חוה

THEN HE SAID TO MOSES, "COME UP TO THE LORD, YOU
AND AARON, NADAB, AND ABIHU, AND SEVENTY OF
THE ELDERS OF ISRAEL, AND WORSHIP FROM AFAR."

EXODUS 24:1

Worship in Hebrew is not just adoration in the head or praise in the heart; it's full-bodied. To *chavah* is to put one's face to the ground, before either God (in worship) or people (in respect). When Abraham saw three visitors approaching, he ran to meet them and "bowed himself [*chavah*] to the earth" (Gen. 18:2; cf. 19:1). God tells Moses at Sinai to "*chavah* from afar" (Exod. 24:1). When the Lord caused his glory to pass before Moses, he "quickly bowed his head toward the earth and *chavah*" (34:8). Hebrew destroys any false notion that humans are just "brains on a stick," as James K. A. Smith puts it, or souls trapped in bodies. Rather, as embodied images of God, we worship our Creator with the totality of who we are—knees, arms, chest, feet, and face included.

The same physicality of worship is continued in the NT. When the Magi see Jesus, they "fell down and worshiped him" (Matt. 2:11). When praying to his Father, Jesus himself "fell on his face and prayed" (26:39). The physicality of worship is itself a confession that our bodies are the gifts of God, with which we serve, worship, and praise him.

Heavenly Father, Creator of our bodies, grant that we may worship you with all of who we are.

The Blood of the Covenant דם הברית

MOSES TOOK THE BLOOD AND THREW IT ON THE PEOPLE AND SAID, "BEHOLD THE BLOOD OF THE COVENANT THAT THE LORD HAS MADE WITH YOU IN ACCORDANCE WITH ALL THESE WORDS."

EXODUS 24:8

This is the only time blood is sprinkled on the Israelites. The closest parallel is at the ordination of Aaron and his sons as priests, when blood is daubed on their ears, thumbs, and big toes (29:20). Since "the life of the flesh is in the blood," and that blood "makes atonement" (Lev. 17:11), God is literally sprinkling life and atonement on his people. By blood, he is making them a "kingdom of priests and a holy nation" (Exod. 19:6). This *dam ha-b'rit* ("blood of the covenant") cements them to himself as his chosen people.

When Jesus gives his disciples the cup on his final Passover, he says, "this is my blood of the covenant, which is poured out for many for the forgiveness of sins" (Matt. 26:28). The parallel is unmistakable. Rather than sprinkling blood on us externally, Christ sprinkles his blood inside us as we drink from his cup, so that "our hearts [are] sprinkled clean from an evil conscience" (Heb. 10:22); we are given the life of God, ordained as his kingdom of priests (1 Pet. 2:5, 9), and made part of the new covenant of God's chosen people (Heb. 12:24).

Sprinkle our hearts with your blood, O Christ, that we may be clean and forgiven, ready for service.

God Goes Tent Camping שָׁכַן

THE GLORY OF THE LORD DWELT ON MOUNT
SINAI, AND THE CLOUD COVERED IT SIX DAYS.
AND ON THE SEVENTH DAY HE CALLED TO
MOSES OUT OF THE MIDST OF THE CLOUD.

EXODUS 24:16

The Lord is not some far-off, hands-off deity in a celestial resort a million miles away. He's in the thick of things, pitching his tent among his people. The Lord's glory *shakan* on Sinai. To *shakan* is to settle, reside, pitch a tent. At this point, Mt. Sinai is God's tent. Its peak is like the Holy of Holies (where only one man, Moses, can go); its slopes are like the Holy Place (where a few, like the priests, can go); and its base is like the fore-court and area around the tabernacle (where the Israelites worship). When God's tent—the tabernacle—is built, it will be a portable Sinai. God's glory cloud will fill it (Exod. 40:34), as that same cloud enveloped Sinai. Every Israelite knew where God had located himself. They knew precisely where to find him.

When the Father's Word became flesh, he pitched his tent (tabernacled) among us (John 1:14). "We have seen his glory," John adds. The glory of God is no longer in a tent but a man. The Messiah is where God has located himself, where we find him. Indeed, the Messiah is Yahweh embodied. He is Emmanuel, God-with-us.

O come, O come, Emmanuel, and dwell among us, that we may find mercy and holiness in you.

Follow the Blueprint תבנית

"AND LET THEM MAKE ME A SANCTUARY, THAT I MAY DWELL IN THEIR MIDST. EXACTLY AS I SHOW YOU CONCERNING THE PATTERN OF THE TABERNACLE, AND OF ALL ITS FURNITURE, SO YOU SHALL MAKE IT."

EXODUS 25:8-9

Any architect will tell you that a sloppy blueprint leads to shoddy construction. God is having none of that. Moses is to ensure every item is made exactly according to "the pattern [*tavnit*]" God shows him. A *tavnit* is a copy, model, image, or plan. The Lord, as it were, has a model that he shows Moses. "Make it like this," he says, "down to the finest detail." When it's done, there will not be two tabernacles—one up in heaven, and one down on earth—but both will exist inside each other: one visible, one invisible. Thus when Isaiah sees the Lord in his temple, he's still on earth, in Jerusalem, only now his eyes are unveiled to gaze on the reality that was there all along (6:1ff.). Worship is heaven on earth. The earthly tabernacle is the heavenly tabernacle, and vice versa.

It is no different today when the church gathers in worship. We are surrounded by angels and saints. Christ and his Father are there with the Spirit. We don't really begin worship but join in the ongoing worship around the throne of God and of the Lamb. We "have come to Mount Zion" (Heb. 12:22).

Direct our hearts, O Lord, to worship you in spirit and in truth.

The Covenant Chest ארון

"THEY SHALL MAKE AN ARK OF ACACIA WOOD.
TWO CUBITS AND A HALF SHALL BE ITS
LENGTH, A CUBIT AND A HALF ITS BREADTH,
AND A CUBIT AND A HALF ITS HEIGHT."

EXODUS 25:10

Though both are translated as "ark," Noah had a *tevah* ("boat") and the tabernacle had an *aron* ("box"). The word *aron* can refer to a coffin (Gen. 50:26) or money chest (2 Kings 12:10). But the vast majority of OT references are to the *aron* of the covenant, so called because the two tables of the law or covenant were deposited inside it (25:16). Thus the "ark of the covenant" is shorthand for "the chest that contained the covenant documents." David also calls the *aron* "the footstool of our God" (1 Chron. 28:2), over which he was enthroned as the divine King of Israel.

The ark of the covenant disappeared around 587 BC, when the Babylonians conquered Jerusalem and razed the temple. When the Messiah came, the Holy of Holies held no ark. Perhaps that was fitting anyway, for the true ark had landed. He was in Mary's womb, then grew into a man—this one in whom God's law resided. Covered not in gold but flesh and blood, he would not be a footstool but would reign alongside his Father, who would make his "enemies [his] footstool" (Ps. 110:1).

Arise, O Lord Jesus, and go to your resting place beside the Father, for you are the ark of our strength (Ps. 132:8)

The Atonement Lid כפרת

"YOU SHALL MAKE A MERCY SEAT OF PURE GOLD . . .
AND YOU SHALL MAKE TWO CHERUBIM OF GOLD; OF
HAMMERED WORK SHALL YOU MAKE THEM, ON THE
TWO ENDS OF THE MERCY SEAT . . . AND YOU SHALL
PUT THE MERCY SEAT ON THE TOP OF THE ARK,
AND IN THE ARK YOU SHALL PUT THE TESTIMONY
THAT I SHALL GIVE YOU. THERE I WILL MEET WITH
YOU, AND FROM ABOVE THE MERCY SEAT."

EXODUS 25:17-18, 21-22

Chests have lids, and the "covenant chest" was no exception. Its *kapporet* or lid, though often translated "mercy seat," is from the verb *kapar*, which means to cover or atone for. Thus a *kapporet* is an atonement cover. Two golden cherubim, their wings outstretched, faced each other across the *kapporet*. Here too the blood of sacrifice was sprinkled on Yom Kippur ("Day of Atonement"—*kippur* too being formed from *kapar*). This was indeed the seat of divine mercy, for from "above the *kapporet*," Yahweh met with Moses to relay his words to Israel.

Paul tells us that we "are justified by his grace as a gift, through the redemption that is in Christ Jesus, whom God put forward as a propitiation by his blood" (Rom. 3:24-25). The Greek for "propitiation" is *hilasterion*, the word used to translate the Hebrew *kapporet*. The Father put forward his Son as our atonement cover. In the Messiah, God meets us and gives us mercy.

Lord, draw us into your holy place and cover us with your mercy.

Bread of the Face לחם פנים

"YOU SHALL MAKE A TABLE OF ACACIA WOOD.
TWO CUBITS SHALL BE ITS LENGTH, A CUBIT ITS
BREADTH, AND A CUBIT AND A HALF ITS HEIGHT . . .
AND YOU SHALL SET THE BREAD OF THE PRESENCE
ON THE TABLE BEFORE ME REGULARLY."

EXODUS 25:23, 30

Bread, *lechem*, is the elemental food staple of the Hebrews. Israelites would have found the petition "Give us this day our daily bread" perfectly fitting to their needs and lifestyle. As his people had bread in their tents, so God had bread on his table inside his tent. Older translations called this "show-bread." It's the *lechem panim*: literally, "bread of the face." When we're in front of someone's face, we are in their presence—so *panim* means presence. This bread, being in front of God's face, was holy. Every Sabbath, the twelve loaves were eaten by the priests (as representatives of the twelve tribes) and replaced with a dozen more. They consumed bread suffused with the holy presence of God. They ingested sanctification.

The Lord used many meals in Israel's history as the backdrop (hors d'oeuvres, if you will) for the meal of meals that he has given his church. We now gather around God's table to eat the bread filled with the presence of Christ. "Take, eat; this is my body," the Messiah says (Matt. 26:26). We ingest his holiness.

Heavenly Father, give us this day, and every day, the Bread of life, Jesus our Savior.

The Illuminating Tree of Life מנורה

"YOU SHALL MAKE A LAMPSTAND OF PURE GOLD.
THE LAMPSTAND SHALL BE MADE OF HAMMERED
WORK: ITS BASE, ITS STEM, ITS CUPS, ITS CALYXES,
AND ITS FLOWERS SHALL BE OF ONE PIECE WITH IT."

EXODUS 25:31

Though Adam and Eve were barred from the tree of life in God's sacred garden (Gen. 3:24), the Lord provided a substitute tree for their descendants in his tabernacle. His sanctuary was a new Eden in the midst of a fallen world. Flora and fauna, as from a garden, adorned its tent curtains. And in its holy place, there was a *menorah* ("lampstand"), with branches, as from a tree, coming out either side. The *menorah* was the replacement tree of life, illuminating God's Eden-like sanctuary with the flaming fruit of light.

The OT *menorah*, iconic of light and life, became symbolic of both God's Spirit (Rev. 4:5) and his churches (Rev. 1:20). The Spirit "has shone in our hearts to give the light of the knowledge of the glory of God in the face of Jesus Christ" (2 Cor. 4:6). And as Christ's church, we let that light "shine before others, so that they may see [our] good works and give glory to [our] Father who is in heaven" (Matt. 5:16). We reflect the Messiah, "the light of the world" (John 9:5), who turned the tree of the cross into the tree of life.

"Lift up the light of your face upon us, O Lord!" (Ps. 4:6).

The Veil פָּרֹכֶת

"AND YOU SHALL MAKE A VEIL OF BLUE AND PURPLE
AND SCARLET YARNS AND FINE TWINED LINEN. IT
SHALL BE MADE WITH CHERUBIM SKILLFULLY WORKED
INTO IT . . . AND THE VEIL SHALL SEPARATE FOR
YOU THE HOLY PLACE FROM THE MOST HOLY."

EXODUS 26:31, 33

In creation, God divided (*badal*) this from that. He *badal* light from darkness (1:4); waters below from waters above (1:6); day from night (1:14). The verb recurs here for the veil *badal* the inner sanctum from the outer sanctum. The tabernacle is a minicosmos in which the Creator is putting everything in its proper place. The *paroket* ("veil") is a lavishly woven, angel-embroidered screen behind which is God's throne room, his "inner heaven" on earth. Only once annually, on the Day of Atonement, did the high priest enter this throne room, and never without blood (Heb. 9:7).

The ripping of the *paroket* during the crucifixion sacrifice of the great high priest, Jesus, meant that division was eradicated (Matt. 27:51). Two-way traffic was now allowed daily. God exited the temple to bring his glory to all nations, beginning at Jerusalem. And all nations, in Christ, enter the holy place by the blood of Jesus, because through the veil of his flesh, a new and living way was opened for us to enter God's presence (Heb. 10:19–20).

Christ, our great high priest over the house of God, give us confidence to come before you and your Father through the grace of your Spirit.

Christ's Vestments בגדי־קדֹשׁ

"THEN BRING NEAR TO YOU AARON YOUR BROTHER,
AND HIS SONS WITH HIM, FROM AMONG THE PEOPLE
OF ISRAEL, TO SERVE ME AS PRIESTS—AARON AND
AARON'S SONS, NADAB AND ABIHU, ELEAZAR AND
ITHAMAR. AND YOU SHALL MAKE HOLY GARMENTS FOR
AARON YOUR BROTHER, FOR GLORY AND FOR BEAUTY."

EXODUS 28:1-2

The *bigdey-qodesh* ("holy garments") of the priests were lifted from the closet of God's Son. In Isaiah's vision, the hem [*shul*] of the Lord's robe filled the temple (6:1)—the same word used to describe the hem of the high priest's robe (Exod. 28:33). And the Lord whom Isaiah saw was Jesus, for Isaiah "saw his glory and spoke of him" (John 12:41). Similarly, when John saw Christ in Revelation, in a temple-like setting full of menorahs, he was "clothed in a long robe and with a golden sash around his chest" (1:13). The same Greek words used in Revelation for "long robe" and "sash" are used in the Septuagint to translate the robe and sash of the high priest (Exod. 25:7; 28:4).

The glory and beauty of these *bigdey-qodesh* were the glory and beauty of the Messiah. The high priests of Israel were vested like Christ our "great priest over the house of God" (Heb. 10:21). Their vestments were vested with the prophecy of the one who would clothe us in his own righteousness.

O Lord Jesus, clothed with splendor and majesty, clothe us with righteousness that we may shout for joy (Ps. 104:1; 132:9).

O Lord, Smell
My Prayer קטרת

"YOU SHALL MAKE AN ALTAR ON WHICH TO BURN
INCENSE; YOU SHALL MAKE IT OF ACACIA WOOD . . .
AND YOU SHALL PUT IT IN FRONT OF THE VEIL
THAT IS ABOVE THE ARK OF THE TESTIMONY, IN
FRONT OF THE MERCY SEAT THAT IS ABOVE THE
TESTIMONY, WHERE I WILL MEET WITH YOU. AND
AARON SHALL BURN FRAGRANT INCENSE ON IT."

EXODUS 30:1, 6–7

A few days ago, we talked about how Hebrew worship was full-bodied. It was also fully sensory: worship was felt, tasted, heard, seen, and smelled. Incense, *q'toret*, involved those last two—sight and smell. Every morning and evening, a priest would burn *q'toret* on the altar directly in front of the veil that screened off the seat of atonement. "Let my prayer be counted as incense before you," the psalmist prayed (141:2), for incense was prayer made visible. Its odor wafted into God's nostrils, so that incense was also prayer made olfactory.

The petitions of Israel, fired by the Spirit, wafted in a cloud of incense in and around his throne of grace. So too in Revelation's heavenly worship there are "golden bowls full of incense, which are the prayers of the saints" (5:8). Our mouths, like censers, breathe out the incense of prayer, which Christ our high priest mingled with his own before the Father's throne.

"Let my prayer be counted as incense before you, and the lifting up of my hands as the evening sacrifice!" (Ps. 141:2).

Melting Down Mirrors כִּיּוֹר

THE LORD SAID TO MOSES, "YOU SHALL ALSO MAKE
A BASIN OF BRONZE, WITH ITS STAND OF BRONZE,
FOR WASHING. YOU SHALL PUT IT BETWEEN THE
TENT OF MEETING AND THE ALTAR, AND YOU SHALL
PUT WATER IN IT, WITH WHICH AARON AND HIS SONS
SHALL WASH THEIR HANDS AND THEIR FEET."

EXODUS 30:17-19

For priests safely to handle holy things and walk on holy ground, they needed to wash. Washing required a basin, so the *kiyyor* was constructed. It was made by melting down "the mirrors of the ministering women who ministered at the entrance of the tent of meeting" (Exod. 38:8). Who these women were, and what they did, we are never told, but their erstwhile mirrors became an object that still reflected—reflected the need for cleansing when one entered God's presence. Unwashed hands and feet were hazardous (30:20-21). This relatively small *kiyyor* would become the huge Bronze Sea at the temple, complete with multiple smaller washbasins on wheels (1 Kings 7:23-39).

Baptism is not just plain water but water with a sacred history. Part of that history is the bronze *kiyyor*. As fellow priests of Jesus, we enter God's presence. Not just our hands and feet but "our bodies [have been] washed with pure water" (10:22), through the "washing of regeneration and renewal of the Holy Spirit" (Titus 3:5), that we may mirror the Messiah.

O heavenly High Priest, "wash me thoroughly from my iniquity, and cleanse me from my sin!" (Ps. 51:2).

From Divine
to Bovine עגל מסכה

AND [AARON] RECEIVED THE GOLD FROM THEIR
HAND AND FASHIONED IT WITH A GRAVING TOOL
AND MADE A GOLDEN CALF. AND THEY SAID,
"THESE ARE YOUR GODS, O ISRAEL, WHO BROUGHT
YOU UP OUT OF THE LAND OF EGYPT!"

EXODUS 32:4

The Lord and his bride were still checked into their Sinai honeymoon suite when she started cheating on him. "Make us a god," the people demanded. And Aaron needed no arm-twisting. We get the impression this wasn't his first rodeo. In no time flat, he had the *egel massekah* ("molten calf") made. This was likely a wooden model overlaid with gold. An *egel* is a young ox, often depicted in ancient art as the platform for a deity—a god throne. Chances are that Israel, having sojourned for centuries in a land inebriated with idolatry, were replicating what they had eyed in the motherland. The Israelites were revealing just how Egyptified they were. One small step from divine to bovine for Aaron; one giant fall for Israel.

What saved the nation from immediate annihilation? Only the mediation of Moses. He pleaded for their lives and God relented (32:11-14). Indeed, God would relent and relent, century after century, until finally the Lamb would take care of Israel's (and our) sin once and for all.

Forgive us, dear Father, for all the times we have strayed from you to worship lies and deceptions. Have mercy and draw us back to you.

Breaking the Law, Literally לחת

THEN MOSES TURNED AND WENT DOWN FROM THE
MOUNTAIN WITH THE TWO TABLETS OF THE TESTIMONY
IN HIS HAND, TABLETS THAT WERE WRITTEN ON
BOTH SIDES; ON THE FRONT AND ON THE BACK THEY
WERE WRITTEN. THE TABLETS WERE THE WORK OF
GOD, AND THE WRITING WAS THE WRITING OF GOD,
ENGRAVED ON THE TABLETS . . . AND AS SOON AS
HE CAME NEAR THE CAMP AND SAW THE CALF AND
THE DANCING, MOSES' ANGER BURNED HOT, AND
HE THREW THE TABLETS OUT OF HIS HANDS AND
BROKE THEM AT THE FOOT OF THE MOUNTAIN.

EXODUS 32:15–16, 19

Moses didn't simply blow his top and start smashing things. His breaking of the *luchot* ("tablets") was a calculated, ritualistic act. Israel had broken the covenant, so Moses literally broke the tablets engraved with the covenant. These *luchot*—which can refer to tablets of stone, boards of wood, or plates of metal—were not massive stones, but smaller slabs, with Hebrew on the front and back. The law now lay in pieces on the ground.

That law, with its unfulfilled demands, would continue to compound a debt that sinners could not pay. But the Messiah could and did. He didn't shatter it on the ground; he "set [that record of debt] aside, nailing it to the cross," where it was paid in full with crimson currency (Col. 2:14).

Forgive us our debts, heavenly Father, and write your love and faithfulness on the tablet of our hearts (Prov. 3:3).

Seeing God's Backside אחור

AND THE LORD SAID, "BEHOLD, THERE IS A PLACE
BY ME WHERE YOU SHALL STAND ON THE ROCK,
AND WHILE MY GLORY PASSES BY I WILL PUT YOU
IN A CLEFT OF THE ROCK, AND I WILL COVER YOU
WITH MY HAND UNTIL I HAVE PASSED BY. THEN I
WILL TAKE AWAY MY HAND, AND YOU SHALL SEE
MY BACK, BUT MY FACE SHALL NOT BE SEEN."

EXODUS 33:21-23

When Moses requests a peek at God's glory, the Lord gives a qualified Yes. He will let his goodness pass by, proclaim his divine name, and blindfold Moses with his hand. Only then will Moses catch a glimpse. Rather than God's face, however, he'll spy his divine *achor* ("back" or "backside"). This odd procedure is necessary for Moses' survival, for the Lord says, "You cannot see my face, for man shall not see me and live" (33:20). When God's goodness passes by, and his name is declared, divine glory looks like the muted, hidden backside of God.

In John 17, Jesus repeatedly refers to when his glory will be revealed (vv. 5, 22, 24). How shocked we are, however, to discover that he is referring to his inglorious execution! This is the ultimate manifestation of God's glory—his *achor* glory—that both reveals his goodness to us and places his name on us.

"Help us, O God of our salvation, for the glory of your name; deliver us, and atone for our sins, for your name's sake!" (Ps. 79:9).

The Jealous God קנא

YOU SHALL WORSHIP NO OTHER GOD, FOR THE LORD,
WHOSE NAME IS JEALOUS, IS A JEALOUS GOD.

EXODUS 34:14

Divinities in the ancient world were fine with the theological equivalent
of sleeping around. Worshipers could hook up with as many deities as
they desired. Offer a goat to Baal, a pinch of incense to Asherah, a splash
of wine to El. That was the religious, polytheistic norm. As long as each
god was getting some of the action, there was no harm, no foul. The God
of the Hebrews could not have been more different. He declared himself to
be the only God, the only God to be worshiped, and a jealous one at that. All
this would have struck the ancient peoples as narrow and nonsensical. But
God's people were his bride. He wasn't about to share her with anyone else.

Yahweh is *qanna* ("jealous")—indeed, he could be nicknamed Jealous—not
because he was domineering, but because he was so intensely, passionately
devoted to Israel. "You shall worship no other god" was him saying to his
wife, "You shall sleep with no other man."

Our one Lord, Jesus the Messiah, loved his bride, the "church and gave
himself up for her" (Eph. 5:25). He would brook no rival. His jealousy, his
unconquerable love, compelled him to go the distance, even the cross, to
make and keep her his spotless bride.

Lord Jesus, sanctify us, cleanse us with water and Word, that we might be
holy and without blemish.

Michelangelo and
Horned Moses קרן

WHEN MOSES CAME DOWN FROM MOUNT SINAI . . .
[HE] DID NOT KNOW THAT THE SKIN OF HIS FACE
SHONE BECAUSE HE HAD BEEN TALKING WITH GOD . . .
AND WHEN MOSES HAD FINISHED SPEAKING WITH
[THE ISRAELITES], HE PUT A VEIL OVER HIS FACE.

EXODUS 34:29, 33

Bad translations sometimes make their way into good art. Look no further than Michelangelo. In his famous sculpture of Moses, horns are poking out of the prophet's head. Why the horns? When Moses descended from Sinai, "his face *qaran* [shone]." The Latin Vulgate, however, translated *qaran* ("shone") as *cornuta* ("horns"). It's an easy mistake. The word *qaran* is very similar to the word *qeren* ("horn"). In all likelihood, the radiance was beaming from his face, like horns protruding from an ox.

Indeed, the word *qaran* was possibly chosen because it sounds like *qeren*. It was an allusion to the golden calf—the story that immediately precedes this account. The message is this: "Listen, Israel, don't go looking for a horned animal to serve as the go-between for me and you. Look to the radiant-faced Moses, with whom I speak face to face. That stupid, idolatrous, lifeless calf can't even moo, but the living and radiant Moses speaks my life-giving words." Or, as the Father will later say of his Son, the Light of the world and the prophet like Moses, "Listen to him" (Matt. 17:5).

Remove the veil over our hearts, O Lord, that we may behold your glory and hear your life-giving words.

Bringing an Offering קרב

THE LORD CALLED MOSES AND SPOKE TO HIM FROM
THE TENT OF MEETING, SAYING, "SPEAK TO THE
PEOPLE OF ISRAEL AND SAY TO THEM, WHEN ANY
ONE OF YOU BRINGS AN OFFERING TO THE LORD,
YOU SHALL BRING YOUR OFFERING OF LIVESTOCK
FROM THE HERD OR FROM THE FLOCK."

LEVITICUS 1:1–2

Almost every Hebrew word is formed from a three-consonant stem/root. Prefixes, suffixes, and other additions to this stem make it a particular kind of verb, noun, adjective, or adverb. Invisible in English translation is the interconnected web of many Hebrew words. For instance, the stem q-r-b is the basis of "approach," "brings," "offering," "midst," and "near." This is vital for understanding Leviticus. Pulling all these q-r-b words together, we might say, "Because the Lord is in Israel's midst (*qereb*), near to them (*qarob*), they approach him (*qarab*), bringing (*hiqrib*) an offering (*qorban*) to him." All five words, like branches of a tree, are from the same q-r-b trunk. And together they teach us that God's nearness makes possible Israel's approach and offerings to him.

All these offerings are the backstory for the Messiah, who drew near to us as both priest and offering. "We have been sanctified through the offering of the body of Jesus Christ once for all" (Heb. 10:10), "for by a single offering he has perfected for all time those who are being sanctified" (v. 14).

Jesus, our priest and offering, make our bodies a living sacrifice in loving service to others.

Not a Holy BBQ עלה

"IF HIS OFFERING IS A BURNT OFFERING FROM THE
HERD, HE SHALL OFFER A MALE WITHOUT BLEMISH.
HE SHALL BRING IT TO THE ENTRANCE OF THE TENT
OF MEETING, THAT HE MAY BE ACCEPTED BEFORE
THE LORD. HE SHALL LAY HIS HAND ON THE HEAD OF
THE BURNT OFFERING, AND IT SHALL BE ACCEPTED
FOR HIM TO MAKE ATONEMENT FOR HIM."

LEVITICUS 1:3-4

The altar was not a BBQ grill. Whatever meat was placed atop it was not cooked to medium rare or well done but to smoke and ashes. The primary and foundational sacrifice for Israel is the *olah* ("[whole] burnt offering"). Formed from the verb *alah* ("to go up"), the *olah* was so named because—except for the hide—it went up entirely in smoke to God. Offered both for the nation and by individuals, this *olah* engendered acceptance before God. And not just acceptance, but all that entailed: purification, forgiveness, blessing, sanctification.

Israel received the Lord's gifts wrapped in the elements of creation. In Leviticus, it's the blood and flesh of an animal. Elsewhere it's manna or water. God's ways remain the same today, for in baptism's water as well as the Lord's Supper's bread and wine, he gives the purification, forgiveness, blessing, and sanctification we need, all acquired for us by the Messiah's offering of himself on the Roman altar of crucifixion.

Blessed are you, O Lord, King of the universe, who gives us gifts we can taste, see, and touch.

Sharing Salt
with Jesus מלח

"YOU SHALL SEASON ALL YOUR GRAIN OFFERINGS
WITH SALT. YOU SHALL NOT LET THE SALT OF
THE COVENANT WITH YOUR GOD BE MISSING
FROM YOUR GRAIN OFFERING; WITH ALL YOUR
OFFERINGS YOU SHALL OFFER SALT."

LEVITICUS 2:13

Since Yahweh was the true owner of the holy land, Israelites "paid rent" to him by offering the fruits and grains from their fields. Part of the grain that was ground into flour was placed on the altar, and the rest given to the priests as part of their paycheck. To this flour was always added *melach* ("salt"). It's called the "salt of the covenant" because in the ancient world two parties would often "share salt" as a way of concretizing their relationship. Thus the allies of the Persian king Artaxerxes said they ate "the salt of the palace" (Ezra 4:14).

Before Jesus ascended, he shared *melach* with his followers. Though Acts 1:4 is usually translated, "while [Jesus was] staying with them," the Greek verb (*sunalizo*) means "sharing salt." Our High Priest was sharing salt with his fellow priests of the new covenant. He was pledging his commitment to them—and to us. We, baptized as priests, dine with the great High Priest around his covenant table. We are thereby sanctified for service in his kingdom as the "salt of the earth" (Matt. 5:13).

O Lord, may our speech always be gracious, seasoned with salt, so that we may know how we ought to answer each person (Col. 4:6).

Shalom Sacrifices שְׁלָמִים

"IF HIS OFFERING IS A SACRIFICE OF PEACE OFFERING,
IF HE OFFERS AN ANIMAL FROM THE HERD, MALE
OR FEMALE, HE SHALL OFFER IT WITHOUT BLEMISH
BEFORE THE LORD. AND HE SHALL LAY HIS HAND
ON THE HEAD OF HIS OFFERING AND KILL IT AT
THE ENTRANCE OF THE TENT OF MEETING, AND
AARON'S SONS THE PRIESTS SHALL THROW THE
BLOOD AGAINST THE SIDES OF THE ALTAR."

LEVITICUS 3:1–2

Shalom, like Amen and Hallelujah, is one of those words at home on the lips of all varieties of non-Hebrew speakers. Shalom is also the root of one of Israel's main sacrifices, the *sh'lamim* ("peace offering"). But shalom encompasses not just peace but wholeness, integrity, well-being. The Greek OT translates *sh'lamim* as "sacrifices of salvation." And salvation, peace, and well-being were, quite literally, something you could sink your teeth into. The *sh'lamim* was the meal God shared with his people. The blood went on the altar, but most of the meat was returned to the worshiper, to be cooked and eaten in a celebratory meal (7:11ff.).

Beginning with the tree of life, God has made his life and blessings edible. "Taste and see that the Lord is good" (Ps. 34:8). "The afflicted shall eat and be satisfied" (Ps. 22:26), for Christ himself is our peace and peace offering (Eph. 2:14). God prepares a table before us, laden with the Lamb himself.

The eyes of all look to you, O Lord, to feed us with the food that endures to eternal life.

Sin and Reparation Offerings חטאת

"IF THE WHOLE CONGREGATION OF ISRAEL SINS
UNINTENTIONALLY AND THE THING IS HIDDEN FROM
THE EYES OF THE ASSEMBLY . . . WHEN THE SIN
WHICH THEY HAVE COMMITTED BECOMES KNOWN,
THE ASSEMBLY SHALL OFFER A BULL FROM THE HERD
FOR A SIN OFFERING AND BRING IT IN FRONT OF THE
TENT OF MEETING . . . AND THE PRIEST SHALL MAKE
ATONEMENT FOR THEM, AND THEY SHALL BE FORGIVEN."

LEVITICUS 4:13-14, 20

The Lord was not naive. He was well aware that Israel would make a mess of things. By theft, lying, fraud, or some other vice they would pollute both themselves and others. To provide a way for atonement and forgiveness, he instituted both the *chattat* ("sin offering") and the *asham* ("reparation [or guilt] offering"). The *asham* differs in that it was offered only by individuals, and in addition to the sacrifice, a 20 percent reparation was tacked onto it. But both sacrifices shared the same goal: cleansing the unholy sinner for reunion with the holy God.

When Isaiah prophesies the death of the messianic Servant, he says, "it was the will of the Lord to crush him; he has put him to grief; when his soul makes an offering for guilt" (53:10). The crucified one is our *asham*, the "offering for guilt," whereby we unholy sinners are made right with our holy Father.

"Have mercy on me, O God, according to your steadfast love, according to your abundant mercy blot out my transgressions" (Ps. 51:1).

A Priestly Handful מלאים

[MOSES SAID TO AARON AND HIS SON,] "AND YOU SHALL NOT GO OUTSIDE THE ENTRANCE OF THE TENT OF MEETING FOR SEVEN DAYS, UNTIL THE DAYS OF YOUR ORDINATION ARE COMPLETED, FOR IT WILL TAKE SEVEN DAYS TO ORDAIN YOU."

LEVITICUS 8:33

When we say, "My hands are full," we mean that we have become busy. When an Israelite said, "My hands are full," he meant that he had become a priest. Though traditionally translated "ordination," *millu'im* means "filling." It's based on the verb *mala* ("fill") and derived from the Hebrew idiom "to fill the hand." Moses took bread, oil, and a sacrifice, "and he put all these in the hands of Aaron and in the hands of his sons" (8:27). This "filling of their hands" placed them in office.

After his resurrection, Jesus showed his disciples "his hands and his feet" (Luke 24:40). Those scarred hands were the priestly insignia of his office. The Father had given all things into his hands (John 13:3). With those almighty hands he washed dirty feet and received piercing nails. Now he lifts those same hands to bless us, intercede for us, and one day to raise our bodies and place us in the New Jerusalem. There each of us, like the high priest of old, shall wear on our foreheads the holy name of God (Exod. 28:36; Rev. 22:4).

Fill our hands, Holy Spirit, with the blessings of our Father, that we might serve as copriests with our great High Priest.

Unclean Doesn't Mean Dirty טמא

THIS IS THE LAW ABOUT BEAST AND BIRD AND EVERY LIVING CREATURE THAT MOVES THROUGH THE WATERS AND EVERY CREATURE THAT SWARMS ON THE GROUND, TO MAKE A DISTINCTION BETWEEN THE UNCLEAN AND THE CLEAN AND BETWEEN THE LIVING CREATURE THAT MAY BE EATEN AND THE LIVING CREATURE THAT MAY NOT BE EATEN.

LEVITICUS 11:46-47

Tame´ ("unclean") is the technical term for ritual impurity. It has nothing to do with being dirty or the "yuck factor." People became temporarily *tame´* (e.g., by touching a corpse; Num. 9:6) and some animals were permanently *tame´* (e.g., pigs). By keeping the God-given distinctions about which foods to place on their table, Israelites were practicing the discipline of keeping the God-given distinctions about which people to invite to their table (Lev. 20:22–26). Food and fellowship were thus baked together.

In his ministry, Jesus "declared all foods clean" (Mark 7:19) and "ate with tax collectors and sinners" (Matt. 9:10–11). He demonstrated, in a vision to Peter, that the old covenant laws between unclean foods and unclean people were now null and void. The command to "eat" (Acts 10:13) was followed by the invitation to visit the home of a Gentile (10:17ff.). Food and fellowship laws of the old covenant are over, for "there is neither Jew nor Greek, there is neither slave nor free, there is no male and female, for you are all one in Christ Jesus" (Gal. 3:28).

Blessed are you, Lord Jesus, for welcoming us to your holy table.

What's Wrong with Natural Body Functions? נדה

"THIS IS THE LAW FOR HIM WHO HAS A DISCHARGE AND FOR HIM WHO HAS AN EMISSION OF SEMEN, BECOMING UNCLEAN THEREBY; ALSO FOR HER WHO IS UNWELL WITH HER MENSTRUAL IMPURITY."

LEVITICUS 15:32-33

To moderns, all this talk about semen and menstruation seems bizarre. Why would a woman in *niddah* ("menstruation") be unclean (*tame´*)? Or a man with a seminal discharge? These are natural bodily functions. Most likely, this was God's way of declaring that a woman's blood and a man's semen were not sacred. In the cultures around them, the opposite was often true, especially in religions that practiced ritual prostitution. To that, God says an emphatic No. His sanctuary must be kept clean of all such pagan ideas and practices. Thus the Lord established ways whereby men and women could purify themselves before entering the holy courts of his tabernacle.

One of the most remarkable stories in the Gospels is when a woman who had been unclean for twelve years due to menstrual bleeding touches the fringe on the garments of our Lord (Mark 5:25-34). This touch would have rendered Jesus ritually unclean. Rather than rebuking the woman, however, Jesus says, "Daughter, your faith has made you well; go in peace, and be healed of your disease" (v. 34). The Messiah absorbs our uncleanness, that in him we might be clean, restored, and healed.

"Purge me with hyssop, and I shall be clean; wash me, and I shall be whiter than snow" (Ps. 51:7).

The Goat for Azazel עֲזָאזֵל

"THEN [AARON] SHALL TAKE THE TWO GOATS AND
SET THEM BEFORE THE LORD AT THE ENTRANCE
OF THE TENT OF MEETING. AND AARON SHALL
CAST LOTS OVER THE TWO GOATS, ONE LOT FOR
THE LORD AND THE OTHER LOT FOR AZAZEL."

LEVITICUS 16:7-8

Older translations understood *Azazel* not as a proper noun but a combination of *ez* ("goat") and *azal* ("to go away"). Thus we get "scapegoat" (short for "escaped goat"). Most scholars today, however, identify Azazel as a desert demon, as indeed some rabbis did, calling him Azael. This goat is not an innocent victim that bears the blame (as we colloquially say, "The boss is using Cindy as a scapegoat for his mistakes"). Rather, on Yom Kippur, the sins *have already been atoned* for by the first goat sacrificed (Lev. 16:15-19). When the high priest lays his hands on the head of the Azazel goat, confesses, and sends him into the wilderness, this goat bears witness not of guilt but of absolution. The goat goes to the devil, as it were, parading the atonement on the accuser's own turf.

When Jesus, after his death, descended into hell, he was parading before the enemy in a victory march that beat the drum of forgiveness. After the final Yom Kippur of Calvary, Satan had no claim on us. It is finished.

Lord Jesus, the Lamb of our absolution, all glory be to you for the atonement by which you trampled underfoot all our foes.

Uncovering Nakedness גלה ערוה

"NONE OF YOU SHALL APPROACH ANY ONE OF HIS CLOSE RELATIVES TO UNCOVER NAKEDNESS. I AM THE LORD. YOU SHALL NOT UNCOVER THE NAKEDNESS OF YOUR FATHER, WHICH IS THE NAKEDNESS OF YOUR MOTHER; SHE IS YOUR MOTHER, YOU SHALL NOT UNCOVER HER NAKEDNESS."

LEVITICUS 18:6–7

Idioms spice up a language, but for nonnative speakers, they're often bewildering. Imagine trying to understand "by the skin of your teeth" or "cost an arm and a leg" as if they were literal! As with English, so with Hebrew. For instance, to *galah ervah* ("uncover [someone's] nakedness") often implicitly refers to sex with Person X while explicitly referring to Person Y. So to "undercover a father's nakedness" is actually to commit incest with the mother. But since she and her husband are "one flesh" (Gen. 2:24), her body is his, and his, hers. All the sexual laws in Leviticus 18 are variations on this theme: family members are our flesh and blood—to be defended against every evil.

"Let marriage be held in honor among all, and let the marriage bed be undefiled, for God will judge the sexually immoral and adulterous" (Heb. 13:4). Our families are gifts of God. Each marriage is an icon of Christ and his bride. May our Father defend us from every attack of the evil one, who seeks to fracture families, including the family of God.

Blessed are you, O Lord, giver of marriage and family; you alone are our rock and salvation.

Tattooed for the Dead קעקע

"YOU SHALL NOT MAKE ANY CUTS ON YOUR BODY FOR
THE DEAD OR TATTOO YOURSELVES: I AM THE LORD."

LEVITICUS 19:28

Every society mourns the dead in their own way. Some wear black; some wail publicly; others leave mementos at the graveside. In the ancient cultures around Israel, inner grief was often expressed in physical alteration. Mourners disfigured their bodies, shaved their heads, or inked a *qa'aqa* ("tattoo") into their skin (e.g., Jer. 16:6). A *qa'aqa* was a cultic action. The ink religiously bonded them with the dead. In Israel, however, the living God erected clear boundaries between the living and dead. With him, even believers who died are alive, for "he is not God of the dead, but of the living" (Matt. 22:32).

This verse is sometimes misapplied as a prohibition against getting inked by your local tattoo artist. As is obvious from the context, however, it concerned Israel maintaining holiness by not fellowshipping with the dead by indulging in pagan practices. Christians do grieve, of course, even as Jesus shed tears at the tomb of his friend Lazarus. But we mourn our dead, not as unbelievers, who have no hope (1 Thess. 4:13). Even through tears, we see Christ's empty tomb and our promised resurrection, thanks to the one who has engraved Zion—and us, her citizens—onto the palms of his hands (Isa. 49:16).

Console us in our grief, Lord Jesus, with the sure and certain hope of your resurrection.

The Feast of Weeks שבעת

"YOU SHALL COUNT SEVEN FULL WEEKS FROM THE DAY AFTER THE SABBATH, FROM THE DAY THAT YOU BROUGHT THE SHEAF OF THE WAVE OFFERING. YOU SHALL COUNT FIFTY DAYS TO THE DAY AFTER THE SEVENTH SABBATH. THEN YOU SHALL PRESENT A GRAIN OFFERING OF NEW GRAIN TO THE LORD."

LEVITICUS 23:15-16

Christians call it Pentecost (Greek for "fiftieth"), but Israelites called it *Shavu'ot* ("weeks"). They counted seven *shavu'ot* after Passover, then began this second annual festival the next day. Originally, *Shavu'ot* was a farming festival in which the firstfruits of the spring wheat harvest were brought to the altar. Well before the first century, however, it had also become the time to celebrate God's giving of the Torah at Sinai. Since the nation had arrived at that mountain on the third month after the original Passover (Exod. 19:1), the seven-weeks-plus-one-day time period lined up. In Acts 2, when Jews from around the world were gathered in Jerusalem, they were there to celebrate the giving of the old covenant.

But the Holy Spirit had other plans. As Sinai had flamed and smoked, so a "mighty rushing wind" and "tongues of fire" appeared at this new *Shavu'ot*. As Israel had offered her firstfruits, now Christ gave his people "the first-fruits of the Spirit" (Rom. 8:23). The tongues of the disciples spoke of the universal message of grace for all in the new covenant.

Holy Spirit, God's fire from above, kindle in our hearts faith, hope, and love.

The Day of Affliction and Atonement ענה

AND THE LORD SPOKE TO MOSES, SAYING, "NOW ON THE TENTH DAY OF THIS SEVENTH MONTH IS THE DAY OF ATONEMENT. IT SHALL BE FOR YOU A TIME OF HOLY CONVOCATION, AND YOU SHALL AFFLICT YOURSELVES AND PRESENT A FOOD OFFERING TO THE LORD. AND YOU SHALL NOT DO ANY WORK ON THAT VERY DAY, FOR IT IS A DAY OF ATONEMENT, TO MAKE ATONEMENT FOR YOU BEFORE THE LORD YOUR GOD."

LEVITICUS 23:26-28

Only once per year, on Yom Kippur ("day of atonement"), are the Israelites are told, "Afflict yourselves." The verb *anah* ("afflict" or "humble") suggests both inner contrition over sins and outer fasting from food, drink, sex, and bathing. Still today, the Jews call the time from Rosh Hashanah to Yom Kippur the "Ten Days of *Teshuvah* [Repentance]." This isn't just about "beating yourself up" but confessing sins and praying for God's mercy. Fasting and repentance do not merit atonement but are God's way of bringing his people to an awareness of their deep and abiding need of his mercy.

The suffering messianic Servant of Isaiah 53 is himself *anah* ("afflicted" v. 7). He fasted even from speech, for "he opened not his mouth." Though he had no sins of his own for which to repent, our sins became his own, for "the LORD has laid on him the iniquity of us all" (v. 6).

O Lord, who takes pleasure in your people, adorn the humble with salvation (Ps. 149:4).

Feast of Huts סכות

"ON THE FIFTEENTH DAY OF THIS SEVENTH MONTH
AND FOR SEVEN DAYS IS THE FEAST OF BOOTHS
TO THE LORD . . . YOU SHALL DWELL IN BOOTHS
FOR SEVEN DAYS. ALL NATIVE ISRAELITES SHALL
DWELL IN BOOTHS, THAT YOUR GENERATIONS MAY
KNOW THAT I MADE THE PEOPLE OF ISRAEL DWELL
IN BOOTHS WHEN I BROUGHT THEM OUT OF THE
LAND OF EGYPT: I AM THE LORD YOUR GOD."

LEVITICUS 23:34, 42-43

The third annual mass gathering of Israelites is the "roughing it" festival in the fall. No comfy beds in the Jerusalem Hilton, but makeshift *sukkot* were their homes for seven days. A *sukka* (plural: *sukkot*) is a hut or booth made from leafy branches. Living in these *sukkot* was Israel's way of remembering that their ancestors lived similarly when God brought them out of Egypt. By the first century, during Sukkot the high priest poured out water around the altar to commemorate God's gift of water during the wilderness wandering and to anticipate the profusion of life-giving water that the Messiah would outpour.

On the last day of Sukkot, Jesus made himself known as the Messiah (John 7:2, 37). Standing in the temple, he proclaimed, "If anyone thirsts, let him come to me and drink" (v. 37). From Christ, the embodied *sukka* of God, rivers of living water flow to all who believe in him (v. 38).

Lord Jesus, may we ever feast on the abundance of your house, and drink from the river of your delights (Ps. 36:8).

Year of the Ram's Horn יובל

"ON THE DAY OF ATONEMENT YOU SHALL SOUND
THE TRUMPET THROUGHOUT ALL YOUR LAND. AND
YOU SHALL CONSECRATE THE FIFTIETH YEAR, AND
PROCLAIM LIBERTY THROUGHOUT THE LAND TO ALL
ITS INHABITANTS. IT SHALL BE A JUBILEE FOR YOU,
WHEN EACH OF YOU SHALL RETURN TO HIS PROPERTY
AND EACH OF YOU SHALL RETURN TO HIS CLAN."

LEVITICUS 25:9-10

Today, "Jubilee" refers to everything from a special anniversary to an X-Men character. It all started with the Hebrew word *yovel*. A *yovel* ("jubilee") is a ram's horn that is hollowed into an instrument (e.g., Josh. 6:5). Every fiftieth year, on Yom Kippur, a blast from the *yovel* would put the brakes on the nation for an extended rest. Debts were forgiven. Ancestral lands returned. Slaves liberated. It was the Sabbath of Sabbaths. Everyone, including the land, enjoyed R&R from labor, captivity, and debt. *Yovel* was a foretaste of the ultimate rest to come in the Messiah.

When Jesus preached his first sermon in Nazareth, he announced that the messianic *Yovel* was on their doorstep. Quoting Isaiah, he told the synagogue that he had come to liberate captives, give sight to blind, give liberty to the oppressed, and proclaim the year of the Lord's favor (Luke 4:18-19). Sins were forgiven. Chains broken. In Jesus, the Spirit blows the horn of salvation to announce that we have entered the ongoing Jubilee that has no end.

All glory to you, O Lord, for bringing us, who are weary and heavy laden, into your rest.

When God Smiles פנים

"THE LORD BLESS YOU AND KEEP YOU; THE LORD MAKE
HIS FACE TO SHINE UPON YOU AND BE GRACIOUS TO
YOU; THE LORD LIFT UP HIS COUNTENANCE UPON YOU
AND GIVE YOU PEACE. SO SHALL THEY PUT MY NAME
UPON THE PEOPLE OF ISRAEL, AND I WILL BLESS THEM."

NUMBERS 6:24-27

Faces pop up frequently in conversation: a face-off, a slap in the face, a poker face. Twice in the priestly blessing, God's *panim* ("face") does something: it shines and is lifted up. This shining face is not the same as our "glowing face" in English. When God's face illumines, he is gracious and saves (Ps. 31:16). He enlightens our darkness. Likewise, when he "lifts up his *panim*" he looks with favor. A smile spreads across his face, filling us with peace. God's shining and smiling face, along with the threefold repetition of his name on us, is how he blesses us.

When Jesus was transfigured before his disciples, his face shone like the sun (Matt. 17:2), "for God, who said, 'Let light shine out of darkness,' has shone in our hearts to give the light of the knowledge of the glory of God in the face of Jesus Christ" (2 Cor. 4:6). In the face of Jesus, we see the Father's smile of grace and favor, for in him we are blessed by the Spirit.

"Restore us, O God of hosts! Let your face shine, that we may be saved!" (Ps. 80:7).

Mouth-to-Mouth Conversation פה אל פה

AND [GOD] SAID, "HEAR MY WORDS: IF THERE IS A
PROPHET AMONG YOU, I THE LORD MAKE MYSELF
KNOWN TO HIM IN A VISION; I SPEAK WITH HIM IN
A DREAM. NOT SO WITH MY SERVANT MOSES. HE
IS FAITHFUL IN ALL MY HOUSE. WITH HIM I SPEAK
MOUTH TO MOUTH, CLEARLY, AND NOT IN RIDDLES,
AND HE BEHOLDS THE FORM OF THE LORD."

NUMBERS 12:6-8

We communicate in a variety of ways—emails, texts, phone calls, video, and face to face. When the Lord wanted to convey a message, he too had options. To Gentiles, like Pharaoh, he ordinarily used dreams (Gen. 41:1). To most prophets he spoke in visions (Isa. 1:1). But to Moses, the apex prophet, he spoke *peh el peh* ("mouth to mouth"). The image is drawn from royalty, for only the king's closest servants had regular dialogues with him. As in 2 Kings 25:19, where the "king's council" are literally "those who see the face of the king." So with Moses, who knew the King of kings "face to face" (Deut. 34:10).

Moses foretold that the Lord would raise up a prophet like himself (Deut. 18:15). Jesus, indeed, was this prophet—but infinitely more, "for the law was given through Moses; grace and truth came through Jesus Christ" (John 1:17). From his mouth comes "a sharp, two-edged sword" by which to defend us, the people who heed his voice (Rev. 1:16).

Open our ears, O Lord, to listen to the voice of your all-wise, all-powerful Word.

Grasshoppers and Giants נפלים

THEY BROUGHT TO THE PEOPLE OF ISRAEL A BAD REPORT OF THE LAND THAT THEY HAD SPIED OUT, SAYING, "THE LAND, THROUGH WHICH WE HAVE GONE TO SPY IT OUT, IS A LAND THAT DEVOURS ITS INHABITANTS, AND ALL THE PEOPLE THAT WE SAW IN IT ARE OF GREAT HEIGHT. AND THERE WE SAW THE NEPHILIM (THE SONS OF ANAK, WHO COME FROM THE NEPHILIM), AND WE SEEMED TO OURSELVES LIKE GRASSHOPPERS, AND SO WE SEEMED TO THEM."

NUMBERS 13:32–33

Goliath may be the best-known giant of the Bible, but he was only one in a long list of herculean men. Centuries before brave-hearted David faced his foe, his fainthearted forefathers cowered before the Nephilim and sons of Anak. Nephilim means "fallen ones" and Anak is from "neck," probably referring to either a long-necked people (i.e., giants) or a necklace-wearing tribe. The Nephilim were known in pre-Flood days as "mighty men . . . men of renown" (Gen. 6:4). Since the average Israelite male was probably between 5⊠ and 5⊠3⊠, the spies probably did feel "like grasshoppers" compared to them. What they failed to believe, however, was that the battle was the Lord's. He himself would fight for them.

As David fought Goliath, so the Son of David wielded his weapon against every monster, every gargantuan foe, who shackles humanity to fear and death. His empty tomb marks the burial plot of our every enemy.

Unsheathe your sword, O Lord, and lift up your shield, to fight on behalf of your people.

The Good News of God's Long Nose ארך אפים

"THE LORD IS SLOW TO ANGER AND ABOUNDING IN STEADFAST LOVE, FORGIVING INIQUITY AND TRANSGRESSION, BUT HE WILL BY NO MEANS CLEAR THE GUILTY, VISITING THE INIQUITY OF THE FATHERS ON THE CHILDREN, TO THE THIRD AND THE FOURTH GENERATION."

NUMBERS 14:18

For the Israelite, God's heart is made visible in his *af* ("nose"). When "the anger of the LORD was kindled against Moses" (Exod. 4:14), the Hebrew says "the *af* of Yahweh burned." Even more graphically, David says smoke billows from divine nostrils (Ps. 18:8). Hot-nosed would be like us saying someone's blood boiled. The opposite, however, is not cold-nosed but long-nosed. Moses says "the LORD is *erek appayim*," literally, "long of nose," just as we use expressions like "short-tempered" versus "long-suffering." In the context of Numbers 14, the Lord was on the verge of annihilating Israel when they stubbornly refused to enter the land of promise. Moses, however, reminds God that he is not a short-nosed deity but the long-nosed covenant King.

The Greek word used to translate this Hebrew expression is found in 1 Corinthians 13:4: "Love is patient." Love is long-nosed. A Hebrew spin on 2 Peter 3:9 would be that the Lord is "long-nosed toward you, not wishing that any should perish, but that all should reach repentance." The long arm of God's law might accuse us, but the long nose of God's grace saves us.

Lengthen your nose toward us, heavenly Father, and grant us your steadfast love.

Resident Aliens
in Israel גר

"AND IF A STRANGER IS SOJOURNING WITH YOU, OR ANYONE IS LIVING PERMANENTLY AMONG YOU, AND HE WISHES TO OFFER A FOOD OFFERING, WITH A PLEASING AROMA TO THE LORD, HE SHALL DO AS YOU DO."

NUMBERS 15:14

Never forget who you once were. That dictum defined how Israelites were to treat a *ger* ("resident alien"). God told them, "You shall not oppress a *ger*. You know the heart of a *ger*, for you were *gerim* in the land of Egypt" (Exod. 23:9). Like refugees today, a *ger* left land, home, and property to seek refuge in a foreign country. Though not given full citizenship in Israel, they were protected and—if they maintained ritual purity—even allowed to participate in the Passover (Exod. 12:47–48) and other sacrifices (Num. 15:14). Israel was proactively to incorporate Gentiles into Yahweh's ways and worship.

God desired foreigners to join themselves to him, minister to him, and offer sacrifices on his altar. Why? Because, he said, "My house shall be called a house of prayer for all peoples" (Isa. 56:7). Jesus quoted these words when he drove the money changers out of the temple (Matt. 21:13). By so doing, he was announcing the death of the old temple and the birth of the new, for the Messiah is the new temple and new Israel, where believing Jews and Gentiles alike have full citizenship.

"O LORD, I love the habitation of your house and the place where your glory dwells" (Ps. 26:8).

A Royal and Priestly Uniform צִיצִת

THE LORD SAID TO MOSES, "SPEAK TO THE PEOPLE
OF ISRAEL, AND TELL THEM TO MAKE TASSELS ON
THE CORNERS OF THEIR GARMENTS THROUGHOUT
THEIR GENERATIONS, AND TO PUT A CORD OF BLUE
ON THE TASSEL OF EACH CORNER. AND IT SHALL BE
A TASSEL FOR YOU TO LOOK AT AND REMEMBER ALL
THE COMMANDMENTS OF THE LORD, TO DO THEM, NOT
TO FOLLOW AFTER YOUR OWN HEART AND YOUR OWN
EYES, WHICH YOU ARE INCLINED TO WHORE AFTER."

NUMBERS 15:37–39

Just as couples wear wedding rings as a sort of miniature uniform to mark us as one bound to another, so *tzitzit* ("tassels") were the uniform of Israel. "To look at" the *tzitzit*, which hung like tassels from their cloaks, was "to remember all the commandments of the LORD," their divine Husband.

Most significantly, a cord of blue was on the *tzitzit*, the same color as on the ephod of the high priest (Exod. 28:6) and inner veil of the tabernacle (26:31). This color meant every Israelite wore "royal blue" as part of "a kingdom of priests and a holy nation" (Exod. 19:6). The *tzitzit* foreshadowed the work of the Messiah, who has "made us a kingdom, priests to his God and Father" (Rev. 1:6). Our royal and holy vestment is Jesus himself, for we, his church, are "clothed with righteousness" (Ps. 132:9) and "with power from on high" (Luke 24:49).

Strip off our filthy garments, O Lord, and vest us with your righteous mercy.

The Ashes of a Red Heifer פרה אדמה

"TELL THE PEOPLE OF ISRAEL TO BRING YOU A RED HEIFER WITHOUT DEFECT, IN WHICH THERE IS NO BLEMISH, AND ON WHICH A YOKE HAS NEVER COME. AND YOU SHALL GIVE IT TO ELEAZAR THE PRIEST, AND IT SHALL BE TAKEN OUTSIDE THE CAMP AND SLAUGHTERED BEFORE HIM."

NUMBERS 19:2-3

For Israel, impurity was contagious. Just like we catch a virus by contact with a sick person, so God's people "caught" impurity by touching unclean things, like a corpse. This was unavoidable, of course, since the bodies of loved ones were to be buried with dignity. So God provided an unusual means of purifying those made unclean by death—he put the remains of death on them. A *parah adummah* ("red heifer") was killed, her body burned to ashes, and the ashes mixed with water and kept outside the camp. When Israelites were made impure by death, this ash-soaked water was sprinkled on them. Death overcame death.

Hebrews directly connects these ashes to the Messiah: "For if the blood of goats and bulls, and the sprinkling of defiled persons with the ashes of a heifer, sanctify for the purification of the flesh, how much more will the blood of Christ, who through the eternal Spirit offered himself without blemish to God, purify our conscience from dead works to serve the living God" (9:13-14). His death "outside the gate" (13:12) overcomes the death inside us.

Sprinkle on us, Lord Jesus, your cleansing blood of life.

Miriam, the First Mary מרים

AND THE PEOPLE OF ISRAEL, THE WHOLE
CONGREGATION, CAME INTO THE WILDERNESS OF ZIN IN
THE FIRST MONTH, AND THE PEOPLE STAYED IN KADESH.
AND MIRIAM DIED THERE AND WAS BURIED THERE.

NUMBERS 20:1

If you've ever wondered who's responsible for all the "Marys" in the New Testament—there are six or seven of them!—all fingers point to Miriam. Her name, *Miryam*, is the Hebrew equivalent of the Greek name *Mariam* or *Maria* ("Mary"). Miriam was thus the first Mary of the Bible. This big sister to baby Moses was there to help rescue him at the Nile. Later, at the Red Sea, now a prophetess, she led the choir in Israel's exultant song. Like almost all the adults who left Egypt, this "Mary" never set foot in the promised land. She died not having received what was promised (Heb. 11:39).

But another Miriam did. Her namesake, a young virgin from Galilee, not only lived in the land of promise; she carried in her womb, bore, and nursed the Promise himself. Like the prophetess sang the Song at the Sea, so Mary sang her psalm, the Magnificat. And like Miriam, she, along with Joseph, rescued the child of promise by whisking him away—ironically, to Egypt. From the old Mary to the new Mary, we trace God's unfolding narrative of salvation.

Our souls magnify you, O Lord, and our spirits rejoice in you, our Savior, for the gift of the Christ child who came to us through Mary.

Serpent of Salvation
נחש נחשת

AND THE LORD SAID TO MOSES, "MAKE A FIERY
SERPENT AND SET IT ON A POLE, AND EVERYONE
WHO IS BITTEN, WHEN HE SEES IT, SHALL LIVE." SO
MOSES MADE A BRONZE SERPENT AND SET IT ON A
POLE. AND IF A SERPENT BIT ANYONE, HE WOULD
LOOK AT THE BRONZE SERPENT AND LIVE.

NUMBERS 21:8-9

Hebrew delights in word plays, even in undelightful, unplayful stories such as this one. The "bronze serpent" is the *n'chash n'choshet*. The word for serpent (*nachash*) sounds like the word for bronze (*n'choshet*). Snakes occupy a pretty low place in the biblical story—from Eden's serpent all the way to the Pharisaic "brood of vipers." How odd, then, that this bronze image of healing and life looked like the real source of the venom and death.

Odd, yes, but also splendidly fitting in light of Christ. He ties himself to this bronze serpent, saying, "As Moses lifted up the serpent in the wilderness, so must the Son of Man be lifted up" (John 3:14). He who is healing and life absorbed the source of venomous sin and death. With eyes of faith we behold our "Serpent of salvation" (Luther). "For our sake [God] made him to be sin who knew no sin, so that in him we might become the righteousness of God" (2 Cor. 5:21).

Lord Jesus, lifted up on the cross, lift us up in union with you, that we might receive healing in your wounds.

The Wise Donkey of a Foolish Prophet פתח

WHEN THE DONKEY SAW THE ANGEL OF THE LORD, SHE LAY DOWN UNDER BALAAM. AND BALAAM'S ANGER WAS KINDLED, AND HE STRUCK THE DONKEY WITH HIS STAFF. THEN THE LORD OPENED THE MOUTH OF THE DONKEY, AND SHE SAID TO BALAAM, "WHAT HAVE I DONE TO YOU, THAT YOU HAVE STRUCK ME THESE THREE TIMES?"

NUMBERS 22:27-28

Balaam is a comic figure. This prophet for hire was blind to the danger his donkey saw with twenty-twenty vision. He was employed to curse Israel, but he couldn't even manage his own beast. Finally, like a toddler who doesn't get his way, Balaam throws a hissy fit and gets into a shouting match with a seemingly wise and stoic donkey. Slapstick humor, biblical style. That God is controlling events is obvious from the language of "opening." God *patach* ("opened") the donkey's mouth, as when God *patach* the mouth of prophets (e.g., Ezek. 33:22). Rather than heehawing, this animal outprophets the prophet!

Balaam was eventually strong-armed by God into blessing Israel rather than cursing them. Israel's army eventually neutralized him (Num. 31:8), but his memory lived on in infamy. Even in the New Testament, he is synonymous with false teaching (Rev. 2:14). He is a vivid reminder that God will always find someone or something to speak his truth, even if stones—or a donkey—does his preaching (Luke 19:40).

O Lord, open our lips, that our mouths may declare your praise (Ps. 51:15).

The Star of Jacob כוכב

[BALAAM SAID,] "I SEE HIM, BUT NOT NOW; I BEHOLD HIM, BUT NOT NEAR: A STAR SHALL COME OUT OF JACOB, AND A SCEPTER SHALL RISE OUT OF ISRAEL; IT SHALL CRUSH THE FOREHEAD OF MOAB AND BREAK DOWN ALL THE SONS OF SHETH."

NUMBERS 24:17

Talk of "stars" in Hollywood has ancient echoes. In Hebrew, "star" is *kokav* and "stars" *kokavim*. Throughout history, people or creatures of renown have been called *kokavim*, including angels (Job 38:7). Believers shall shine "like the stars forever and ever" in the resurrection (Dan. 12:3). In the Jewish revolt in AD 132–135, Rabbi Akiva thought the leader was the messiah, so he called him by the Aramaic name Bar Kokhba ("son of a star"). Akiva based that name on the well-known interpretation of "a star [*kokav*]" coming "out of Jacob" as the Anointed One (Num. 24:17).

Akiva was a hundred years late, of course, and dead wrong, for the true Messiah had already arrived. Magi followed a star to this Star of Jacob. Of himself he testified, "I am the root and the descendant of David, the bright morning star" (Rev. 22:16). By the scepter of his Word, he rules. He crushes the foreheads of all his foes—especially the ancient serpent—by trampling them under his resurrection feet.

Blessed are you, Lord Jesus Christ, our bright morning star, for you shine on us to lead us in the path of peace.

The Regal Shepherd רעה

MOSES SPOKE TO THE LORD, SAYING, "LET THE LORD,
THE GOD OF THE SPIRITS OF ALL FLESH, APPOINT
A MAN OVER THE CONGREGATION WHO SHALL GO
OUT BEFORE THEM AND COME IN BEFORE THEM,
WHO SHALL LEAD THEM OUT AND BRING THEM
IN, THAT THE CONGREGATION OF THE LORD MAY
NOT BE AS SHEEP THAT HAVE NO SHEPHERD."

NUMBERS 27:15-17

"Like sheep without a shepherd." Jesus used that image to describe the crowds on whom he had compassion (Matt. 9:36). But Jesus, a student of Moses and the prophets, wasn't inventing the simile; he was reusing an ancient scriptural analogy. Its first occurrence is when Moses asks God for a leader (Joshua) to replace him, so Israel "may not be as sheep that have no *ro'eh* [shepherd]." Later, Micaiah "saw all Israel scattered on the mountains, as sheep that have no *ro'eh*" (1 Kings 22:17). And Ezekiel saw God's people "scattered, because there was no *ro'eh*" (34:5).

For a king (like David) or leader (like Joshua) to be called a *ro'eh* was common (2 Sam. 5:2). So when Jesus calls himself "the good shepherd," he's doing more than painting a quaint picture. He's proclaiming himself king. He is the ruler of Israel. Rather than lording it over us, however, in sacrificial love he "lays down his life for the sheep" (John 10:11).

"Give ear, O Shepherd of Israel, you who lead Joseph like a flock . . . Stir up your might and come to save us!" (Ps. 80:1-2).

Low Idolatry in High Places במה

[THE LORD SAID TO ISRAEL,] "WHEN YOU PASS OVER THE JORDAN INTO THE LAND OF CANAAN, THEN YOU SHALL DRIVE OUT ALL THE INHABITANTS OF THE LAND FROM BEFORE YOU AND DESTROY ALL THEIR FIGURED STONES AND DESTROY ALL THEIR METAL IMAGES AND DEMOLISH ALL THEIR HIGH PLACES."

NUMBERS 33:51–52

Though translated "high place," the word *bamah* is a language knot that's hard to untie. It can refer to the back of something as well as a ridge (Deut. 33:29). Since a religious *bamah* could be located in a valley (Ezek. 6:3), the translation "high place" doesn't quite fit. One thing is clear: whatever they looked like, every Canaanite cultic *bamah* was subject to Israelite bulldozing. Just as we clean up an oil spill lest it pollute the soil, so Israel was to "clean up" the polluting influence of pagan worship on God's sacred turf. A pagan *bamah* was no more to be tolerated than would be the statue of a Hindu deity in a church.

Every idol is a demon's religious mask. Therefore, Paul warns, "Flee from idolatry" (1 Cor. 10:14), for what pagans sacrifice they offer to demons (v. 20). The only "high place" for true godly worship is where the cross is lifted high, on which reigns our God and Lord, Jesus the Messiah.

We do not lift our eyes to the hills, O Lord, but to you, from whence our help comes (Ps. 121:1–2).

A Burr in Your
Backside צנינים

"BUT IF YOU DO NOT DRIVE OUT THE INHABITANTS OF
THE LAND FROM BEFORE YOU, THEN THOSE OF THEM
WHOM YOU LET REMAIN SHALL BE AS BARBS IN YOUR
EYES AND THORNS IN YOUR SIDES, AND THEY SHALL
TROUBLE YOU IN THE LAND WHERE YOU DWELL."

NUMBERS 33:55

From nursery rhymes ("Peter Piper picked a peck of pickled peppers") to lyrics ("Whisper words of wisdom"), alliteration is everywhere. All you need is a series of the same consonants. Hebrew can play that game too. In Numbers 33:55, three words in a row have a "tz" sound: *tz'ninim* (thorns), *tzad* (side), and *tzarar* (trouble). We might say, "A burr in your backside to bother you." But this is no laughing matter. Should Israel not purge the land of idolaters, idolaters will poke and provoke them toward their own pagan ways.

The Lord did allow some Canaanites to remain in the land, however, to teach his people how to fight and to follow his word (Judg. 3:1–4). Isn't this God's approach with Paul? Three times he pleaded with God to extract his own "thorn in the flesh" (2 Cor. 12:7), but God said No. His grace was all Paul needed, for divine power is made perfect in human weakness. Sometimes God's soldiers and preachers must endure thorns. Indeed, at one time, a thatch of thorns topped our enthroned King.

Our Savior, crowned with thorns, perfect in our weakness the power of your grace.

Redeemer of Blood גאל הדם

"WHEN YOU CROSS THE JORDAN INTO THE LAND OF CANAAN, THEN YOU SHALL SELECT CITIES TO BE CITIES OF REFUGE FOR YOU, THAT THE MANSLAYER WHO KILLS ANY PERSON WITHOUT INTENT MAY FLEE THERE. THE CITIES SHALL BE FOR YOU A REFUGE FROM THE AVENGER, THAT THE MANSLAYER MAY NOT DIE UNTIL HE STANDS BEFORE THE CONGREGATION FOR JUDGMENT."

NUMBERS 35:10-12

Not every biblical redeemer (*go'el*) was the same; some were out for blood. The *go'el hadam* ("avenger of blood," 35:19) would avenge the killing of a family member, even if it was an accidental death. To protect the slayer long enough for his guilt or innocence to be determined, God established "cities of refuge" to which the slayer could hightail it before the *go'el hadam* caught up with him. If found guilty, he would be executed. But if innocent, to remain safe, he resided in the city of refuge "until the death of the high priest" (Num. 35:25). In this way, rather than the relative exacting his vengeful redemption, the death of God's anointed priest paid the price, as it were, for his merciful redemption.

If the death of a high priest, who was a sinner, nevertheless liberated another sinner stuck in a city of refuge, then how much more does the death and resurrection of Christ, our perfect high priest, liberate us that we might walk in newness of life?

Blessed are you, Jesus Christ, our merciful high priest, for paying the price for our redemption.

Latter Days אחרית הימים

"WHEN YOU ARE IN TRIBULATION, AND ALL THESE THINGS
COME UPON YOU IN THE LATTER DAYS, YOU WILL RETURN
TO THE LORD YOUR GOD AND OBEY HIS VOICE. FOR
THE LORD YOUR GOD IS A MERCIFUL GOD. HE WILL NOT
LEAVE YOU OR DESTROY YOU OR FORGET THE COVENANT
WITH YOUR FATHERS THAT HE SWORE TO THEM."

DEUTERONOMY 4:30–31

In car racing, officials wave flags of various colors to alert drivers. White usually means they're entering the last lap. The preacher in Hebrews waves his own white flag: "Long ago, at many times and in many ways, God spoke to our fathers by the prophets, but in these last days he has spoken to us by his Son" (Heb. 1:1–2). The "white flag" is the phrase "these last days," which in the OT is *acharit hayyamim* ("the latter days"). In Deuteronomy 4, Moses speaks of these "latter days," as does Isaiah: "It shall come to pass in the latter days [*acharit hayyamim*] that the mountain of the house of the LORD shall be established as the highest of the mountains" (2:2).

Since the Father spoke to us by his Son "in these last days," we have been living in the *acharit hayyamim* for the last two millennia. We are in the messianic era of world history. In these days, Jesus expands his kingdom until he comes again to establish the everlasting day of the resurrection.

O Lord, our shield, defend us during these latter days with your gracious protection.

The Shema שְׁמַע

"HEAR, O ISRAEL: THE LORD OUR GOD, THE
LORD IS ONE. YOU SHALL LOVE THE LORD YOUR
GOD WITH ALL YOUR HEART AND WITH ALL
YOUR SOUL AND WITH ALL YOUR MIGHT."

DEUTERONOMY 6:4-5

The center of daily worship for Jews is the recitation of the *Shema* ("hear"). But it is far from just a Jewish confession. The *Shema* is at heart of the Christian faith. These words are recited by Jesus himself to indicate love for God as the foremost commandment (Mark 12:29-30). James, the brother of Jesus and leader of the Jerusalem church, quotes them (2:19), as does Paul (1 Cor. 8:4). Divine unity ("the LORD is one") calls for a unified and undivided love ("with all your heart and with all your soul and with all your might"). As God is one, so let our love be one. Although several passages have spoken of God's love for us, this is the first time in the Scriptures that our love for God is mentioned.

The proscription "You have no other gods" is balanced by this prescription: "You shall love the LORD." Our God wants the totality of who we are. Belonging wholly to him is the only way we will truly flourish in this world. His Spirit shapes this love within us as he reshapes us in the image of Jesus, who is the embodiment of the Father's heart.

Most merciful God, grant that with all our hearts, all our souls, and all our might, we love you.

Words between Your Eyes טוטפות

"AND THESE WORDS THAT I COMMAND YOU TODAY
SHALL BE ON YOUR HEART. YOU SHALL TEACH THEM
DILIGENTLY TO YOUR CHILDREN, AND SHALL TALK OF
THEM WHEN YOU SIT IN YOUR HOUSE, AND WHEN YOU
WALK BY THE WAY, AND WHEN YOU LIE DOWN, AND
WHEN YOU RISE. YOU SHALL BIND THEM AS A SIGN
ON YOUR HAND, AND THEY SHALL BE AS FRONTLETS
BETWEEN YOUR EYES. YOU SHALL WRITE THEM ON THE
DOORPOSTS OF YOUR HOUSE AND ON YOUR GATES."

DEUTERONOMY 6:6-9

God wants the lives of his people to be so permeated with his Word that everywhere they go or look, his words loom large before their eyes. Sitting or lying down? Yes. In between their eyes? Yes. On their doorposts? Yes. Our lives are to be awash with God-words. Many Jews interpret these verses literally. They write select verses on tiny scrolls and place them in black leather boxes called *tefillin*, which they wrap around their arms and forehead during daily prayers. What Jews today call *tefillin*, the Bible calls *totafot* ("frontlets").

Our ears are ever to be open to our Father, so that we live "by every word that comes from the mouth of the Lord" (Deut. 8:3). Every word is from the Father's Word, the Logos, who has bound his very nature and life to our own and has written our names with crucifixion ink in the Lamb's Book of Life.

Blessed are you, O Lord, King of the world, who has enriched us with your Word.

Stiff-Necked קְשֵׁה עֹרֶף

"KNOW, THEREFORE, THAT THE LORD YOUR
GOD IS NOT GIVING YOU THIS GOOD LAND TO
POSSESS BECAUSE OF YOUR RIGHTEOUSNESS,
FOR YOU ARE A STUBBORN PEOPLE."

DEUTERONOMY 9:6

"Sly as a fox. Busy as a bee. Drunk as a skunk." We encounter human-to-animal comparisons like these all over the Bible as well. In the beginning, Adam named the animals; so, in turn, the animals began to describe Adam's children—and often it's a put-down. For example, Israel is frequently depicted as *q'sheh-oref*—a people "stiff-of-neck." It all started after the golden calf debacle (Exod. 32:9). Why? Because the people were behaving like the stiff-necked beast they worshiped. "Dumb as an ox," we might say.

The Bible teaches this truth over and over: we take on the characteristics of what we worship. As one scholar put it, "What you revere you resemble, either for ruin or for restoration" (G. K. Beale). The psalmist says, "Those who make [idols] become like them; so do all who trust in them" (Ps. 115:8). "They went after false idols and became false" (2 Kings 17:15).

Since Christ is the image of God, to worship him is to become like him, and like the Father, in the power of the Spirit. To revere Christ is to mirror him, so that, as the sheep of his flock, we will follow the Lamb, who is our shepherd (Rev. 7:17).

O Lamb of God, who takes away the sin of the world, restore us to your image.

Goat Milk and
Date Syrup חלב ודבש

"YOU SHALL THEREFORE KEEP THE WHOLE
COMMANDMENT THAT I COMMAND YOU TODAY,
THAT YOU MAY BE STRONG, AND GO IN AND TAKE
POSSESSION OF THE LAND THAT YOU ARE GOING
OVER TO POSSESS, AND THAT YOU MAY LIVE LONG
IN THE LAND THAT THE LORD SWORE TO YOUR
FATHERS TO GIVE TO THEM AND TO THEIR OFFSPRING,
A LAND FLOWING WITH MILK AND HONEY."

DEUTERONOMY 11:8-9

Goats were the main source of *chalav* ("milk") for Israelites. And since there's no evidence of beekeeping in ancient Canaan, *d'vash* ("honey") is probably a syrupy liquid made from dates. Thus the "land flowing with milk and honey" is the "land flowing with goat milk and date syrup." Not as romantic sounding, to be sure, but more accurate. The promise of these protein- and carbohydrate-rich products of the land doubtlessly fed the hopes of Israelites while they were in the wilderness.

The land of Israel was like an expanded Eden. Vines, herds, and flocks in abundance. On this soil, God was preparing the world for an even more expanded Eden, when the blessing of Abraham would flow to all peoples. When Jesus came, he sent out his disciples to the ends of the earth to plant little "Edens" all over the world, where the milk of his Word slakes parched souls and the honey of his grace feeds hungry hearts.

O Lord, "how sweet are your words to my taste, sweeter than honey to my mouth!" (Ps. 119:103).

Ear-Piercing, Hebrew Style רצע

"IF [YOUR HEBREW SERVANT] SAYS TO YOU, 'I WILL NOT GO OUT FROM YOU,' BECAUSE HE LOVES YOU AND YOUR HOUSEHOLD, SINCE HE IS WELL-OFF WITH YOU, THEN YOU SHALL TAKE AN AWL, AND PUT IT THROUGH HIS EAR INTO THE DOOR, AND HE SHALL BE YOUR SLAVE FOREVER."

DEUTERONOMY 15:16-17

When hard times fell on the Israelites, they would sometimes willingly become temporary servants of their fellow believers. Every seventh year (the Sabbath year), they would be liberated. Sometimes, however, if they grew to love the people for whom they labored, they chose to remain lifelong servants in that household. In such cases, they received an ear-piercing, Hebrew style. The verb *ratza* ("pierce") occurs only once: "His master shall *ratza* his ear through with an awl" (Exod. 21:6). This ear-piercing marked him or her as a willing permanent servant. The ear was especially fitting because, henceforth, the servant would "give ear" to the instructions of his master.

The Messiah says to his Father, you have "given me an open ear" (Ps. 40:6). What the ear-piercing of servants symbolized, Christ made a reality. He had no need of piercing, for the ears of this anointed Servant were always open to the voice of his Father, willingly and everlastingly doing his will to accomplish the salvation and freedom of humanity.

Open our ears, heavenly Father, to hear the voice of the Spirit of your Son speaking through your Word.

The Equestrian Christ סוּס

[THE ISRAELITE KING WHOM GOD CHOOSES] MUST NOT ACQUIRE MANY HORSES FOR HIMSELF OR CAUSE THE PEOPLE TO RETURN TO EGYPT IN ORDER TO ACQUIRE MANY HORSES, SINCE THE LORD HAS SAID TO YOU, "YOU SHALL NEVER RETURN THAT WAY AGAIN."

DEUTERONOMY 17:16

The Bible saddles the *sus* ("horse") with both positive and negative connections. Positively, Jeremiah promises that the sons of David will sit on his throne, "riding in chariots and on horses" if they "do justice and righteousness" (22:1–4). Negatively, however, Israelite kings "must not acquire many horses" (Deut. 17:16). Solomon shattered this law to smithereens, for he "had 40,000 stalls of horses for his chariots, and 12,000 horsemen" (1 Kings 4:26)! The *sus* also embodied the rush to evil ("like a horse plunging headlong into battle" Jer. 8:6) and lust ("they were well-fed, lusty stallions, each neighing for his neighbor's wife" 5:8).

Jesus rode a donkey into the city where he was crucified, but he will return on a different animal. A white warhorse will appear from heaven, with the King, the Messiah, astride him (Rev. 19:11). His eyes are aflame. A diadem crown adorns his brow. On his robe and thigh is written, "King of Kings and Lord of Lords" (v. 16). Celestial armies trail behind him on their own white mounts (v. 14). They ride to destroy, for all time, every foe that faces us.

Ride to our rescue, faithful and true Warrior, when enemies encircle and attack us.

Forthtelling and Foretelling נביא

"THE LORD YOUR GOD WILL RAISE UP FOR YOU A PROPHET LIKE ME FROM AMONG YOU, FROM YOUR BROTHERS—IT IS TO HIM YOU SHALL LISTEN."

DEUTERONOMY 18:15

Some people envision a biblical *navi* ("prophet") isolated in a cave, meditating, waiting for God to whisper an oracle into his ears that he will carry to Israel so they'll be privy to the future. Granted, some *n'vi'im* ("prophets") had ecstatic experiences. And, yes, the Word of the Lord would come to them, often in visions. But a *navi* was primarily a preacher. God's mouth to Israel's ears. At times they would foretell the future, but the main duty of their vocation was forthtelling. They interpreted and preached on the Scriptures, especially the Torah. In Jewish tradition, even the authors of books like Joshua, Judges, and Kings were prophetic historians.

Moses was a forthtelling prophet, but near the end of his life, he also foretold the advent of the Prophet of prophets. As a true prophet, Jesus did not speak on his own authority, but he said what the Father had told him to say (John 12:49–50). Indeed, many people thought he was just a prophet or an OT prophet come back to life (Matt. 16:14). But as Peter confessed, he was much more: "You are the Christ, the Son of the living God" (v. 16).

Jesus, Son of the living God, give us ears to listen to you, and enliven us with your grace, that we might boldly confess your name.

An Eye for an Eye עַיִן תַּחַת עַיִן

"YOUR EYE SHALL NOT PITY. IT SHALL BE LIFE FOR LIFE, EYE FOR EYE, TOOTH FOR TOOTH, HAND FOR HAND, FOOT FOR FOOT."

DEUTERONOMY 19:21

Leviticus first informs us of this law: "whatever injury he has given a person shall be given to him . . . *ayin tachat ayin* ['eye for eye']" (24:20; cf. Exod. 21:22–25). This so-called law of retaliation (Latin: *lex talionis*) should not be read with wooden legalism. Rather, it's a general principle that the punishment should fit the crime. It's not "two arms and two legs for an eye" or "a firstborn child for an eye" but *ayin tachat ayin*. This principle was well known in ancient times; laws such as this are also found in the famous eighteenth-century BC Babylonian Code of Hammurabi.

Jesus quotes the "eye for eye" law but proceeds to add: "But I say to you, Do not resist the one who is evil. But if anyone slaps you on the right cheek, turn to him the other also" (Matt. 5:39). Jesus, rather than undoing the law, actually doubles down on it, for it is much easier to seek retribution than to demonstrate mercy. We are much more prone to rip our enemy's head off than offer him our cheek in love. And so we are caught. Even the keeping of *ayin tachat ayin* shows we have an eye only to self-interest. And so we pray:

Lord have mercy. Christ have mercy. Lord have mercy.

Hung on a Tree תלה

"IF A MAN HAS COMMITTED A CRIME PUNISHABLE BY DEATH AND HE IS PUT TO DEATH, AND YOU HANG HIM ON A TREE, HIS BODY SHALL NOT REMAIN ALL NIGHT ON THE TREE, BUT YOU SHALL BURY HIM THE SAME DAY, FOR A HANGED MAN IS CURSED BY GOD. YOU SHALL NOT DEFILE YOUR LAND THAT THE LORD YOUR GOD IS GIVING YOU FOR AN INHERITANCE."

DEUTERONOMY 21:22-23

Stoning was the ordinary way of execution among the Israelites. Sometimes, however, the body of the criminal would be temporarily exposed to public view. They would *talah* ("hang [him] up") on a tree. Joshua, for instance, *talah* the body of the king of Ai "on a tree until evening" (Josh. 8:29; cf. 10:26). Death on a tree marked him as one "cursed by God."

When Paul wanted to double down on just how far Christ went to redeem us, he turned to the Torah: "Christ redeemed us from the curse of the law by becoming a curse for us—for it is written, 'Cursed is everyone who is hanged on a tree'" (Gal. 3:13). How great is the Great Exchange! The Messiah becomes a curse that we might receive a blessing, and dies that we might live. The Son of God is emptied of everything so that we might overflow with his Father's love and gifts.

Lord of the tree, who underwent the curse for us, fill us with your blessings that we might live in you.

Blotting out Names מחה

"REMEMBER WHAT AMALEK DID TO YOU ON THE WAY AS YOU CAME OUT OF EGYPT, HOW HE ATTACKED YOU ON THE WAY WHEN YOU WERE FAINT AND WEARY, AND CUT OFF YOUR TAIL, THOSE WHO WERE LAGGING BEHIND YOU, AND HE DID NOT FEAR GOD. THEREFORE WHEN THE LORD YOUR GOD HAS GIVEN YOU REST FROM ALL YOUR ENEMIES AROUND YOU, IN THE LAND THAT THE LORD YOUR GOD IS GIVING YOU FOR AN INHERITANCE TO POSSESS, YOU SHALL BLOT OUT THE MEMORY OF AMALEK FROM UNDER HEAVEN; YOU SHALL NOT FORGET."

DEUTERONOMY 25:17-19

Among Hebrew curses, *yimach shmo* ranks near the top. *Shmo* is "his name" and *yimach* is from *machah* ("obliterate" or "blot out")—thus "may his name be blotted out." God *machah* all life in the flood (Gen. 6:7). David asks the Lord to *machah* his iniquities (Ps. 51:9). Because the Amalekites ambushed the most vulnerable, God commands that the memory of this people be *machah* from under heaven.

To the church in Sardis, Jesus puts a positive spin on this image: "The one who conquers will be clothed thus in white garments, and I will never blot his name out of the book of life. I will confess his name before my Father and before his angels" (Rev. 3:5). Our names in the book of life are written not in pencil but in indelible ink. Jesus will never *machah* them.

Blot out our iniquities, Lord Jesus, and joyfully speak our names before your heavenly host.

The Farmer's Creed

ארמי אבד אבי

"A WANDERING ARAMEAN WAS MY FATHER. AND HE WENT
DOWN INTO EGYPT AND SOJOURNED THERE, FEW IN NUMBER,
AND THERE HE BECAME A NATION, GREAT, MIGHTY, AND
POPULOUS. AND THE EGYPTIANS TREATED US HARSHLY
AND HUMILIATED US AND LAID ON US HARD LABOR."

DEUTERONOMY 26:5-6

These sentences are part of a longer confession that Israelites spoke when they presented a basket of produce at the sanctuary. Early rabbis called it the *Mikra Bikkurim* ("the firstfruits recitation"); we might call it the Farmer's Creed. It wasn't just thanksgiving for crops but joy over redemption. The opening alliterative words are poetic: *"Arammi oved avi* [A wandering Aramean was my father]." "My father" is Abraham, who came from Aram (Gen. 24:4, 10) and, at God's behest, wandered from his homeland (Gen. 12:1). When Abraham's family grew and eventually were enslaved, the Lord of the covenant redeemed them. He brought them to the land that now flourished with crops. Wandering no longer, they were rooted in holy soil.

God does blush over being the Creator. He loves physicality. His redeeming work and his creating words are two sides of the same coin. After all, our salvation is a flesh-and-blood man, who himself would have confessed not only that God was his heavenly Father but also that "a wandering Aramean was [his] father." Jesus, Son of God and son of Abraham, is our Creator and Redeemer.

Blessed are you, Jesus Christ, who has both made us and remade us as your own.

Keep the Iron Away ברזל

"AND THERE [ON MT. EBAL] YOU SHALL BUILD AN ALTAR
TO THE LORD YOUR GOD, AN ALTAR OF STONES. YOU
SHALL WIELD NO IRON TOOL ON THEM; YOU SHALL
BUILD AN ALTAR TO THE LORD YOUR GOD OF UNCUT
STONES. AND YOU SHALL OFFER BURNT OFFERINGS ON
IT TO THE LORD YOUR GOD, AND YOU SHALL SACRIFICE
PEACE OFFERINGS AND SHALL EAT THERE, AND YOU
SHALL REJOICE BEFORE THE LORD YOUR GOD."

DEUTERONOMY 27:5-7

God doesn't always fully explain his "thou shalt nots." Take, for instance, the prohibition of using *barzel* ("iron") to hew stones for the altar. At Sinai, he said, "If you make me an altar of stone, you shall not build it of hewn stones, for if you wield your tool on it you profane it" (Exod. 20:25; cf. 1 Kings 6:7). What did God have against iron? A likely explanation is offered in the Mishnah, an early Jewish collection of oral laws: "Iron was created to shorten man's days, while the altar was created to lengthen man's days; what shortens may not rightly be lifted up against what lengthens" (Middoth 3:4).

The altar was created to lengthen life. Through it the Lord cleansed, forgave, and sustained his people. But even the altar was temporary, awaiting the final sacrifice to be made—the Messiah's offering of himself, by which the Father has given us everlasting days in his kingdom.

Draw us to your altar, gracious Savior, that we may rejoice before you.

Nephew Wormwood לַעֲנָה

"BEWARE LEST THERE BE AMONG YOU A MAN OR
WOMAN OR CLAN OR TRIBE WHOSE HEART IS TURNING
AWAY TODAY FROM THE LORD OUR GOD TO GO AND
SERVE THE GODS OF THOSE NATIONS. BEWARE LEST
THERE BE AMONG YOU A ROOT BEARING POISONOUS
AND BITTER FRUIT, ONE WHO, WHEN HE HEARS THE
WORDS OF THIS SWORN COVENANT, BLESSES HIMSELF
IN HIS HEART, SAYING, 'I SHALL BE SAFE, THOUGH
I WALK IN THE STUBBORNNESS OF MY HEART.'"

DEUTERONOMY 29:18-19

C. S. Lewis was indebted to the word *la'anah* for the name of Wormwood, the junior tempter in *The Screwtape Letters*. And a devilish name it is, for *la'anah* refers to a plant that produces an intensely bitter oil. The OT uses *la'anah* metaphorically for idolatry (Deut. 29:18), an adulteress (Prov. 5:4), and divine chastisement (Jer. 9:15). Its Greek name is given to a great blazing star that plummets from heaven: "The name of the star is Wormwood. A third of the waters became wormwood, and many people died from the water, because it had been made bitter" (Rev. 8:11).

The psalmist sings, "How sweet are your words to my taste, sweeter than honey to my mouth!" (119:103). God crafted us in his image for the honey of his Word, not the wormwood of lies. Open your lips to taste how sweet his salvation and mercy are!

Feed us with your grace, Lord Jesus, and see that no root of bitterness springs up among us (Heb. 12:15).

Wheat, Kidneys, and Fat חלב

[GOD] MADE [ISRAEL] RIDE ON THE HIGH PLACES OF
THE LAND, AND HE ATE THE PRODUCE OF THE FIELD,
AND HE SUCKLED HIM WITH HONEY OUT OF THE ROCK,
AND OIL OUT OF THE FLINTY ROCK. CURDS FROM
THE HERD, AND MILK FROM THE FLOCK, WITH FAT OF
LAMBS, RAMS OF BASHAN AND GOATS, WITH THE VERY
FINEST OF THE WHEAT—AND YOU DRANK FOAMING
WINE MADE FROM THE BLOOD OF THE GRAPE.

DEUTERONOMY 32:13-14

Fat has a bad reputation in western cultures. Not so in Israel. The *chelev* ("fat") of something is the best and finest part. For instance, "the very finest of the wheat" is literally the "fat of the kidneys of wheat." Pharaoh also tells Joseph that his family "shall eat the *chelev* of the land" of Egypt (Gen. 45:18). Even in some modern societies, which, like Israel, regularly suffer through famines, fat is a sign of health and well-being. There are a few negative uses of fat in the OT ("fat hearts" = callousness in Ps. 17:10), but most are positive.

In the biblical world, having a few extra inches on your waistline was not a reason for dieting but for dancing. So smile and thank God you have food on your table. And rejoice that one fine day we'll dine and enjoy desserts at the fat-laden, wine-rich wedding feast of the Lamb.

All praise to you, O Lord, for daily bread, daily delights, and the delicious food you provide for us.

Jeshurun: Israel's Nickname יְשֻׁרוּן

"BUT JESHURUN GREW FAT, AND KICKED; YOU GREW FAT, STOUT, AND SLEEK; THEN HE FORSOOK GOD WHO MADE HIM AND SCOFFED AT THE ROCK OF HIS SALVATION."

DEUTERONOMY 32:15

Giving the name "Jeshurun" to Israel is like nicknaming an NFL linebacker "Tiny." The name derives from *yashar*, which means "straight" or "upright." Israel may have been many things, but upright? No, not in their moral resumé. In fact, in this verse, Jeshurun acts not upright but downright bad. Like an overweight and unruly calf, they kick at their owner. Forsake God. Scoff at the Rock of their salvation. In the three other occurrences of the name, Jeshurun has nothing to do with Israel's uprightness and everything to do with the rightness of the true *Yashar*—God himself (Deut. 33:5, 26; Isa. 44:2).

Doesn't Jeshurun sum up our entire existence as God's gifted people? We are holy (as a gift from the Holy God); we are righteous (as a gift from our righteous Savior); we are beloved (as a gift from our loving Father); we are upright (as a gift from our upright Lord). Our lives are "hidden with Christ in God" (Col. 3:3). Who we are, and who we are named, is reflected 100 percent in who he is and what he gives us by grace. We too are Jeshurun, because we are Christ's people.

O Lord, who made us and helps us, praise be to you, for all we have is from your hand of mercy.

The Kiss of Death נְשִׁיקָה

SO MOSES THE SERVANT OF THE LORD DIED THERE
IN THE LAND OF MOAB, ACCORDING TO THE WORD
OF THE LORD, AND HE BURIED HIM IN THE VALLEY
IN THE LAND OF MOAB OPPOSITE BETH-PEOR; BUT
NO ONE KNOWS THE PLACE OF HIS BURIAL TO THIS
DAY. MOSES WAS 120 YEARS OLD WHEN HE DIED.
HIS EYE WAS UNDIMMED, AND HIS VIGOR UNABATED.

DEUTERONOMY 34:5-7

According to an old Jewish legend, God took the soul of Moses by a kiss (*n'shiqah*) on the mouth. This gave rise to the Hebrew expression *mitat n'shiqah* ("death by a kiss"), referring to a sudden and peaceful death in old age. The rabbis derived this from Moses' death "according to the word of the LORD," or, literally, "according to the *peh* [mouth] of Yahweh." God's mouth gave Moses the kiss of death. A fanciful interpretation, yes, but one that is quite beautiful and hopeful in its message.

Moses, the beloved servant of God, was kissed from this life while his eyes beheld the promised land. That is a picture for us as well: while our eyes are locked on the resurrection, the everlasting promised land, we die with the kiss of God on our lips—the very same lips that, at the end, will say, "Behold, I am making all things new" (Rev. 21:5).

Until our journey's end, O Christ, keep us in your grace and, at your trumpet's blast, raise us to life eternal.

Growling over God's Word הגה

"THIS BOOK OF THE LAW [I.E., TORAH] SHALL NOT
DEPART FROM YOUR MOUTH, BUT YOU SHALL MEDITATE
ON IT DAY AND NIGHT, SO THAT YOU MAY BE CAREFUL
TO DO ACCORDING TO ALL THAT IS WRITTEN IN IT."

JOSHUA 1:8

The Hebrew verb for meditate is *hagah*. But don't conjure up the image of a Buddhist monk sitting in the lotus position chanting "Om." Picture a lion growling over his prey (Isa. 31:4). Picture a dove cooing or moaning in distress (Isa. 38:14). The prophet Isaiah uses *hagah* to describe the sounds of both these animals. This is the voice of meditation.

Meditation, in other words, is not all about closing your eyes, saying nothing, and disappearing inside yourself. It is about focusing your eyes on the Bible, saying the words, and disappearing inside Christ. When you meditate, you are a lion crouching over its prey. You are the eater and the Word is your food. Take a bite, chew it, taste it, crunch the verbs, salivate over the nouns. There's no rush. This is not McDonald's. Savor the feast. Growl over the words you swallow. Let them echo from the chambers of your body. Let each one have its say. No word is unimportant. Each has a voice. Let them roll off your tongue. What you are eating is what you are saying. God's Word becomes your word.

O Lord, teach us to delight in your Word, that we may meditate in it day and night.

A Cord of Hope תקוה

[THE SPIES SAID TO RAHAB], "BEHOLD, WHEN WE COME INTO THE LAND, YOU SHALL TIE THIS SCARLET CORD IN THE WINDOW THROUGH WHICH YOU LET US DOWN, AND YOU SHALL GATHER INTO YOUR HOUSE YOUR FATHER AND MOTHER, YOUR BROTHERS, AND ALL YOUR FATHER'S HOUSEHOLD."

JOSHUA 2:18

Homographs are words with the same spellings but different meanings, like "bat" (baseball equipment or animal) or "bass" (deep voice or fish). The word *tiqvah* is a Hebrew homograph, meaning "cord" or "hope." In fact, everywhere in the OT, *tiqvah* refers to "hope" except in the case of Rahab, where it refers to the scarlet cord that was the agreed-upon sign between her and the spies she protected in Jericho. Joshua 2:18 is strongly hinting that this cord, which is a flag of security for Rahab, is also symbolic of the hope she has in coming redemption, when she and her family will be spared. She who a hung a *tiqvah* (cord) in her window also hung her *tiqvah* (hope) on the one true God of Israel.

This Gentile prostitute, a woman of faith (Heb. 11:31), not only was adopted into God's family but also formed part of the family tree of the Messiah (Matt. 1:5). Her hope—hope in the Lord of the covenant, his mercy, and his Messiah—runs likes a scarlet cord through the entire Scriptures.

"For you, O Lord, are my hope, my trust, O LORD, from my youth" (Ps. 71:5).

The Salt Sea ים המלח

THE WATERS [OF THE JORDAN] COMING DOWN FROM
ABOVE STOOD AND ROSE UP IN A HEAP VERY FAR
AWAY, AT ADAM, THE CITY THAT IS BESIDE ZARETHAN,
AND THOSE FLOWING DOWN TOWARD THE SEA OF THE
ARABAH, THE SALT SEA, WERE COMPLETELY CUT OFF.
AND THE PEOPLE PASSED OVER OPPOSITE JERICHO.

JOSHUA 3:16

At over 1,400 feet below sea level, the shore of the Dead Sea is the lowest land elevation on earth. At about 34 percent salinity, it's also one of the saltiest bodies of water on the globe. Though its name befits this near-lifeless place, it's called by different names in the Bible: Sea of the Arabah, Eastern Sea, and *Yam Hammelach* ("the Sea of Salt"). In a remarkable vision, Ezekiel is shown a trickle of water emerging from the side of a temple, growing deeper and broader as it streams from Zion toward the *Yam Hammelach*. When it empties into the sea, "the water will become fresh [literally, 'healed']" (47:8). The Sea of Salt will be desalinated; the Dead Sea resurrected.

Using this prophecy, John says that this vivifying "river of the water of life" flows from "the throne of God and of the Lamb" (22:1). The same water of God that desalinates one of the saltiest seas in the world flows onto us in baptism. Though once dead, we are made alive in Christ.

Blessed are you, O Lord, for giving us a river whose streams make glad the city of God (Ps. 46:4).

Dry Ground . . . Again חרבה

NOW THE PRIESTS BEARING THE ARK OF THE COVENANT
OF THE LORD STOOD FIRMLY ON DRY GROUND IN
THE MIDST OF THE JORDAN, AND ALL ISRAEL WAS
PASSING OVER ON DRY GROUND UNTIL ALL THE
NATION FINISHED PASSING OVER THE JORDAN.

JOSHUA 3:17

Two water crossings, the Red Sea and Jordan River, serve as bookends for the Israelite journey from slavery to freedom. In the first, they left the land of menace and humiliation; in the second, they entered the land of milk and honey. In the first, their enemies were destroyed; after the second, they destroyed their enemies. Common to both crossings is that they didn't swim, wade, or raft across, but walked on *charavah* ("dry ground"). Their Lord, who said, "Let the dry land appear" on the third day of creation (Gen. 1:9), spoke his almighty Word once more to usher his people on *charavah* into the new creation of liberation and joy.

When Jesus was baptized in the Jordan, it wasn't the waters that were parted; the heavens themselves were rent asunder (Matt. 3:16). The Messiah, as Israel-reduced-to-one, indeed, all humanity in one man, is welcomed by the Father as his beloved Son in whom he is well pleased. Baptized into Christ, we are wet with grace and yet also stand on the dry ground that leads to freedom and joy as the beloved children of God.

Plant our feet firmly, dear Father, on the ground of faith, hope, and love.

A Healthy, Holistic Fear ירא

"YOU SHALL LET YOUR CHILDREN KNOW, 'ISRAEL PASSED OVER THIS JORDAN ON DRY GROUND.' FOR THE LORD YOUR GOD DRIED UP THE WATERS OF THE JORDAN FOR YOU UNTIL YOU PASSED OVER, AS THE LORD YOUR GOD DID TO THE RED SEA, WHICH HE DRIED UP FOR US UNTIL WE PASSED OVER, SO THAT ALL THE PEOPLES OF THE EARTH MAY KNOW THAT THE HAND OF THE LORD IS MIGHTY, THAT YOU MAY FEAR THE LORD YOUR GOD FOREVER."

JOSHUA 4:22-24

Not all fears are created equal. And not all fears are bad. One is the very beginning and essence of wisdom itself: to *yare* the Lord. This fear is holistic. In some ways, it sums up our life with God better than faith, hope, love, and worship because it encompasses all of these. To fear God is to know that "the hand of the LORD is mighty" to save (Josh. 4:24). Later in Joshua, to "worship the LORD" is literally to "fear the LORD" (22:25). And in Psalm 115:11, "fear" and "trust" parallel each other.

Echoing words from Psalm 103:17, Mary sings in the Magnificat that God's "mercy is for those who fear him from generation to generation" (Luke 1:50). That mercy is found in the child she carried in her womb—the Savior whom we fear, love, and trust above all things.

"Teach me your way, O LORD, that I may walk in your truth; unite my heart to fear your name" (Ps. 86:11).

Circumcision and Golgotha גלל

WHEN THE CIRCUMCISING OF THE WHOLE NATION WAS FINISHED, THEY REMAINED IN THEIR PLACES IN THE CAMP UNTIL THEY WERE HEALED. AND THE LORD SAID TO JOSHUA, "TODAY I HAVE ROLLED AWAY THE REPROACH OF EGYPT FROM YOU." AND SO THE NAME OF THAT PLACE IS CALLED GILGAL TO THIS DAY.

JOSHUA 5:8-9

What do circumcision, Gilgal, and Golgotha have in common? Because Israelites boys were not circumcised in the wilderness, this ceremony was performed when Israel reached Canaan (Josh. 5:2-9). This circumcision *galal* ("rolled away") the reproach of Egypt. They therefore named this place Gilgal (the "rolling away" place). At Gilgal, through circumcision, God rolled away all the stain and pain of his people's slavery. Every vestige of their past captivity was gone.

Because the root *galal* refers to round things or actions, *galal* is also the root of *gulgolet* ("skull"), paralleled by the Aramaic word *Golgotha*, "the place of the skull." On Golgotha, Jesus rolled away all our reproach. He took on himself all the stain and pain of our sin and slavery. *Galal* also refers to the rolling of a stone (Josh. 10:18). On Easter morning, when the stone was *galal* from Christ's tomb, the removal of reproach was complete. Every hint of our past shame and guilt is gone. Both Hebrew words for "roll away" and "reproach" from Joshua 5:9 are used in Psalm 119:22, which we pray:

"Take away from me scorn and contempt, for I have kept your testimonies."

General Jesus שׂר

WHEN JOSHUA WAS BY JERICHO, HE LIFTED UP HIS
EYES AND LOOKED, AND BEHOLD, A MAN WAS STANDING
BEFORE HIM WITH HIS DRAWN SWORD IN HIS HAND. AND
JOSHUA WENT TO HIM AND SAID TO HIM, "ARE YOU FOR
US, OR FOR OUR ADVERSARIES?" AND HE SAID, "NO; BUT
I AM THE COMMANDER OF THE ARMY OF THE LORD. NOW
I HAVE COME." AND JOSHUA FELL ON HIS FACE TO THE
EARTH AND WORSHIPED AND SAID TO HIM, "WHAT DOES
MY LORD SAY TO HIS SERVANT?" AND THE COMMANDER
OF THE LORD'S ARMY SAID TO JOSHUA, "TAKE OFF YOUR
SANDALS FROM YOUR FEET, FOR THE PLACE WHERE
YOU ARE STANDING IS HOLY." AND JOSHUA DID SO.

JOSHUA 5:13-15

A *sar* is a leader, prince, or representative of a king. Isaiah calls the Messiah *Sar Shalom*, "Prince of peace" (Isa. 9:6). When joined to *tzava* ("army"), the *sar* is a military commander. The *sar* who appears to Joshua repeats, almost verbatim, what the divine messenger told Moses at the burning bush: to remove his footwear on holy ground (Exod. 3:5).

In both cases, the one who speaks is the Son of God, who visited his people of old in various guises. General Jesus, who will marshal the forces of heaven in the final battle (Rev. 19:11ff.), leads them here also, for he is the Warrior who always fights on our behalf.

"Contend, O LORD, with those who contend with me; fight against those who fight against me!" (Ps. 35:1).

Under the Ban חרם

JOSHUA SAID TO THE PEOPLE, "SHOUT, FOR THE LORD
HAS GIVEN YOU THE CITY. AND THE CITY AND ALL
THAT IS WITHIN IT SHALL BE DEVOTED TO THE LORD
FOR DESTRUCTION. ONLY RAHAB THE PROSTITUTE AND
ALL WHO ARE WITH HER IN HER HOUSE SHALL LIVE,
BECAUSE SHE HID THE MESSENGERS WHOM WE SENT."

JOSHUA 6:16-17

When a governing authority declares a building "condemned," they mean it is no longer safe or fit for human habitation. God had his own method of condemning: he declared things *cherem*. If a city or person was *cherem*, they were "put under the ban" or "devoted to destruction." Because everything in Jericho was *cherem* (except Rahab and her family), nothing was to be left alive. As the story unfolds, we learn that Achan absconded with some of the things under *cherem* (7:1), resulting in Israel herself falling under the ban (v. 12)! Only when Achan finally confessed, and was executed, did the Lord's judgment cease.

Cherem illustrates that God does not deal with sin and evil fractionally but wholly. And that is very good news for us. Jesus did not die for 50 percent of sins, or even 99.9 percent. He dealt with evil in totality. No sins remained outside of Jesus on the cross, so that no sins remain on us. Christ became *cherem* for us, so we become cherished in him.

O Lamb of God, who takes away the sin of the world, have mercy on us.

Trouble Valley and Hope's Doorway עכור

AND JOSHUA SAID [TO ACHAN], "WHY DID YOU BRING TROUBLE ON US? THE LORD BRINGS TROUBLE ON YOU TODAY." AND ALL ISRAEL STONED HIM WITH STONES. THEY BURNED THEM WITH FIRE AND STONED THEM WITH STONES. AND THEY RAISED OVER HIM A GREAT HEAP OF STONES THAT REMAINS TO THIS DAY. THEN THE LORD TURNED FROM HIS BURNING ANGER. THEREFORE, TO THIS DAY THE NAME OF THAT PLACE IS CALLED THE VALLEY OF ACHOR.

JOSHUA 7:25-26

Israel's map memorializes sin. Achan, who brought trouble (*akar*) on Israel, whom the Lord troubled (*akar*), is buried in the Valley of Trouble (*Akor*). In what should have been a jubilant time of celebration, Achan's sin cast a pall over Israel's party. In an unexpected twist, however, later prophets point to Trouble Valley as Hope's Doorway. Hosea predicts a second exodus, led by the Messiah, when God will bring Israel out of the wilderness and "make the Valley of Achor a door of hope" (2:15). Isaiah too, when depicting the future blessings of God's people in Christ, says that God will make "the Valley of Achor a place for herds to lie down" (65:10).

No trouble is bigger than God's ability to overturn it. His Spirit breathes on the ashes of despair to kindle the flame of hope, for he is the Lord who brings Easter out of Good Friday.

"Let your steadfast love, O LORD, be upon us, even as we hope in you" (Ps. 33:22).

Mounds of Memory תל

BUT JOSHUA DID NOT DRAW BACK HIS HAND WITH
WHICH HE STRETCHED OUT THE JAVELIN UNTIL
HE HAD DEVOTED ALL THE INHABITANTS OF AI TO
DESTRUCTION. ONLY THE LIVESTOCK AND THE SPOIL
OF THAT CITY ISRAEL TOOK AS THEIR PLUNDER,
ACCORDING TO THE WORD OF THE LORD THAT HE
COMMANDED JOSHUA. SO JOSHUA BURNED AI AND MADE
IT FOREVER A HEAP OF RUINS, AS IT IS TO THIS DAY.

JOSHUA 8:26–28

Dotting the landscape of the Middle East are thousands of hill-shaped mounds that archaeologists call *tels* (or "tells"). In Hebrew, *tel* means "heap," as when Joshua demolished Ai, making it a "*tel* of ruins." Over the centuries, a *tel* was formed when a city was destroyed and rebuilt atop the ruins, adding layer to layer. Some cities in the OT have the word added to their name, such as Tel Aviv (Ezek. 3:15) and Tel Harsha (Neh. 7:61).

Each *tel* is a mound of memory. They bear silent witness to the transitory nature of earthly cities, each one teetering on the brink of war, fire, or earthquake. Along with Abraham, we look "forward to the city that has foundations, whose designer and builder is God" (Heb. 11:10). This is no *tel*, built from below, but "the holy city, new Jerusalem, coming down out of heaven from God, prepared as a bride adorned for her husband" (Rev. 21:2).

Open to us the gates of righteousness, O Lord, that we may reside forever within Zion's walls.

Reading Aloud קרא

AFTERWARD [JOSHUA] READ ALL THE WORDS OF THE
LAW, THE BLESSING AND THE CURSE, ACCORDING TO
ALL THAT IS WRITTEN IN THE BOOK OF THE LAW. THERE
WAS NOT A WORD OF ALL THAT MOSES COMMANDED
THAT JOSHUA DID NOT READ BEFORE ALL THE ASSEMBLY
OF ISRAEL, AND THE WOMEN, AND THE LITTLE ONES,
AND THE SOJOURNERS WHO LIVED AMONG THEM.

JOSHUA 8:34–35

Until modern times, reading silently, even when alone, was virtually unheard
of. To read was to read aloud. To "read or recite aloud from a scroll or doc-
ument" is one of many meanings of the verb *qara*. The noun form, *miqra*,
could designate "the reading" from Scripture (Neh. 8:8). When Joshua publicly and orally read from the Torah to "all the assembly of Israel," he established a tradition that continues to this day in church. Men, women, and
children have the Word of God poured into their ears.

In a synagogue in Nazareth, Jesus was handed the scroll of the prophet
Isaiah. Like Joshua before him, Jesus read before the people. Only when
he was finished, he didn't say, "This is the word of the Lord." He said, in
essence, "I am the word of the Lord," for he told the worshipers, "Today
this Scripture has been fulfilled in your hearing" (Luke 4:21). He who stood
before them, reading Scriptures, was Scripture's author and goal.

Open our eyes, O Lord, that we may behold wondrous things out of your
Word (Ps. 119:18).

Pray for the Peace
of Jerusalem ירושלם

AS SOON AS ADONI-ZEDEK, KING OF JERUSALEM, HEARD
HOW JOSHUA HAD CAPTURED AI AND HAD DEVOTED
IT TO DESTRUCTION, DOING TO AI AND ITS KING AS
HE HAD DONE TO JERICHO AND ITS KING, AND HOW
THE INHABITANTS OF GIBEON HAD MADE PEACE WITH
ISRAEL AND WERE AMONG THEM, HE FEARED GREATLY.

JOSHUA 10:1–2

Yerushalayim ("Jerusalem") is formed from two words: "Jeru-" is from *yara*
("found" or "establish"), and "-salem" is from *shalom* ("peace" or "wholeness"). It is sadly fitting, though, that the Bible's first use of this name
(Josh. 10:1) is in the context of war, for this "foundation of peace" rarely
lived up to its name. From time immemorial, it's been rocked by civil war,
insurrection, coup, and siege. Yet it was the city of David and hometown of
Yahweh. Though stained by millennia of tragedy and death, *Yerushalayim*
was the mountainous city where, of all other dwelling places on earth, God
chose to hang his hat.

Jesus knew he must die in Jerusalem. No other zip code would do. In this
"foundation of peace," he himself would become our peace (Eph. 2:14),
bridging the gap between Jews and Gentiles in his own body. In him we
have *shalom* beyond understanding. And we await, in faith and hope, when
the Lord will "create Jerusalem to be a joy, and her people to be a gladness"
(Isa. 65:18).

"Blessed be the LORD from Zion, he who dwells in Jerusalem! Praise the
LORD!" (Ps. 135:21).

Canaanites' Superior Weaponry רכב

AND THEY CAME OUT WITH ALL THEIR TROOPS, A GREAT HORDE, IN NUMBER LIKE THE SAND THAT IS ON THE SEASHORE, WITH VERY MANY HORSES AND CHARIOTS. AND ALL THESE KINGS JOINED THEIR FORCES AND CAME AND ENCAMPED TOGETHER AT THE WATERS OF MEROM TO FIGHT AGAINST ISRAEL.

JOSHUA 11:4-5

Six chariots were found in the tomb of Tutankhamen ("King Tut"), witness to the popularity of chariotry in ancient Egypt. The *rekev* ("chariot"), from the verb *rakav* ("to ride"), was used for warfare, hunting, and transportation. In Israel's story and song, chariots were linked with Pharaoh and his army, whom God "cast into the sea" (Exod. 15:4). Shortly after Israel began the conquest of the land, they faced more chariots—a vast and powerful army, led by the king of Hazor. God's people were simply outgunned. Yet the Lord, who battled for them at the Red Sea, brandished his sword for them here as well. The much-feared chariotry of the enemy was reduced to ashes in the aftermath (Josh. 11:9).

In a strange twist, the *rekev*, so closely associated with war in Israel's past, became the location of evangelism after Pentecost. Using prophecies from Isaiah, Philip witnessed of Christ to the Ethiopian eunuch inside a moving chariot (Acts 8:28). Like swords beaten into plowshares, the chariot was transformed into a vehicle of Gospel.

Some trust in chariots and some in horses, but we, O Lord our God, put our trust in your saving name (Ps. 20:7).

Welded to God דבק

[JOSHUA SAID,] "ONLY BE VERY CAREFUL TO
OBSERVE THE COMMANDMENT AND THE LAW THAT
MOSES THE SERVANT OF THE LORD COMMANDED
YOU, TO LOVE THE LORD YOUR GOD, AND TO WALK
IN ALL HIS WAYS AND TO KEEP HIS COMMANDMENTS
AND TO CLING TO HIM AND TO SERVE HIM WITH
ALL YOUR HEART AND WITH ALL YOUR SOUL."

JOSHUA 22:5

For a husband to "hold fast" or "cleave" to his wife is to *davaq* (Gen. 2:24). This picturesque word illustrates many intimate attachments: bones clinging to skin (Job 19:20), tongues sticking to jaws (Ps. 22:15), the scales of a beast closely joined (Job 41:17), and Ruth's attachment to Naomi (Ruth 1:14). In Joshua 22 and other places, Israel is admonished to *davaq* to Yahweh (e.g., Deut. 10:20). The noun form, *deveq*, describes iron that's been soldered or welded together (Isa. 41:7). In modern Hebrew, *deveq* means glue or adhesive.

When Paul says, "He who is joined to the Lord becomes one spirit with him," he uses a Greek equivalent of *davaq* for "joined to" (1 Cor. 6:17). We are joined to, glued, welded to the Lord Jesus because we are "members of his body," his bride, the church (Eph. 5:30–32). We cleave to him by faith even as he cleaves to us by love. Welded together by the fire of the Spirit, we are forever united to the Lord.

O Lord, my Savior, "my soul clings to you; your right hand upholds me" (Ps. 63:8).

Terrain of Tears בכה

AS SOON AS THE ANGEL OF THE LORD SPOKE
THESE WORDS TO ALL THE PEOPLE OF ISRAEL, THE
PEOPLE LIFTED UP THEIR VOICES AND WEPT. AND
THEY CALLED THE NAME OF THAT PLACE BOCHIM.
AND THEY SACRIFICED THERE TO THE LORD.

JUDGES 2:4-5

We may be grossed out by most bodily fluids, but tears have the opposite effect. We wipe or even kiss them away from the faces of our loved ones. Tears elicit compassion—and often sympathetic tears of our own. When the divine messenger delivered a chilling rebuke to Israel for their disobedience, they "lifted up their voices and *bakah* [wept]." This place of *bakah* was thus named Bochim ("Weeping"). The Lord, "moved to pity by their groaning" (Judg. 2:18), no doubt put these tears in his bottle of mercy (Ps. 56:8).

Isaiah foretells the resurrection banquet at which the Lord not only will "swallow up death forever" and serve to us the richest of foods and wines, but "will wipe away tears from all faces" (25:8). John reaffirms this promise when he says that Christ "will wipe away every tear from their eyes, and death shall be no more, neither shall there be mourning, nor crying, nor pain anymore, for the former things have passed away" (Rev. 21:4). There will be no terrain of tears in the new creation.

All praise to you, Lord Jesus, for "you have delivered my soul from death, my eyes from tears, my feet from stumbling" (Ps. 116:8).

Warrior Judges שֹׁפְטִים

THEN THE LORD RAISED UP JUDGES, WHO SAVED
THEM OUT OF THE HAND OF THOSE WHO PLUNDERED
THEM. YET THEY DID NOT LISTEN TO THEIR JUDGES,
FOR THEY WHORED AFTER OTHER GODS AND
BOWED DOWN TO THEM. THEY SOON TURNED ASIDE
FROM THE WAY IN WHICH THEIR FATHERS HAD
WALKED, WHO HAD OBEYED THE COMMANDMENTS
OF THE LORD, AND THEY DID NOT DO SO.

JUDGES 2:16-17

We would have been spared some muddied thinking about the book of
Judges if it had been titled "Saviors" instead. When the author calls them
shofetim ("judges"), he describes their vocation this way: they "saved [Israel]
out of the hand of those who plundered them" (2:16-18). Their calling was
not judicial; they were to *yasha* ("save") God's people. They wore swords,
not black robes. And their "courtroom" was the battlefield. Almost all of
them did some dastardly deeds—they too often did what was right in their
own eyes—but God still used these broken vessels for his kingdom's work.
Indeed, Hebrews remembers them for their faith (11:32-34).

Each "savior" served as a black-and-white sketch that Jesus filled in with
full, holy, and rich color. Not just another one of the *shofetim*, this almighty
Judge and Savior redeemed humanity by overthrowing the overlord of hell
who had plundered us of life itself. And the rest that Christ bestows on us
will never end.

"Oh, save your people and bless your heritage! Be their shepherd and carry
them forever" (Ps. 28:9).

Forget You! שכח

AND THE PEOPLE OF ISRAEL DID WHAT WAS EVIL IN THE
SIGHT OF THE LORD. THEY FORGOT THE LORD THEIR
GOD AND SERVED THE BAALS AND THE ASHEROTH.

JUDGES 3:7

Not all forgetting is the same. For example, if I forget to pick up my wife's dry cleaning, that's one thing. But if later, while fighting about this, I yell, "Forget you!" that's vastly different. The former is a foible, the latter an affront. In Hebrew, to *shakach* ("forget") often belongs to the second category. When God's people spiritually prostituted themselves to Canaanite deities, their Lord didn't simply fade from their memories. They actively rejected him and spurned his exclusive worship. To *shakach*, in this sense, is not a slip of the mind but an adulteration of the heart. It's saying, "Forget you!" to God.

Paul considered his former religious achievements as "rubbish" (Greek: *skubala* [slang for "excrement"]) compared to gaining Christ (Phil. 3:8). A few verses later, he says, "One thing I do: forgetting what lies behind and straining forward to what lies ahead"—namely, to "the upward call of God in Christ" (3:13-14). In Hebrew fashion, Paul is saying, "Forget you!" to his past. He desires—as do we—to know Christ and the power of his resurrection (3:10). Faith is to *shakach* all that would keep us from life and salvation in the Messiah, who remembers us in his mercy.

"Arise, O LORD; O God, lift up your hand; forget not the afflicted" (Ps. 10:12).

God as Merchant מכר

THE ANGER OF THE LORD WAS KINDLED AGAINST ISRAEL,
AND HE SOLD THEM INTO THE HAND OF CUSHAN-
RISHATHAIM KING OF MESOPOTAMIA. AND THE PEOPLE
OF ISRAEL SERVED CUSHAN-RISHATHAIM EIGHT YEARS.

JUDGES 3:8

When Joseph's brothers opted not to murder him, they *makar* ("sold") him to Ishmaelites (Gen. 37:28). If an Israelite soldier brought home a prisoner of war and married her, he could not later *makar* her (Deut. 21:14). In addition to selling people, *makar* also covers many commercial transactions, like selling land (Gen. 47:20). Multiple times, to discipline his people for their idolatry, God would *makar* them to foreign kings, such as Cushan-rishathaim (Judg. 3:8), Jabin (4:2), and the Philistines (10:7). The goal was to bring them to repentance, that they might remember the covenant and trust again in him as their redeeming God.

But ultimately there was only one way to deal, finally and fully, with the evil that bedevils humanity: the Son of God himself was sold out for a measly "thirty pieces of silver" by Judas Iscariot (Matt. 26:15). Yet the result of that sale was priceless redemption for us. We were ransomed not with "silver or gold, but with the precious blood of Christ, like that of a lamb without blemish or spot" (1 Pet. 1:18-19).

Heavenly Father, though our sins are as scarlet, make them white as snow in the blood of the Lamb.

The Fat Calf King עֶגֶל

AND THE PEOPLE OF ISRAEL AGAIN DID WHAT
WAS EVIL IN THE SIGHT OF THE LORD, AND
THE LORD STRENGTHENED EGLON THE KING OF
MOAB AGAINST ISRAEL, BECAUSE THEY HAD
DONE WHAT WAS EVIL IN THE SIGHT OF THE
LORD . . . NOW EGLON WAS A VERY FAT MAN.

JUDGES 3:12, 17

Some expressions that we deem politically incorrect or highly offensive today are used without reservation in the Old Testament to mock Israel's enemies. The short story of Eglon is a raw and sarcastic farce intended to poke fun at the foe. The comedy begins with Eglon's name, a form of the Hebrew word *egel*, meaning young bull, ox, or calf. It also sounds and looks like the word *agol*, which means "round" or "rotund." This enemy king lived up to his name, for he was indeed "a very fat man"—"fat as a cow," as the insult goes. At the end of the story, he who filled his paunch with too much food will eat the dagger that spells his doom.

As both inspiration and heir to this sharp-tongued, in-your-face Hebrew rhetoric, Jesus will not shy away from calling Herod a fox and the Pharisees a brood of vipers. Paul too will tell his Judaizing opponents that they should castrate themselves (Gal. 5:12)! Sometimes, when life and truth are at stake, only the sharpest and boldest language will do.

Even in our speech, O Lord, makes us wise as serpents and innocent as doves (Matt. 10:16).

The Dangerous
Hebrew Southpaw אטר

THEN THE PEOPLE OF ISRAEL CRIED OUT TO THE LORD,
AND THE LORD RAISED UP FOR THEM A DELIVERER,
EHUD, THE SON OF GERA, THE BENJAMINITE, A
LEFT-HANDED MAN. THE PEOPLE OF ISRAEL SENT
TRIBUTE BY HIM TO EGLON THE KING OF MOAB.
AND EHUD MADE FOR HIMSELF A SWORD WITH
TWO EDGES, A CUBIT IN LENGTH, AND HE BOUND
IT ON HIS RIGHT THIGH UNDER HIS CLOTHES.

JUDGES 3:15-16

Unlike modern literature, the Bible typically provides us with no physical description of its characters. On those rare occasions when it does, sit up and take notice; it'll be important. Ehud, for instance, is "a left-handed man," literally, "a man bound [*itter*] in his right hand." This could mean either "left-handed" or, more likely, ambidextrous (cf. Judg. 20:16). Either way, the paradox is amusing, for Ehud, who employs his left hand to kill Eglon with a hidden dagger, hails from the tribe of Benjamin, whose name means "son of the right hand"! Leave it to God to use a most unlikely deliverer to shatter his people's chains.

Ehud is, in fact, from a long line of paradoxical saviors—a line ending with the Savior himself. He is man but also God, rejected yet glorified, whose execution is the death of death itself. Such are the ways of God whose foolishness is wiser than men (1 Cor. 1:25).

"Into your hand I commit my spirit; you have redeemed me, O LORD, faithful God" (Ps. 31:5).

Prophetic Mother Bee דבורה

NOW DEBORAH, A PROPHETESS, THE WIFE OF LAPPIDOTH,
WAS JUDGING ISRAEL AT THAT TIME. SHE USED TO SIT
UNDER THE PALM OF DEBORAH BETWEEN RAMAH AND
BETHEL IN THE HILL COUNTRY OF EPHRAIM, AND THE
PEOPLE OF ISRAEL CAME UP TO HER FOR JUDGMENT.

JUDGES 4:4-5

The name Deborah means "bee" (*d'vorah*) in Hebrew (Deut. 1:44). During a time in Israel's history that was soured by fear, the sweet honey of her leadership, wisdom, and courage was direly needed. She was a *neviah*, a prophetess, one of several in the Bible, including Miriam (Exod. 15:20), Huldah (2 Kings 22:14), Noadiah (Neh. 6:14), the wife of Isaiah (Isa. 8:3), Anna (Luke 2:36), and a false prophetess in the church of Thyatira (Rev. 2:20). The people of God came to Deborah for *mishpat* (justice or judgment). She was the mouthpiece of God, as were the other prophets, the ones through whom the Lord revealed his will to his people. When she called Barak to lead Israel into battle, and he waffled and wavered, she bravely marched with the troops alongside him.

In the song she wrote about the battle, she calls herself "a mother in Israel" (5:7). She birthed hope for the nation once more. In her footsteps followed another mother in Israel, one named after the prophetess Miriam (= Mary), who birthed hope incarnate—the Savior who "brings justice to victory" (Matt. 12:20).

Blessed are you, O Lord, for raising up women to be mouthpieces of your wisdom and grace.

Hammer Time מקבת

JAEL THE WIFE OF HEBER TOOK A TENT PEG, AND TOOK
A HAMMER IN HER HAND. THEN SHE WENT SOFTLY TO
[SISERA] AND DROVE THE PEG INTO HIS TEMPLE UNTIL
IT WENT DOWN INTO THE GROUND WHILE HE WAS
LYING FAST ASLEEP FROM WEARINESS. SO HE DIED.

JUDGES 4:21

When Sisera, the enemy of Israel, was on the run, Jael tricked him into entering her tent to get some shut-eye. He never woke up. Having quenched his thirst with milk and covered him with a blanket, Jael waited till he was fast asleep, then this housewife became a warrior. Tent peg and *maqqevet* ("hammer") in hand, she stole upon this general and staked his head to the ground. "Most blessed of women be Jael," Deborah sings, for she shattered the skull of the foe (5:24–27). In the second century BC, when the Jews rebelled against their Seleucid overlords, the leading family was called the Maccabees or "The Hammers." But Jael beat them to the punch. This *maqqevet*-wielding woman deserves the title Matriarch of the Maccabees.

Once more, through a woman, God crushed the skull of an enemy. Once more, we have a preview of the ultimate crushing of the ultimate enemy by the seed of the woman (Gen. 3:15). Jael's short story sits squarely within the long story of the Gospel of the skull-crushing Messiah.

"O LORD, my Lord, the strength of my salvation, you have covered my head in the day of battle" (Ps. 140:7).

The Locust ארבה

[THE MIDIANITES AND THE AMALEKITES AND THE
PEOPLE OF THE EAST] WOULD ENCAMP AGAINST THEM
AND DEVOUR THE PRODUCE OF THE LAND, AS FAR AS
GAZA, AND LEAVE NO SUSTENANCE IN ISRAEL AND NO
SHEEP OR OX OR DONKEY. FOR THEY WOULD COME
UP WITH THEIR LIVESTOCK AND THEIR TENTS; THEY
WOULD COME LIKE LOCUSTS IN NUMBER—BOTH THEY
AND THEIR CAMELS COULD NOT BE COUNTED—SO THAT
THEY LAID WASTE THE LAND AS THEY CAME IN.

JUDGES 6:4-5

The *arbeh* ("locust") crawls all over the pages of the Bible. We first encounter this insect in Egypt, during the eighth plague (Exod. 10). Later, in the harrowing list of curses with which God will smite Israel should they scorn his covenant, devouring locusts are included (Deut. 28:38). The prophet Joel preaches in the aftermath of a locust infestation (1:4). When the author of Judges was looking for a metaphor to depict how hordes of neighboring peoples had gobbled up the produce of the land, he says they were "like locusts in number." Finally, in Revelation, ghoulish locusts cast woe on earth (9:1–12).

Yet there stands the forerunner of Jesus, chewing on the *arbeh*. John made locusts his prophetic lunch (Matt. 3:4). The one who prepared the way for the Messiah, even in his food choice, indicated that our Lord would devour the devourer, swallow the curse, and provide us with the food of blessing.

Lord of creation, be our tower of defense against everything that might harm body or soul.

The Canaanite
Consorts בעל אשרה

THAT NIGHT THE LORD SAID TO [GIDEON], "TAKE YOUR FATHER'S BULL, AND THE SECOND BULL SEVEN YEARS OLD, AND PULL DOWN THE ALTAR OF BAAL THAT YOUR FATHER HAS, AND CUT DOWN THE ASHERAH THAT IS BESIDE IT AND BUILD AN ALTAR TO THE LORD YOUR GOD ON THE TOP OF THE STRONGHOLD HERE, WITH STONES LAID IN DUE ORDER. THEN TAKE THE SECOND BULL AND OFFER IT AS A BURNT OFFERING WITH THE WOOD OF THE ASHERAH THAT YOU SHALL CUT DOWN."

JUDGES 6:25-26

Baal and Asherah were a popular couple in the Canaanite pantheon. Baal, a junior god, was the sky deity; Asherah was the fertility goddess. Worshipers sacrificed to Baal for good weather and good crops, and to Asherah for fertility and children. A fruitful earth and fruitful wombs—those were elementary needs, especially in the ancient world. The Israelites, sharing those needs, and suffering from a chronic case of the wandering idolatrous eye, often became devotees of Baal and Asherah. That was the case in Gideon's family, who had an altar to Baal and an Asherah pole smack-dab in their backyard.

Syncretism—worshipping the true God alongside faux deities—was, and still is, humanity's premier temptation. Thus "You shall have no other gods" always accuses us, driving us to repentance and faith. In the Father, Son, and Spirit alone do we, with ever wandering hearts, find peace and abiding rest.

Teach us, Father, to fear, love, and trust in you above all things.

Gideon's Nickname ירבעל

BUT JOASH SAID TO ALL WHO STOOD AGAINST HIM,
"WILL YOU CONTEND FOR BAAL? OR WILL YOU SAVE
HIM? WHOEVER CONTENDS FOR HIM SHALL BE PUT TO
DEATH BY MORNING. IF HE IS A GOD, LET HIM CONTEND
FOR HIMSELF, BECAUSE HIS ALTAR HAS BEEN BROKEN
DOWN." THEREFORE ON THAT DAY GIDEON WAS CALLED
JERUBBAAL, THAT IS TO SAY, "LET BAAL CONTEND
AGAINST HIM," BECAUSE HE BROKE DOWN HIS ALTAR.

JUDGES 6:31–32

Multiple forms of the little word *riv* occur in this brief exchange. It often means to contend or quarrel. It also carries a legal connotation, as in "act as a defense attorney." When the townspeople tell Joash his son must be executed for tearing down Baal's shrine, he scoffs, as if to ask, "Are you Baal's attorneys? What kind of lousy god needs to hire a law firm?" Seemingly won over by this argument, the citizens, using a pun, later give this altar-wrecker the nickname Jerubbaal, which means "Let Baal contend [against him]." After all, if a deity can't manage to rescue himself, he must be a big, fat failure at being a god.

How different is the true God! "Surely his salvation is near to those who fear him" (Ps. 85:9). His Son is called Jesus, "for he will save his people from their sins" (Matt. 1:21). In him, "we have an advocate with the Father, Jesus Christ the righteous" (1 John 2:1).

Jesus, friend of sinners, our advocate and brother, defend us by your almighty power.

God the Refiner צרף

AND THE LORD SAID TO GIDEON, "THE PEOPLE ARE STILL
TOO MANY. TAKE THEM DOWN TO THE WATER, AND I WILL
TEST THEM FOR YOU THERE, AND ANYONE OF WHOM I
SAY TO YOU, 'THIS ONE SHALL GO WITH YOU,' SHALL
GO WITH YOU, AND ANYONE OF WHOM I SAY TO YOU,
'THIS ONE SHALL NOT GO WITH YOU,' SHALL NOT GO."

JUDGES 7:4

God wanted Gideon's military force outmanned. Otherwise, when victorious, they might boast, "My own hand has saved me" (7:2). So first he whittled his forces down from thirty-two thousand to ten thousand, but that was still too many. So the Lord *tzaraf* ("refined") the remainder. The translation "test" is a bit misleading. The Lord is a metalworker, smelting away the dross. His method, however, involves not fire but water. Every soldier who lapped water from his hand like a dog was chosen. These remaining three hundred men were Gideon's dog soldiers.

God's Word is "refined," that is, pure (2 Sam. 22:31), "like silver refined in a furnace on the ground, purified seven times" (Ps. 12:6). With that same Word he smelts "my heart and my mind" (26:2). Indeed, the Messiah himself is like "a refiner's fire" (Mal. 3:2). He burns away the dross of our sin in the fires of baptism (Matt. 3:11), that we may "be pure and blameless for the day of Christ" (Phil. 1:10).

Gracious Father, refine us in the fires of your mercy, that pure in heart, we may see you.

Shofar שׁוֹפָר

AND [GIDEON] DIVIDED THE 300 MEN INTO THREE
COMPANIES AND PUT TRUMPETS INTO THE HANDS OF ALL OF
THEM AND EMPTY JARS, WITH TORCHES INSIDE THE JARS.

JUDGES 7:16

Gideon's itty-bitty army looked like students leaving pottery class on their way to band practice. No AR-15s, no grenades, just clay jars, torches, and a shofar in hand. The shofar, a well-known Hebrew instrument crafted from a hollowed-out ram's horn, was used in Israelite worship and battle. Under cover of night, Gideon's army broke their jars, raised high their torches, and blasted the shofar. The Midianite military, berserk with panic, turned swords on one another. Israel vanquished their foe without even unsheathing their swords.

The Messiah's final victory will happen when "he will send out his angels with a loud trumpet call" (Matt. 24:31). "The Lord himself will descend from heaven with a cry of command, with the voice of an archangel, and with the sound of the trumpet of God" (1 Thess. 4:16). All this will happen "in a moment, in the twinkling of an eye, at the last trumpet. For the trumpet will sound, and the dead will be raised imperishable, and we shall be changed" (1 Cor. 15:52). That blast from the celestial shofar will sound from one end of creation to the other, to announce the defeat of death and the unending triumph of our resurrected Lord.

Ready our ears, O Lord, and prepare our hearts to rejoice at the shofar blast of resurrection.

The Harlot's Ephod אֵפוֹד

AND THE WEIGHT OF THE GOLDEN EARRINGS THAT
[GIDEON] REQUESTED WAS 1,700 SHEKELS OF GOLD,
BESIDES THE CRESCENT ORNAMENTS AND THE PENDANTS
AND THE PURPLE GARMENTS WORN BY THE KINGS OF
MIDIAN, AND BESIDES THE COLLARS THAT WERE AROUND
THE NECKS OF THEIR CAMELS. AND GIDEON MADE
AN EPHOD OF IT AND PUT IT IN HIS CITY, IN OPHRAH.
AND ALL ISRAEL WHORED AFTER IT THERE, AND IT
BECAME A SNARE TO GIDEON AND TO HIS FAMILY.

JUDGES 8:26-27

Gideon started out well but ended poorly. The Spirit of the Lord had clothed him for victory (6:34). Then what did he do? Like a dog that bites the hand that feeds it, he turned on his divine master. Power bloated his head. He who had been clothed in the Spirit, reveling in his own success, then clothed an idol with an ephod made from the spoils of war. An ephod is a special vestment of a priest, worn over his chest (Exod. 28:6-14). This one, probably draped over a pagan image, was a harlot's ephod, for "all Israel whored after it there" in spiritual adultery.

Gideon, a man of faith (Heb. 11:32), was also a man of selfish ambition—a deliverer direly in need of deliverance himself. Thank God that at the foot of Christ's cross is a whole wardrobe, filled with the garments of salvation, in which Christ's one size fits all.

Strip off our filthy garments, merciful Lord, and robe us in your absolving love.

The Bramble King אטד

"THEN ALL THE TREES SAID TO THE BRAMBLE, 'YOU COME AND REIGN OVER US.' AND THE BRAMBLE SAID TO THE TREES, 'IF IN GOOD FAITH YOU ARE ANOINTING ME KING OVER YOU, THEN COME AND TAKE REFUGE IN MY SHADE, BUT IF NOT, LET FIRE COME OUT OF THE BRAMBLE AND DEVOUR THE CEDARS OF LEBANON.'"

JUDGES 9:14-15

Compared to the NT and early rabbinic writings, which are full of *mashalim* ("parables" or "allegories"), the OT has relatively few. Jotham's fable, in Judges 9, is one of the more memorable. The trees, in the market for a king, offer to anoint the olive tree, fig, and vine, but they all refuse. But not the *atad* ("bramble," a species of buckthorn); it's all gung-ho for the job. This scrawny bush, riddled with thorns, represents the lowlife, brother-murdering Abimelech, whom the foolish citizens of Shechem had crowned. In the end, as Jotham predicted, this bramble king torched his own people. Afterward, his skull was crushed when a woman weaponized a millstone and brained him with it. Not all fables, it seems, end with "happily ever after."

The crown of thorns topping the head of the King of kings was meant as a mockery, but how fitting it was, for the Messiah died for lowlifes too. For murderers and thieves and—most menacing of all—the self-righteous. His bramble crown marks true, selfless, divine royalty.

O thorn-crowned King, lover of humanity, reign over us in the power of your absolution.

Shibboleth שבלת

THE GILEADITES CAPTURED THE FORDS OF THE JORDAN
AGAINST THE EPHRAIMITES. AND WHEN ANY OF THE
FUGITIVES OF EPHRAIM SAID, "LET ME GO OVER," THE
MEN OF GILEAD SAID TO HIM, "ARE YOU AN EPHRAIMITE?"
WHEN HE SAID, "NO," THEY SAID TO HIM, "THEN SAY
SHIBBOLETH," AND HE SAID, "SIBBOLETH," FOR HE COULD
NOT PRONOUNCE IT RIGHT. THEN THEY SEIZED HIM AND
SLAUGHTERED HIM AT THE FORDS OF THE JORDAN.

JUDGES 12:5-6

Today a shibboleth is in-group speech that's purposefully exclusionary. It builds linguistic or ideological walls that declare, "You're in" or "You're out." The Hebrew word originally meant "ear of corn" or "flow of water" (scholars are divided on this), but the definition is peripheral. What mattered was whether your tongue was able to pronounce it with a Gileadite accent. What renders the bloodbath from Judges so depressing is that it was a war between brother Israelites. Not knowing the "password" meant not seeing another sunrise. Speech and slaughter have a long and ragged history in humanity.

On the night of Jesus' arrest, Peter was recognized by his Galilean accent (Matt. 26:73). This brother would thrice deny his brother, the student his rabbi. Thank God that though the body of Jesus was bruised and battered from head to toe, his tongue remained uninjured, that he might intercede for us with words his Father would hear, understand, and answer.

"O LORD, you hear the desire of the afflicted; you will strengthen their heart; you will incline your ear" (Ps. 10:17).

No Barbers, Bars, and Bodies נזיר

AND THE ANGEL OF THE LORD APPEARED TO THE WOMAN AND SAID TO HER, "BEHOLD, YOU ARE BARREN AND HAVE NOT BORNE CHILDREN, BUT YOU SHALL CONCEIVE AND BEAR A SON. THEREFORE BE CAREFUL AND DRINK NO WINE OR STRONG DRINK, AND EAT NOTHING UNCLEAN, FOR BEHOLD, YOU SHALL CONCEIVE AND BEAR A SON. NO RAZOR SHALL COME UPON HIS HEAD, FOR THE CHILD SHALL BE A NAZIRITE TO GOD FROM THE WOMB, AND HE SHALL BEGIN TO SAVE ISRAEL FROM THE HAND OF THE PHILISTINES."

JUDGES 13:3-5

The name Nazarite (*Nazir*) is from *nazar* ("separate"). They vowed to *nazar* themselves from haircuts, consumption of vine products, and contact with any corpse (Num. 6:1–21). This vow was usually temporary, though Samson's was lifelong. He was a total Nazarite flunky, however, not only in eating honey from a lion corpse but in getting buzzed by Delilah.

John the Baptist may have been a Nazarite, since he was not to consume "wine or strong drink" (Luke 1:15). Both Samson and John gave their lives in the service of the Lord. Samson "saved Israel" and John rolled out the prophetic carpet for the Messiah. Both were agents in the divine plan that culminated in the one who loves us so intimately that he counts even the hairs of our heads.

"Even to old age and gray hairs, O God, do not forsake me, until I proclaim your might to another generation, your power to all those to come" (Ps. 71:18).

Skirt-Chasing
Sunny Boy שִׁמְשׁוֹן

AND THE WOMAN BORE A SON AND CALLED HIS
NAME SAMSON. AND THE YOUNG MAN GREW,
AND THE LORD BLESSED HIM. AND THE SPIRIT
OF THE LORD BEGAN TO STIR HIM IN MAHANEH-
DAN, BETWEEN ZORAH AND ESHTAOL.

JUDGES 13:24-25

The English spelling of biblical names is usually derived from Greek and Latin translations, so they often don't sound like the original Hebrew. Samson is a case in point. In Hebrew, his name is Shimshon, which is a diminutive form of *shemesh* ("sun"). Samson is Sunny Boy. But the bright hopes attached to Shimshon were often eclipsed by his lunatic addiction to skirt-chasing.

> Samson was a weak, strong man.
> A weak, strong man was he.
> Just one hot-bodied damsel
> Could squash him like a flea.

Shimshon's lust and power were his undoing—the chinks in the armor of many a man. Blessed and Spirit-driven, he was simultaneously cursed and passion-driven. Saint and sinner, a motley mixture of divine weal and human woe. Sunny Boy, like all of us self-destructive mortals, stood in need of the rays of mercy that shine from Sun of righteousness, the Messiah, who rises with healing in his wings (Mal. 4:2).

O Lord God, our sun and shield, bestow favor and honor upon us (Ps. 84:11).

Samson Has the Last Laugh שחק

NOW THE HOUSE WAS FULL OF MEN AND WOMEN. ALL THE LORDS OF THE PHILISTINES WERE THERE, AND ON THE ROOF THERE WERE ABOUT 3,000 MEN AND WOMEN, WHO LOOKED ON WHILE SAMSON ENTERTAINED.

JUDGES 16:27

Hebrew is a language of ambiguity, playful at times, winking at possibilities. We see a masterful example in Samson's final act. The letters שׁ (*sh*) and שׂ (*s*) are distinguished only by the dot on the upper right or left. In the original scrolls, those dots were absent; the reader just had to know how to pronounce the word. The verb translated here as "entertained," *sachaq* (with a שׂ), could also be read as "crushed," with the verb *shachaq* (with a שׁ). So while the Philistines looked on, did Samson entertain them or crush them? Yes! Both. With a clever sort of double entendre, the biblical author is suggesting to us that Samson may have been blinded and mocked, but it was he who had the last laugh.

For all his faults, Samson fulfilled his vocation of delivering Israel with great gusto and sacrifice. He killed more of the enemy by dying than he had killed by living (v. 30). We see here a preview of the Redeemer himself, by whose sacrifice all our foes have been crushed underfoot, so that we, not the devil, have the last laugh.

Lord of sacrifice and God of joy, stir within our hearts the laughter of faith that rejoices in your saving work.

Slingshots and Sin חטא

AMONG ALL THESE WERE 700 CHOSEN MEN
WHO WERE LEFT-HANDED; EVERY ONE COULD
SLING A STONE AT A HAIR AND NOT MISS.

JUDGES 20:16

These highly accurate southpaw slingers give us an insight into the meaning of the verb *chata*, commonly translated "to sin." That they did "not miss," in Hebrew, is they did not *chata*. To *chata* is to miss the mark. Similarly, in Proverbs 19:2, the man in a hurry "*chata* his way," misses his way. To sin, therefore, is to fail to live up to an expectation or duty, to be less than what God has targeted for us. One cannot *chata* unless there is an objective standard, a law, a goal. The Lord's target for us is to image him fully on earth, to be what he created us to be. As sinners, it's not that we don't aim—we are always aiming for something. It's just that our targets are usually self-serving, self-devised schemes of self-righteousness rather than the life of sacrificial love encapsulated in divine laws.

Not only did Jesus never miss the target; he hit God's bull's-eye for all of us. He was not simply a "good boy" who never broke the rules. He was fully, perfectly human as his Father intended all of us to be. Baptized into his body, we are thereby restored to the image God desires us all to share.

"O Lord, be gracious to me; heal me, for I have sinned against you!" (Ps. 41:4).

Bethlehem:
House of Bread בית לחם

IN THE DAYS WHEN THE JUDGES RULED THERE WAS
A FAMINE IN THE LAND, AND A MAN OF BETHLEHEM
IN JUDAH WENT TO SOJOURN IN THE COUNTRY OF
MOAB, HE AND HIS WIFE AND HIS TWO SONS.

RUTH 1:1

The long, frigid winters in Hell, Michigan, make that town's name choice rather paradoxical. At one time, the same applied to *Beth Lechem* ("House of Bread"). During a famine, there was no bread in the House of Bread. Much like the famine in Abraham and Sarah's day led to their journey to Egypt, so this one led to Naomi and her family's trek to Moab. Behind the scenes of both exiles was the hand of the Redeemer, orchestrating events that would lead, after several generations, to acts of salvation: first, the exodus of Israel from Egypt, and, second, the birth of Israel's king David in Bethlehem. A situation of hopeless discord was, in the hands of the divine musician, a perfect opportunity to pen a ballad of liberation and joy.

In perfect tune with this divine music was the birth of the Messiah in *Beth Lechem*. The bread of God, the bread of life, celebrates his nativity in the House of Bread. Into this cosmos of darkness and hopelessness, the whisper of an ancient song of liberation and joy was in the wind once more.

Good Shepherd, who prepares a table before us in the presence of our enemies, feed us with the bread of life.

Untranslatable Love חסד

BUT NAOMI SAID TO HER TWO DAUGHTERS-IN-LAW, "GO, RETURN EACH OF YOU TO HER MOTHER'S HOUSE. MAY THE LORD DEAL KINDLY WITH YOU, AS YOU HAVE DEALT WITH THE DEAD AND WITH ME."

RUTH 1:8

Multiple Hebrew words have simply migrated into English, such as amen, hallelujah, cherub, and hosanna. I wish the same had happened with *chesed*, for there is no simple equivalent in our language. It's been translated as "unfailing love, steadfast love, mercy, loving-kindness, faithfulness, goodness, graciousness." But attempting to squeeze a huge word like *chesed* into one tiny English word is like trying to catch a waterfall in a cup. Naomi uses it when speaking to her daughters-in-law ("may the LORD deal in *chesed* with you"), as she will later use it in thanks to God that his *chesed* has not forsaken the living or the dead (2:20).

Chesed is truly untranslatable love. No-holds-barred mercy. Covenant faithfulness even if it costs God the lifeblood of his beloved Son. *Chesed* is the beating heart of God in cruciform display. The kind of love that chases us to the ends of the earth, picks us up, places us atop divine shoulders, and dances all the way home. There really is only one word that encompasses the totality of what *chesed* is—Christ himself. He is the *chesed* of the Father made flesh.

"Remember your mercy, O LORD, and your *chesed*, for they have been from of old" (Ps. 25:6).

Call Me Bitter מרר

SHE SAID TO THEM, "DO NOT CALL ME NAOMI; CALL ME
MARA, FOR THE ALMIGHTY HAS DEALT VERY BITTERLY
WITH ME. I WENT AWAY FULL, AND THE LORD HAS
BROUGHT ME BACK EMPTY. WHY CALL ME NAOMI,
WHEN THE LORD HAS TESTIFIED AGAINST ME AND
THE ALMIGHTY HAS BROUGHT CALAMITY UPON ME?"

RUTH 1:20-21

No Hallmarkish platitudes exit Naomi's mouth. She's blunt. She's honest. God's hand has struck her (v. 13); embittered her; emptied her of everything; brought calamity (literally, "evil") upon her; and testified against her. He who is supposed to defend widows (Ps. 68:5) has demolished her life. Because she is hardly the same woman anymore, she renames herself (the only person in Scripture to do so). No longer will she be Pleasant ("Naomi") but Bitter ("Mara"), "for the LORD has dealt very *marar* with her."

Naomi personifies the lamenter. God does not want brownnosers or bootlickers. He wants honest children. That's why he's given us the lament psalms—bitter and raw prayers for suffering people. Like Naomi, we lay at the Lord's feet our bruised and bleeding hearts. We cry to the same one who "offered up prayers and supplications, with loud cries and tears, to him who was able to save him from death" (Heb. 5:7). And he listens, loves, and—when the time is right—acts to heal and console us, as he did for Naomi.

Place the healing balm of your mercy, O Lord, into the wounds of our broken hearts.

Noticing the Unnoticed נכר

THEN BOAZ SAID TO RUTH, "NOW, LISTEN, MY
DAUGHTER, DO NOT GO TO GLEAN IN ANOTHER FIELD
OR LEAVE THIS ONE, BUT KEEP CLOSE TO MY YOUNG
WOMEN. . . ." THEN SHE FELL ON HER FACE, BOWING
TO THE GROUND, AND SAID TO HIM, "WHY HAVE I
FOUND FAVOR IN YOUR EYES, THAT YOU SHOULD
TAKE NOTICE OF ME, SINCE I AM A FOREIGNER?"

RUTH 2:8, 10

As both a widow and a foreigner, Ruth was dangerously vulnerable. She could be mistreated or maligned. Or she could be ignored as worthless, a persona non grata. Mercy was the last thing she expected to receive. So when she "found favor" in the eyes of Boaz, she was shocked that he should take notice of her, a foreigner. Ruth used a lovely rhetorical expression. "Take notice" is a form of the verb *nakar*, and a female "foreigner" is a *nokriya*. To capture the pun, we might say Ruth is asking Boaz, her redeemer and future husband, "Why have you noticed the unnoticed?"

Our lives often feel meaningless and worthless. Do we even matter? Does anyone truly see us? Our Redeemer, the Bridegroom of the church, certainly does. He *nakars* the *nokriya*. He notices the unnoticed. "Even the hairs of your head are all numbered" (Matt. 10:30). He counts your teardrops (Ps. 56:8). In his eyes, we have all found abundant favor.

O Lord, whose eyes are toward the righteous and whose ears toward their cry, see and hear us, your children (Ps. 34:15).

A Risqué Marriage Proposal כנף

AND WHEN BOAZ HAD EATEN AND DRUNK, AND HIS HEART WAS MERRY, HE WENT TO LIE DOWN AT THE END OF THE HEAP OF GRAIN. THEN [RUTH] CAME SOFTLY AND UNCOVERED HIS FEET AND LAY DOWN. AT MIDNIGHT THE MAN WAS STARTLED AND TURNED OVER, AND BEHOLD, A WOMAN LAY AT HIS FEET! HE SAID, "WHO ARE YOU?" AND SHE ANSWERED, "I AM RUTH, YOUR SERVANT. SPREAD YOUR WINGS OVER YOUR SERVANT, FOR YOU ARE A REDEEMER."

RUTH 3:7-9

Under cover of darkness, Ruth tiptoed to Boaz, who was snoozing after a hard day's work and some refreshing beverages. Since "feet" are often a biblical euphemism for private parts, she may have pulled back his cloak and lay down next to his partly naked body. Startled, he awoke and gasped, "Who are you?" It was the moment Ruth was waiting for. After identifying herself, she—in Hebrew fashion—popped the question: she asked him to "spread [his] wings" over her. A *kanaf* ("wing") refers to the corner of a garment. To "spread the *kanaf*" is to take a wife (Ezek. 16:8). Ruth is asking her *go'el*, her redeemer, to make her his bride.

This risqué marriage proposal exemplifies Ruth's courage and boldness. This woman of faith, who banked on the grace that her redeemer had already shown her (2:10), models for us the undaunted boldness with which we can approach our redeeming Lord.

Embolden our hearts, gracious Redeemer, to ask, seek, and knock, knowing you will answer.

Mr. So-and-So פלני אלמני

NOW BOAZ HAD GONE UP TO THE GATE AND SAT
DOWN THERE. AND BEHOLD, THE REDEEMER, OF
WHOM BOAZ HAD SPOKEN, CAME BY. SO BOAZ
SAID, "TURN ASIDE, FRIEND; SIT DOWN HERE."
AND HE TURNED ASIDE AND SAT DOWN. AND HE
TOOK TEN MEN OF THE ELDERS OF THE CITY AND
SAID, "SIT DOWN HERE." SO THEY SAT DOWN.

RUTH 4:1–2

The Latin abbreviation N.N. (*nomen nescio*, "I do not know the name") is used to refer to an anonymous person. In English we say, "Mr. So-and-So" or refer to "John Doe." The Hebrew equivalent is *p'loni almoni*. Though translated "friend" in Ruth 4:1, it's more like "Hey, you." This *p'loni almoni*, though first in line to redeem Ruth, opts not to fulfill his duty. This was good news for Ruth and Boaz, of course, but also a black mark against this man. So in a book packed with names and deeply concerned with genealogy, this very unredemptive fellow will forever be known simply as *p'loni almoni*.

This narrative that began with a sadness concludes with joy as Boaz and Ruth have a baby boy—a boy named Obed, who will grow up to be the father of Jesse, who in turn will father David. No *p'loni almoni*, his name will forever be etched into Israel's memory, as will his heir: the Son of David, the Messiah, Christ our Redeemer.

O saving King, all praise be to you for knowing and calling us each by name.

The Compassionate Womb רחם

"ON THE DAY WHEN ELKANAH SACRIFICED, HE WOULD GIVE PORTIONS TO PENINNAH HIS WIFE AND TO ALL HER SONS AND DAUGHTERS. BUT TO HANNAH HE GAVE A DOUBLE PORTION, BECAUSE HE LOVED HER, THOUGH THE LORD HAD CLOSED HER WOMB."

1 SAMUEL 1:4-5

The Israelites pole-vaulted over (what we call) scientific or physical causes of events. They beelined straight to the source: "God did it." Thus Hannah had no children because "the Lord had closed her *rechem* ['womb']." But in time, the same God who had closed her *rechem* opened his heart to *racham* ("be compassionate toward") her. To *racham* someone is to "womb" them—that is, to show the same compassion toward them that a woman does to the baby inside her. In the Hebrew mind, to be in utero is to be in compassion. Indeed, there is no place in the world more iconic of compassion than the womb. Here God weaves together life. And here compassion too has its birth.

When Mary, in the Magnificat, sang of God's mercy, that mercy was growing fingers and toes inside her. In her *rechem* was the compassion of God in the flesh, for "as a father shows compassion to his children, so the LORD shows compassion to those who fear him" by sending to us his own dear Son (Ps. 103:13).

Heavenly Father, do not be angry or hide your face from us, but with everlasting love have compassion on us (Isa. 54:8).

An Outpouring of Soul שָׁפַךְ

AND ELI SAID TO HER, "HOW LONG WILL YOU GO
ON BEING DRUNK? PUT YOUR WINE AWAY FROM
YOU." BUT HANNAH ANSWERED, "NO, MY LORD, I
AM A WOMAN TROUBLED IN SPIRIT. I HAVE DRUNK
NEITHER WINE NOR STRONG DRINK, BUT I HAVE
BEEN POURING OUT MY SOUL BEFORE THE LORD."

1 SAMUEL 1:14–15

Hannah couldn't catch a break. Her cowife mocked Hannah's childlessness. Her obtuse husband argued that he was better to her than ten sons. And now her priest accused her of being liquored up! But she hadn't been pouring drinks. Rather, she *"shafak* ['poured out'] her soul before the LORD." *Shafak*, a word borrowed from the temple, is used for pouring out the blood of sacrifice (e.g., Lev. 4:7). Job's soul is *shafak* within him (30:16) as the psalmist *shafak* his heart before God (62:8). Paul, in Hebrew fashion, says, "I am already being poured out as a drink offering, and the time of my departure has come" (2 Tim. 4:6).

The Messiah says, "I am *shafak* like water" (Ps. 22:14). Indeed, at his death, water will pour from his side, along with blood (John 19:34). This is the blood "poured out for many for the forgiveness of sins" (Matt. 26:28)—the blood that, having purified us, gives us confidence to cry out to God and know we are heard.

O God, our refuge, as we pour out our complaint before you, hear and answer us (Ps. 142:2).

Heard-by-God שְׁמוּאֵל

ELKANAH KNEW HANNAH HIS WIFE, AND THE LORD
REMEMBERED HER. AND IN DUE TIME HANNAH CONCEIVED
AND BORE A SON, AND SHE CALLED HIS NAME SAMUEL,
FOR SHE SAID, "I HAVE ASKED FOR HIM FROM THE LORD."

1 SAMUEL 1:19-20

Mothers may name their children after family members, friends, or even Hollywood actors. But not Hannah; she named her baby boy after God's open ear. Though scholars have differing opinions on this, it seems simplest to take the name from *shama* ("hear") and *El* ("God"). Hannah poured out her heart before the Lord, asking him for a son. When God answered her petition, she named her newborn, Shmuel ("heard by God"), for he was the answer to her prayers. Like Samson before him, Shmuel (= Samuel) would be both a judge (1 Sam. 7:15) and a Nazirite (1:11). In addition, he was a prophet (3:20). In fact, from this faithful woman's prayer was conceived one of the greatest, most devout, and faithful leaders Israel ever had.

Hannah's song (2:1-10) was the poetic basis of Mary's song (Luke 1:46-55). And rightly so. Two faithful women bore two faithful sons who would grow up to be bright lights in benighted times. And Mary's Son, Light of Light, true God of true God, is our very own "Shmuel," for he is the answer to every prayer that's ever been prayed. In Jesus, we are heard by God.

"O God, hear my prayer; give ear to the words of my mouth" (Ps. 54:2).

Sheol שְׁאוֹל

"THE LORD KILLS AND BRINGS TO LIFE; HE BRINGS DOWN
TO SHEOL AND RAISES UP. THE LORD MAKES POOR
AND MAKES RICH; HE BRINGS LOW AND HE EXALTS."

1 SAMUEL 2:6-7

Imagine being down in the dumps, feeling trapped, smothered by darkness, dead but alive, and shackled to misery. Hebrew sums all that up in a single word: you're in Sheol. This word doesn't mean hell—as in everlasting punishment—but our slang phrase "going through hell" is close. Sheol occurs overwhelmingly in poetry, as in Hannah's song, which fits with its metaphorical meaning. Its open mouth is never satiated. Silence, death, and hopelessness permeate this grave-like place. Sheol democratizes; rich and poor, righteous and wicked, descend there. Sheol is, in essence, those times and places in life where we suffer the deepest pangs—and plead for deliverance.

When we cry out from the depths (130:1), the Lord hears, for he is not absent. "If I make my bed in Sheol, you are there!" the psalmist says to God (139:8). The Messiah himself was there not only metaphorically but in a real grave, but God did not abandon his soul to Sheol or let his body undergo decay (Ps. 16:10). His resurrection was the Father's exclamation point that he will not leave us in Sheol either. He will hear. He will answer. He will raise us up, just as Hannah sang.

Lord Jesus, "great is your steadfast love toward me; you have delivered my soul from the depths of Sheol" (Ps. 86:13).

The Anointed One משיח

"THE ADVERSARIES OF THE LORD SHALL BE BROKEN
TO PIECES; AGAINST THEM HE WILL THUNDER IN
HEAVEN. THE LORD WILL JUDGE THE ENDS OF
THE EARTH; HE WILL GIVE STRENGTH TO HIS KING
AND EXALT THE HORN OF HIS ANOINTED."

1 SAMUEL 2:10

Though written differently—Meshiach, Moshiach, Mashiach, Messiah—all refer to "someone anointed." In Israel, there were many (small *m*) messiahs— that is, leaders over whose heads oil was poured to set them apart. Up until Hannah's song, all of them had been priests (e.g., Lev. 4:3), but she sings of the anointed king. This is *Melek Meshiach*, King Messiah, heralded in this prophetic song. To "exalt the horn" of the Messiah is to strengthen him for a victorious battle in which he will break in pieces the adversaries of his Father.

This ultimate enemy-shattering event took place at a recently vacated stone tomb in Jerusalem. All antihuman forces were dashed to smithereens by the risen and anointed Son (Ps. 2:1, 9). He rose to put all his enemies beneath his feet, to reign over the ends of the earth as the ruler of the kingdom of God, and to bless his beloved servants with the peace that passes understanding. In this Messiah, we are anointed with oil of the Spirit and the fragrance of joy.

"O LORD God of hosts, hear my prayer; give ear, O God of Jacob! Behold our shield, O God; look on the face of your anointed!" (Ps. 84:8–9).

Sons of Belial בני בליעל

NOW THE SONS OF ELI WERE WORTHLESS
MEN. THEY DID NOT KNOW THE LORD.

1 SAMUEL 2:12

Worthless men, good-for-nothings, ne'er-do-wells—so we label those whose only contribution to society is negative. Hebrew uses the colorful expression *b'ne Belial*, "sons of Belial," to describe such people. The sons of Eli, for instance, were "the sons of Belial." Hannah defended herself when Eli assumed she was drunk, saying, "Do not regard your servant as a *bat-Belial* [daughter of Belial]" (1:16). Wisdom literature equates a "person of Belial" with a "wicked man" (Prov. 6:12). The origin of the word "Belial" is uncertain. Over time it became another name for Satan, as in the Dead Sea Scrolls and other Jewish literature.

This Hebrew phrase carried over into the NT as well. Paul says, "Do not be unequally yoked with unbelievers. For what partnership has righteousness with lawlessness? Or what fellowship has light with darkness? What accord has Christ with Belial? Or what portion does a believer share with an unbeliever? What agreement has the temple of God with idols?" (2 Cor. 6:14–16). Christ has called us out of darkness to walk in the light of his love, wisdom, and holiness. We are not *b'ne Belial* but "sons of the living God" (Rom. 9:26), brothers and sisters of Christ.

Lord Jesus Christ, Son of God, when the cords of death encompass us and the torrents of Belial assail us, be near to save us by your abundant mercy (Ps. 18:4).

Kicking at God בָּעַט

[GOD SAID TO ELI,] "WHY THEN DO YOU SCORN MY
SACRIFICES AND MY OFFERINGS THAT I COMMANDED
FOR MY DWELLING, AND HONOR YOUR SONS ABOVE
ME BY FATTENING YOURSELVES ON THE CHOICEST
PARTS OF EVERY OFFERING OF MY PEOPLE ISRAEL?"

1 SAMUEL 2:29

Hebrew prefers words you can sink your teeth into, see, smell. So, very often, behind an abstract word in English translation is a concrete Hebrew word. For instance, the verb for Eli "scorning" God's sacrifices is *ba'at* ("kick at"). He kicked at them like garbage, treating them as unholy. Significantly, *ba'at* occurs only once more, in a description of how Jeshurun (Israel) "grew fat and kicked . . . then he forsook God who made him" (Deut. 32:15). The picture of Eli is thereby rounded out: as Israel got fat and kicked, so Eli and his sons kick at God's offerings by fattening themselves. In the end, Eli dies by falling backward and breaking his neck, because he was "old" and—you guessed it—"heavy" (1 Sam. 4:18). This kicking priest, whose god was his belly (Phil. 3:19), finally digested his own destruction.

When persecuting Christians, Paul too, like a recalcitrant ox, was kicking "against the goads" (Acts 26:14). Thank God that Paul's end, unlike Eli's, was that of a faithful martyr. Rather than continuing to kick, he preached the Messiah who has "all things under his feet" (Eph. 1:22).

O holy and most merciful Lord, create in us new hearts that treat you and your gifts as holy.

Given Eyes to See חזון

NOW THE BOY SAMUEL WAS MINISTERING TO THE LORD IN THE PRESENCE OF ELI. AND THE WORD OF THE LORD WAS RARE IN THOSE DAYS; THERE WAS NO FREQUENT VISION.

1 SAMUEL 3:1

Much like our word "vision" is derived from the act of seeing, the Hebrew equivalent, *chazon*, is from *chazah* ("see" or "perceive"). Related to this is the title Seer or *Ro'eh* (from *ra'ah*, "see"), which was the former name for prophets (1 Sam. 9:9). To have a vision, a *chazon*, necessarily involves the eyes. But notice: in Samuel's day, "no frequent vision" is synonymous with "the word of the LORD was rare." We link vision to the eye and word to the ear, but in the OT, God's Word is sometimes seen, not just heard. It—or, rather, *he*—makes himself visible. So it was with Samuel. When God's Word was revealed to him in this vision, "the LORD came and stood" (3:10). This is a coming-and-standing word. This Word is his messenger, his Son, who both speaks and appears.

These appearances of the Word readied our hearts for when "the Word became flesh and dwelt among us" (John 1:14). No longer a temporary vision, this flesh-and-blood Word got dust on his feet, breathed our air, and emptied out his veins that, in him, we might feast our eyes on the love of God for us.

O Holy Spirit, give us eyes to see the mercy of the Father embodied in his Son.

Ichabod אִי־כָבוֹד

SHE NAMED THE CHILD ICHABOD, SAYING, "THE
GLORY HAS DEPARTED FROM ISRAEL!" BECAUSE THE
ARK OF GOD HAD BEEN CAPTURED AND BECAUSE
OF HER FATHER-IN-LAW AND HER HUSBAND. AND
SHE SAID, "THE GLORY HAS DEPARTED FROM ISRAEL,
FOR THE ARK OF GOD HAS BEEN CAPTURED."

1 SAMUEL 4:21-22

Ichabod did not have a playground-safe name. It memorialized the death of his grandfather and father, Israel's black eye from the Philistine fist, and—most significantly—the ark of the covenant taken as spoils of war. Ichabod is actually a two-word name, I-Chabod. The *I* can mean either "where" or "no," and *kavod/chabod* means "glory." I-chabod is thus either "Where is the glory?" or "No glory." The *kavod* of God dwelt between the cherubim atop the ark. With it gone, "the glory has departed [or been exiled] from Israel." The dearest treasure, the most sacred item of God's people, had fallen into the hands of their foe.

At the transfiguration, Moses and Elijah, appearing in glory, spoke of another departure ("exodus" in Greek)—the exile of Jesus himself to death and the grave (Luke 9:31). It was Ichabod all over again, for the enfleshed glory of God, the new ark of the covenant, would fall into the hands of the Philistinish Romans. But there was no cause for fear, for his exile would conclude three days later with an even more glorious repatriation to life.

Lord Jesus Christ, the glory of the Father, all praise to you for restoring us to life in your resurrection.

Golden Hemorrhoids עֹפֶל

THE HAND OF THE LORD WAS HEAVY AGAINST THE
PEOPLE OF ASHDOD, AND HE TERRIFIED AND AFFLICTED
THEM WITH TUMORS, BOTH ASHDOD AND ITS TERRITORY.
AND WHEN THE MEN OF ASHDOD SAW HOW THINGS
WERE, THEY SAID, "THE ARK OF THE GOD OF ISRAEL
MUST NOT REMAIN WITH US, FOR HIS HAND IS HARD
AGAINST US AND AGAINST DAGON OUR GOD."

1 SAMUEL 5:6–7

Little did the Philistines realize that, in capturing the ark, they had grabbed the tiger by the tail. Thinking to exhibit the ark as a trophy of war, they paraded it into the temple of their god, Dagon. On successive nights, however, their idol fell flat on his face before the ark, then later was found decapitated and his hands chopped off. Then a plague of mice ravaged the land. And by far the worst, individuals began to be afflicted with *'ofel* ("tumors" or, more likely, "hemorrhoids"). The ark had become a literal pain in the Philistine posterior! Finally, to end the epidemic, they shipped the ark back to Israel, along with five images of golden hemorrhoids and golden mice as a guilt offering (6:4).

What the enemy thought would be a trophy of war ended up defeating them. So it was too when death confiscated the life of Jesus. Death ended up dying. The supposed messianic trophy of war signaled the defeat of all our foes.

Blessed are you, Lord Jesus, for you have trampled down death by death.

Kiriath-jearim קְרִית יְעָרִים

AND THE MEN OF KIRIATH-JEARIM CAME AND TOOK
UP THE ARK OF THE LORD AND BROUGHT IT TO
THE HOUSE OF ABINADAB ON THE HILL. AND THEY
CONSECRATED HIS SON ELEAZAR TO HAVE CHARGE
OF THE ARK OF THE LORD. FROM THE DAY THAT
THE ARK WAS LODGED AT KIRIATH-JEARIM, A LONG
TIME PASSED, SOME TWENTY YEARS, AND ALL THE
HOUSE OF ISRAEL LAMENTED AFTER THE LORD.

1 SAMUEL 7:1-2

Since *qiryat* means "city of" and *y'arim* means "woods" or "thickets," Qiryat-Yearim or Kiriath-jearim is the City of Woods. Located about seven miles west of Jerusalem, this town's claim to fame is that the ark of the covenant was housed there in the hilltop dwelling of Abinadab. There it remained until David's reign, when it would eventually—with a devastating stumble along the way—be transported to Jerusalem (1 Chron. 13, 15).

In 2019, archaeologists determined, with high likelihood, that Kiriath-jearim is the town known as Emmaus in the NT. In this village, on the day of his resurrection, Jesus revealed himself to two of his disciples while he was breaking bread with them (Luke 24:30–31). The ark of God had come to Kiriath-jearim once more. Only this time, it was the Christ-ark, the embodied place of divine glory, who was on the move so that he might bring life to all through his resurrection victory.

O Lord, our blessed ark of mercy, open our eyes to see you in the breaking of the bread.

Be Careful What You Wish For מלך

THEN ALL THE ELDERS OF ISRAEL GATHERED TOGETHER
AND CAME TO SAMUEL AT RAMAH AND SAID TO
HIM, "BEHOLD, YOU ARE OLD AND YOUR SONS DO
NOT WALK IN YOUR WAYS. NOW APPOINT FOR US
A KING TO JUDGE US LIKE ALL THE NATIONS."

1 SAMUEL 8:4–5

Israel's clamoring for a monarchy is a case of "be careful what you wish for." They wanted a *melek*, which, though usually translated "king," has a wide range of meanings, from the magistrate of a city-state, to a prince, to a national leader. Why they wanted a *melek* is more important: "to judge us like all the nations" and "go out before us and fight our battles" (vv. 5, 20). Samuel warned them that a *melek* would tyrannize them by arrogating to himself their children, servants, crops, and animals, but they mulishly refused to listen. So God gave them what they wished for. They wanted to be like the Gentiles, and like the Gentiles they became.

Divine judgment usually looks like getting exactly what we want—and suffering the consequences. God "gives us over to it," as Paul says (Rom. 1:24). In all this he's disciplining us as a father does his son. He's drawing us into repentance, back to the King of kings, who (as an old prayer puts it) "declares his almighty power most chiefly in showing mercy and pity."

King of kings and Lord of lords, lavish on us, your servants, mercy and pity.

High or Haughty? גבה

THERE WAS A MAN OF BENJAMIN WHOSE NAME
WAS KISH, THE SON OF ABIEL, SON OF ZEROR, SON
OF BECORATH, SON OF APHIAH, A BENJAMINITE, A
MAN OF WEALTH. AND HE HAD A SON WHOSE NAME
WAS SAUL, A HANDSOME YOUNG MAN. THERE WAS
NOT A MAN AMONG THE PEOPLE OF ISRAEL MORE
HANDSOME THAN HE. FROM HIS SHOULDERS UPWARD
HE WAS TALLER THAN ANY OF THE PEOPLE.

1 SAMUEL 9:1–2

When the Bible tells us someone is short, long-haired, or handsome, it's not a literary incidental. Their physicality will feature in the narrative. Saul is tall and handsome. That sounds attractive, but let the reader beware. First, "handsome" is *tov*, the generic word for "good." Is Saul morally good or just easy on the eyes? We find out as we read on. Second, he's *gavoah*, which means "tall" but also can mean "arrogant." Which will it be, high or haughty—or both? Saul may appear the ideal political candidate, but remember: "the LORD sees not as man sees: man looks on the outward appearance, but the LORD looks on the heart" (1 Sam. 16:7).

The Messiah "had no form or majesty that we should look at him, and no beauty that we should desire him" (Isa. 53:2). Appearances are deceptive. He of no outward beauty nor majesty would accomplish a redemption so stunning that words do not suffice to describe it.

Look on us, heavenly Father, as those robed in the beauty of your Son's grace.

Divine Regret נחם

THE WORD OF THE LORD CAME TO SAMUEL: "I
REGRET THAT I HAVE MADE SAUL KING, FOR HE HAS
TURNED BACK FROM FOLLOWING ME AND HAS NOT
PERFORMED MY COMMANDMENTS." AND SAMUEL WAS
ANGRY, AND HE CRIED TO THE LORD ALL NIGHT.

1 SAMUEL 15:10-11

The form of the verb *nacham* used here usually comes into English as one of three "re-" words: repent, regret, or relent (also as "change one's mind"). Sometimes, when God *nacham*, it's good news, such as when he "*nacham* of the disaster" he would bring on Nineveh (Jon. 3:10) or Israel (Exod. 32:14). Other times, however, it's dark and depressing news, such as when he "regretted that he had made man on the earth" (Gen. 6:6) or that he "made Saul king." Divine regret is not over "making a bad decision," but it's like the *nacham* that parents feel when their children go astray and wreck their lives. It is a form of love—grieved, pained love—that regrets that the beloved has spurned the heart of the lover.

There is one action the Lord will surely never regret: loving us. Indeed, "the LORD has sworn and will not change his mind [*nacham*]" that he has made his Son our high priest forever after the order of Melchizedek (Ps. 110:4). In love, in mercy, in compassion, our priestly Messiah intercedes for us.

O merciful Lord, relent from punishing us as we deserve and uphold us by your grace.

The Redheaded King אדמוני

THEN SAMUEL SAID TO JESSE, "ARE ALL YOUR SONS
HERE?" AND HE SAID, "THERE REMAINS YET THE
YOUNGEST, BUT BEHOLD, HE IS KEEPING THE SHEEP."
AND SAMUEL SAID TO JESSE, "SEND AND GET HIM, FOR
WE WILL NOT SIT DOWN TILL HE COMES HERE." AND
HE SENT AND BROUGHT HIM IN. NOW HE WAS RUDDY
AND HAD BEAUTIFUL EYES AND WAS HANDSOME. AND
THE LORD SAID, "ARISE, ANOINT HIM, FOR THIS IS HE."

1 SAMUEL 16:11–12

Tall and handsome Saul made a good first impression but later botched the whole king thing. Now along comes David, who, with his "beautiful eyes" and "handsome" face, makes us wonder if we're in for Saul #2. Worse, the only other person in Scripture who is described as *admoni* ("ruddy" or "red-haired") is Esau, who was born *admoni* (Gen. 25:25). Either way, to have Saul-like and Esau-like characteristics doesn't bode well for David. But once more we are deceived, for this red-haired or ruddy-complected, good-looking young man will become the greatest earthly king ever to reign over Israel.

This shepherd boy from Bethlehem, anointed as king, is the premier preview of another boy from Bethlehem, anointed from eternity, who would ride into Jerusalem, David's city, to assume his cross-throne. The only *admoni* on him, however, would be the blood in which we wash our robes to make them white in the blood of the Lamb (Rev. 7:14).

"Lord, have mercy on us, Son of David!" (Matt. 20:30).

Music Man כנור

AND WHENEVER THE HARMFUL SPIRIT FROM GOD WAS
UPON SAUL, DAVID TOOK THE LYRE AND PLAYED IT
WITH HIS HAND. SO SAUL WAS REFRESHED AND WAS
WELL, AND THE HARMFUL SPIRIT DEPARTED FROM HIM.

1 SAMUEL 16:23

Music has graced the homes and sanctuaries of humanity from the dawn of history. The first musical instrument mentioned is the *kinnor*, a stringed instrument variously translated as "zither," "lyre," or "harp" (Gen. 4:21). It was played during celebrations (Gen. 31:27), prophesying (1 Sam. 10:5), and temple worship (1 Chron. 15:16). David's skill with the *kinnor* earned him a place alongside Saul as his "music man." Behold the power of music. Sounds soothing to troubled hearts were like fingernails on the chalkboard to this "harmful spirit." The devil loathes concord and beauty, for he is the father of discord and lies. Still today, who has not had their spirits unexpectedly lifted, a frown upended into a smile, by music and song?

Were it not for this Israelite music man, this expert on the *kinnor*, how impoverished we would be, since his psalms would never have been composed. As it is, his melodious words have been, for over three thousand years, a balm to wounded hearts, light to darkened lives, and poetic testimony to the Lord's anointed, in whose presence the saints and angels sing.

"I will go to the altar of God, to God my exceeding joy, and I will praise you with the lyre, O God, my God" (Ps. 43:4).

Single Combat לחם

[GOLIATH] STOOD AND SHOUTED TO THE RANKS OF ISRAEL, "WHY HAVE YOU COME OUT TO DRAW UP FOR BATTLE? AM I NOT A PHILISTINE, AND ARE YOU NOT SERVANTS OF SAUL? CHOOSE A MAN FOR YOURSELVES, AND LET HIM COME DOWN TO ME. IF HE IS ABLE TO FIGHT WITH ME AND KILL ME, THEN WE WILL BE YOUR SERVANTS. BUT IF I PREVAIL AGAINST HIM AND KILL HIM, THEN YOU SHALL BE OUR SERVANTS AND SERVE US."

1 SAMUEL 17:8-9

Goliath isn't hankering for a brawl but challenging Israel to engage in what the Greeks would later call *monomachia* ("single combat"). Rather than two entire armies battling it out, each side pitted their #1 fighter against the other. The last man standing determined which army stood victorious. There was only one problem: no Israelite dared throw his hat into the ring with this gargantuan Philistine foe. Until David showed up. "Your servant will go and *lacham* ['fight'] with this Philistine" (v. 32). This young boy remembered the words of Moses, "The LORD will *lacham* for you" (Exod. 14:14).

One man embodying a whole people—that is precisely what the Son of David is for us. He threw his hat into the ring. In fact, he threw himself, body and soul, into the ring. He in us and we in him, so that his victory over the Goliath of the grave is ours as well.

Son of David, heavenly Warrior, fight against those who fight against us.

No Mere Child's Toy קֶלַע

THEN [DAVID] TOOK HIS STAFF IN HIS HAND AND
CHOSE FIVE SMOOTH STONES FROM THE BROOK AND
PUT THEM IN HIS SHEPHERD'S POUCH. HIS SLING WAS
IN HIS HAND, AND HE APPROACHED THE PHILISTINE.

1 SAMUEL 17:40

The *qela* ("sling") was a lethal weapon, used all over the world in warfare
and hunting. Armies included *qalla'im* ("slingers"), famous for their accu-
racy (Judg. 20:16; 2 Kings 3:25). So when David marched to meet Goliath,
he wore no armor, but he was certainly armed—armed with a weapon he'd
used to defend his flock from bears and lions (vv. 34-35). More importantly,
though Goliath came with sword, spear, and javelin, David came armed with
"the name of the LORD of hosts, the God of the armies of Israel," whom
Goliath had defied (v. 45). Written on that stone projectile, as it were, was
the name of Yahweh himself. When David slew Goliath, everyone would
know that "the LORD saves not with sword and spear. For the battle is the
LORD's" (v. 47).

Daniel foretold the uncut stone—the Messiah—who would strike the statue
of the kingdoms of the world, crush it, and become a great mountain that
filled the whole earth (2:34-35). The cosmic Goliath fell because this Christ-
Stone bears the name of God. His kingdom has spread—and continues to
spread—for the battle for our salvation is the Lord's.

"The LORD lives, and blessed be my rock, and exalted be the God of my salvation" (Ps. 18:46).

Knit Soul to Soul קָשַׁר

AS SOON AS HE HAD FINISHED SPEAKING TO SAUL,
THE SOUL OF JONATHAN WAS KNIT TO THE SOUL
OF DAVID, AND JONATHAN LOVED HIM AS HIS OWN
SOUL. AND SAUL TOOK HIM THAT DAY AND WOULD
NOT LET HIM RETURN TO HIS FATHER'S HOUSE. THEN
JONATHAN MADE A COVENANT WITH DAVID, BECAUSE
HE LOVED HIM AS HIS OWN SOUL. AND JONATHAN
STRIPPED HIMSELF OF THE ROBE THAT WAS ON
HIM AND GAVE IT TO DAVID, AND HIS ARMOR, AND
EVEN HIS SWORD AND HIS BOW AND HIS BELT.

1 SAMUEL 18:1-4

Jonathan's soul was *qashar* ("knit") to the soul of David. The verb means to bind or tie together, as Rahab *qashar* a piece of scarlet to her window (Josh. 2:18). The same verb is used to describe how the Israelites were to *qashar* God's words to their foreheads and hands (Deut. 6:8). It's also applied to how love binds people together, as Jacob's soul was *qashar* to the soul of his youngest son, Benjamin (Gen. 44:30), or Jonathan's was to David. Inwardly (soul) and outwardly (robe, armor, weapons), Jonathan emptied himself in love to David.

Jonathan's brotherly love (Greek: *philia*) is a picture of Jesus' perfect, selfless love (Greek: *agape*). He "emptied himself" (Phil. 2:7) to fill us. Inwardly and outwardly, in soul and sweat, he gave all he had that we might receive "grace upon grace" (John 1:16).

Jesus, bind us, heart and body and soul, to you, our Brother and Friend.

The Madman שָׁגַע

[DAVID] CHANGED HIS BEHAVIOR BEFORE THEM AND
PRETENDED TO BE INSANE IN THEIR HANDS AND
MADE MARKS ON THE DOORS OF THE GATE AND LET
HIS SPITTLE RUN DOWN HIS BEARD. THEN ACHISH
SAID TO HIS SERVANTS, "BEHOLD, YOU SEE THE MAN
IS MAD. WHY THEN HAVE YOU BROUGHT HIM TO ME?
DO I LACK MADMEN, THAT YOU HAVE BROUGHT THIS
FELLOW TO BEHAVE AS A MADMAN IN MY PRESENCE?"

1 SAMUEL 21:13-15

Discrediting someone by questioning their sanity is an age-old trick. Jeremiah's opponents slandered him as *m'shugga* ("raging" or "mad" [from *shaga*]) because he foretold the Babylonian destruction of Jerusalem (29:26; cf. 2 Kings 9:11). In David's case, he pretended to be among the *m'shugga'im* ("madmen") to save his own skin—discrediting himself, as it were, to appear a nonthreat. God threatened true madness to Israel, however, should she forsake the covenant. So devastating would be her punishment that the nation would be *m'shugga* ("driven mad") by what they saw (Deut. 28:34).

Jesus' own family once thought he was "out of his mind" (Mark 3:21). Oftentimes the truth is so shockingly opposed to our deepest and dearest assumptions that it appears folly and madness. We need therefore to let God's Word incessantly transform and renew our minds (Rom. 12:2) that we think and speak not as children of the world, but as children of our heavenly Father.

"Teach me your way, O LORD, that I may walk in your truth; unite my heart to fear your name" (Ps. 86:11).

Razor Tongue לָשׁוֹן

THEN THE KING [SAUL] SAID TO DOEG, "YOU TURN AND
STRIKE THE PRIESTS." AND DOEG THE EDOMITE TURNED
AND STRUCK DOWN THE PRIESTS, AND HE KILLED ON
THAT DAY EIGHTY-FIVE PERSONS WHO WORE THE LINEN
EPHOD. AND NOB, THE CITY OF THE PRIESTS, HE PUT
TO THE SWORD; BOTH MAN AND WOMAN, CHILD AND
INFANT, OX, DONKEY AND SHEEP, HE PUT TO THE SWORD.

1 SAMUEL 22:18-19

Doeg ranks as one of the coldest, most despicable men in the Bible. When
Saul wanted intel about David's whereabouts, Doeg not only complied, thus
stabbing the priests in the back; with bloodthirsty zeal, he literally stabbed
those same eighty-five priests to death, along with every living thing in Nob.
And where did it all begin? In his mouth. In a psalm about this slaughter,
David says, "Your *lashon* ['tongue'] plots destruction, like a sharp razor, you
worker of deceit" (52:2). Doeg's *lashon* was "staining the whole body, setting
on fire the entire course of life, and set on fire by hell" (James 3:6).

The rabbis use the phrase *lashon hara* ("evil tongue") to describe the use of
defamatory or derogatory speech designed to harm another person. Our
tongues are gifts from God, full of incredible potential for good but also
harm. Before we ever open our lips, let us first pray to the Father . . .

"Let the words of my mouth and the meditation of my heart be acceptable in
your sight, O LORD, my rock and my redeemer" (Ps. 19:14).

Saul and His Spear חנית

SO DAVID AND ABISHAI WENT TO THE ARMY BY
NIGHT. AND THERE LAY SAUL SLEEPING WITHIN THE
ENCAMPMENT, WITH HIS SPEAR STUCK IN THE GROUND AT
HIS HEAD, AND ABNER AND THE ARMY LAY AROUND HIM.

1 SAMUEL 26:7

Some storytelling swims right below the surface of the narrative. Saul and his *chanit* ("spear") illustrate this well. This weapon was never far from Saul's hand. He threw it at his son, Jonathan, as well as David. It was stuck in the ground as he slept. And no doubt this *chanit* lay beside his body after he'd fallen on his own sword. David, however, does not carry a *chanit*. Who does? Goliath the Gentile, who also threatens to kill David with his spear. It's the narrator's way of nudging us readers, suggesting by this weapon in Saul's hand that he is a king who wants to be like Gentile kings, unfaithful to his vocation as Israel's ruler.

The *chanit* of this wannabe-Gentile never pierced David, but a Gentile's spear went deep inside the Son of David (John 19:34). The blood and water that flowed out of his side are the regal marks of God's kingdom. With these he washes us clean and fills our cups, that we might taste and see that this King of Jews and Gentiles is good, indeed.

Blessed are you, Lord God, for you have delivered us from foes "whose teeth are spears and arrows, whose tongues are sharp swords" (Ps. 57:4).

The Necromancer
of En-dor בעלת־אוב

AND WHEN SAUL INQUIRED OF THE LORD, THE LORD DID
NOT ANSWER HIM, EITHER BY DREAMS, OR BY URIM, OR
BY PROPHETS. THEN SAUL SAID TO HIS SERVANTS, "SEEK
OUT FOR ME A WOMAN WHO IS A MEDIUM, THAT I MAY
GO TO HER AND INQUIRE OF HER." AND HIS SERVANTS
SAID TO HIM, "BEHOLD, THERE IS A MEDIUM AT EN-DOR."

1 SAMUEL 28:6–7

Isaiah encapsulates the Torah's ban on necromancy: "Should they inquire of the dead on behalf of the living?" (8:19). Yet people did, despite repeated "thou shalt nots" from God (e.g., Lev. 19:31; 20:6). In the twilight of his life, when the walls were closing in around him, Saul too was among them. He visited the *ba'alat-ov* (literally, "mistress of the spirits of the dead") when all divine channels of communicate fell silent. When this *ba'alat-ov* summoned Samuel from the dead, Saul must have rued his decision, for Samuel foretold that, very soon, Saul and his sons would join him in the grave. And indeed, soon they did.

Isaiah's words are faintly echoed by the angels on resurrection day: "Why do you seek the living among the dead?" (Luke 24:5). Why seek guidance from the dead? Why seek life in the graveyard? Rather, seek the Living One. Seek his face, his Word, his kingdom, for there God has promised to be for you.

"You have said, 'Seek my face.' My heart says to you, 'Your face, LORD, do I seek'" (Ps. 27:8).

Hebrew Gospel בשׂר

THE NEXT DAY, WHEN THE PHILISTINES CAME TO
STRIP THE SLAIN, THEY FOUND SAUL AND HIS THREE
SONS FALLEN ON MOUNT GILBOA. SO THEY CUT
OFF HIS HEAD AND STRIPPED OFF HIS ARMOR AND
SENT MESSENGERS THROUGHOUT THE LAND OF THE
PHILISTINES, TO CARRY THE GOOD NEWS TO THE
HOUSE OF THEIR IDOLS AND TO THE PEOPLE.

1 SAMUEL 31:8-9

The word "gospel" comes from the Greek word *euangelion* ("good news").
Hebrew has a similar, more neutral word, *b'sorah*, which means "message"
or "news." To announce this *b'sorah* is to *basar*. So when the Philistines
killed Saul, they *basar* ("carried the good news") back home. This word for
"proclaim the news" is repeatedly used in military contexts, when messengers return from a battle. Beautiful are the feet of those who bring the
good news (*basar*) to Zion that "God reigns" over all nations (Isa. 52:7).
The Messiah brings good news (*basar*) to the poor and liberates prisoners of
war (Isa. 61:1; Luke 4:18). When he comes with might, Zion will herald the
good news by proclaiming, "Behold, your God!" (40:9).

This is extremely important for our understanding of the gospel of Christ.
To *basar*—or, as we might say, to evangelize—is to announce a military victory, to proclaim that King Messiah has won. The cross and tomb decorate a
battlefield; and they are trophies of triumph.

"Sing to the LORD, bless His name; Proclaim the good news of his salvation
from day to day" (Ps. 96:2 NKJV).

Do Not Touch אחז

AND WHEN THEY CAME TO THE THRESHING FLOOR OF
NACON, UZZAH PUT OUT HIS HAND TO THE ARK OF GOD
AND TOOK HOLD OF IT, FOR THE OXEN STUMBLED. AND
THE ANGER OF THE LORD WAS KINDLED AGAINST UZZAH,
AND GOD STRUCK HIM DOWN THERE BECAUSE OF HIS
ERROR, AND HE DIED THERE BESIDE THE ARK OF GOD.

2 SAMUEL 6:6-7

Having your name on the map is not always a welcome accomplishment. Just ask Uzzah. His sudden death was memorialized at a place called Perez-Uzzah ("the breaking out against Uzzah"). A non-Levite, Uzzah should not have been transporting the ark to begin with, and it should have been carried with poles, not in a cart. But Uzzah's fatal offense was to *achaz* ("seize" or "take hold of") God's throne. His intentions were good, but human intentions do not always equate with divine will. "There is a way that seems right to a man, but its end is the way to death" (Prov. 14:12). Uzzah *achaz* the untouchable epicenter of holiness.

When God's Son became human, a seismic shift occurred. Whereas Uzzah died when he touched the ark, when people touched Christ, they were healed. He is the messianic ark that "we looked upon and have touched with our hands" (1 John 1:1). Jesus, the epicenter of holiness, beckons us to reach out and *achaz* him.

To you, O Lord, we reach out hands of faith, even as your hand upholds us (Ps. 139:10).

Dancing before the Ark כרר

SO DAVID WENT AND BROUGHT UP THE ARK OF GOD
FROM THE HOUSE OF OBED-EDOM TO THE CITY OF DAVID
WITH REJOICING. AND WHEN THOSE WHO BORE THE
ARK OF THE LORD HAD GONE SIX STEPS, HE SACRIFICED
AN OX AND A FATTENED ANIMAL. AND DAVID DANCED
BEFORE THE LORD WITH ALL HIS MIGHT. AND DAVID
WAS WEARING A LINEN EPHOD. SO DAVID AND ALL THE
HOUSE OF ISRAEL BROUGHT UP THE ARK OF THE LORD
WITH SHOUTING AND WITH THE SOUND OF THE HORN.

2 SAMUEL 6:12-15

David's first attempt to transfer the ark to Jerusalem exploded in anger and death, but his second attempt sparked music and dancing. Sacrifice abounded. Trumpets, cymbals, harps, and lyres painted the air with song (1 Chron. 15:28). All the people feasted afterward. And David *karar* ("danced") with exuberance before the LORD. The verb *karar*, which occurs only in the Bible's descriptions of this particular event, is derived from the word for "round," thus probably meaning to spin around or whirl about in dance. David's happiness before God was so irrepressible that his legs became Alleluias and his arms Amens.

Sometimes our joy before God swells to such heights that language will not suffice. We clap. We laugh. We lift high our heads. We raise our arms. "Great is the LORD and greatly to be praised!" (Ps. 48:1).

"Praise the LORD . . . Praise him with tambourine and dance . . . Let everything that has breath praise the LORD!" (Ps. 150:1, 4, 6).

God the Housebuilder בית

> "MOREOVER, THE LORD DECLARES TO YOU THAT THE
> LORD WILL MAKE YOU A HOUSE. WHEN YOUR DAYS
> ARE FULFILLED AND YOU LIE DOWN WITH YOUR
> FATHERS, I WILL RAISE UP YOUR OFFSPRING AFTER
> YOU, WHO SHALL COME FROM YOUR BODY, AND I
> WILL ESTABLISH HIS KINGDOM. HE SHALL BUILD
> A HOUSE FOR MY NAME, AND I WILL ESTABLISH
> THE THRONE OF HIS KINGDOM FOREVER."

2 SAMUEL 7:11-13

Second Samuel 7 is a mountaintop text, towering high over the Bible's narrative terrain. From its peak, our eyes can scan a thousand-year distance. David wants to be God's housebuilder, to replace his tent with a cedar structure (v. 2). But God has a much better idea. Rather than David building a *bayit* ("physical house") for him, he will build a *bayit* ("lineage house") for David. David's sons shall sit on his throne. But God has even more planned: the Lord will establish the throne of one offspring of the *bayit* of David forever. This hopeful expectation of the Son of David, the Messiah, runs like a vein of gold from 2 Samuel 7 to the opening pages of the Gospels.

There we meet Mary and Joseph, "of the house of David" (Luke 1:27). And there we hear old Zechariah sing that God "has raised up a horn of salvation for us in the house of his servant David" (1:69). Promise fulfilled!

"Let the heavens praise your wonders, O LORD, your faithfulness in the assembly of the holy ones!" (Ps. 89:5).

Rooftop Ogling גג

IT HAPPENED, LATE ONE AFTERNOON, WHEN DAVID
AROSE FROM HIS COUCH AND WAS WALKING
ON THE ROOF OF THE KING'S HOUSE, THAT
HE SAW FROM THE ROOF A WOMAN BATHING;
AND THE WOMAN WAS VERY BEAUTIFUL.

2 SAMUEL 11:2

Since the *gag* ("roof") of an Israelite home was flat, it was well suited for storage (Josh. 2:6), sleeping (1 Sam. 9:25), or—in David's case—strolling and ogling. Mosaic law required homes to have a parapet (small wall) on the edge of their roofs, lest someone fall off (Deut. 22:8). But David fell anyway; he plunged headlong into the bonfires of lust while still atop his *gag*. Zephaniah rebuked "those who bow down on the roofs to the host of heaven" (1:5), but David bowed down on his roof to the host of earth: power, passion, and control. His lament over Saul and Jonathan, "How the mighty have fallen!" (2 Sam. 1:27), became eerily autobiographical.

When the friends of a paralytic tore apart a roof to lower him down in front of Jesus, the first words from our Lord were "Your sins are forgiven you" (Luke 5:20). From a roof down to an absolution—so it was eventually with David: "The LORD also has put away your sin" (2 Sam. 12:13). Not David, not us—no one can outsin the limitless grace of God.

"Have mercy on me, O God, according to your steadfast love; according to your abundant mercy blot out my transgressions" (Ps. 51:1).

The Hebrew Fabio שֵׂעָר

NOW IN ALL ISRAEL THERE WAS NO ONE SO MUCH TO BE PRAISED FOR HIS HANDSOME APPEARANCE AS ABSALOM. FROM THE SOLE OF HIS FOOT TO THE CROWN OF HIS HEAD THERE WAS NO BLEMISH IN HIM. AND WHEN HE CUT THE HAIR OF HIS HEAD (FOR AT THE END OF EVERY YEAR HE USED TO CUT IT; WHEN IT WAS HEAVY ON HIM, HE CUT IT), HE WEIGHED THE HAIR OF HIS HEAD, TWO HUNDRED SHEKELS BY THE KING'S WEIGHT.

2 SAMUEL 14:25-26

Hair is *se'ar*. Long-haired Absalom seems ridiculously vain (who weighs their hair?). He was a man who loved the mirror. A regular Hebrew Fabio. David loved this son, but he was also David's nightmare come true. Nathan had forewarned him that God would "raise up evil against you out of your own house" (2 Sam. 12:11). By the time this man of celebrated *se'ar* was through with his evil, he was suspended, most likely, from the hair on his head "under the thick branches of a great oak" (18:9).

A much better use of hair was made by a humble, repentant woman who "wet [Jesus'] feet with her tears and wiped them with the hair of her head" (Luke 7:38). In this Son of David, she found a man of mercy who, suspended between heaven and earth, gave to her—and all of us—life everlasting.

"Arise, O LORD! Save me, O my God!" (Ps. 3:7).

Springing Up צמח

[DAVID SAID,] "FOR DOES NOT MY HOUSE STAND
SO WITH GOD? FOR HE HAS MADE WITH ME AN
EVERLASTING COVENANT, ORDERED IN ALL
THINGS AND SECURE. FOR WILL HE NOT CAUSE
TO PROSPER ALL MY HELP AND MY DESIRE?"

2 SAMUEL 23:5

In the beginning, God caused "to *tzamach* ['spring up'] every tree that is pleasant to the sight and good for food" (Gen. 2:9). After humanity's rebellion, however, God warned "thorns and thistles it shall *tzamach* for you" (3:18). This verb, *tzamach*, therefore, encapsulates our story: from good trees to thorny thistles, from paradise to pain. In his famous "last words," however, David sings of a coming welcome change. God will cause something else to spring up: "all my help and my desire," literally, "all my salvation and desire." Our Father's saving desire will blossom, spring forth, according to the "everlasting covenant" that he made with David.

The Messiah is this "righteous Branch [*tzemach*]" of David (Jer. 23:5) whom God causes to branch up (*tzamach*; 33:15) for our salvation. "Like a root out of dry ground" (Isa. 53:2), he will spring forth to blossom and grow into our new and better Tree of Life. In the shade of this Christ Tree, we find rest. And from his branches hangs the fruit of life and forgiveness, so that we might sink our teeth into paradise once more.

Open our lips, O Lord, to feed us the fruit that grows from the tree of the Son of David.

A Heart with Ears לב שׁמע

[SOLOMON PRAYED], "GIVE YOUR SERVANT THEREFORE
AN UNDERSTANDING MIND TO GOVERN YOUR PEOPLE,
THAT I MAY DISCERN BETWEEN GOOD AND EVIL, FOR
WHO IS ABLE TO GOVERN THIS YOUR GREAT PEOPLE?"

1 KINGS 3:9

If you could ask God for anything, what would you choose? In a dream, there stood the Lord, telling Solomon, "Ask what I shall give you" (3:5). He could have asked for long life, to grow rich, or to get a pound of flesh from his enemies—anything. Instead, this rookie king wisely requested a *lev shomea*. "Understanding mind" is too abstract; I prefer the more literal rendering: "listening heart." Not just ears that hear but a heart with open ears. In the Bible, the heart (*lev*) is the epicenter of a human being, so to ask for a *lev shomea* is to ask that all of who we are be in tune with every word of the Lord.

Solomon often squandered this gift of a listening heart. But "something greater than Solomon" (Matt. 12:42), the human and divine Son of David, had a heart perpetually in tune with the frequency of his Father's word. His *lev shomea* makes him able "to govern this your great people," the church, with perfect justice and love, for he is "gentle and lowly in heart, and you will find rest for your souls" in him (Matt. 11:29).

"Prove me, O LORD, and try me; test my heart and my mind" (Ps. 26:2).

The Gift of Wisdom חכמה

GOD GAVE SOLOMON WISDOM AND UNDERSTANDING
BEYOND MEASURE, AND BREADTH OF MIND LIKE
THE SAND ON THE SEASHORE, SO THAT SOLOMON'S
WISDOM SURPASSED THE WISDOM OF ALL THE PEOPLE
OF THE EAST AND ALL THE WISDOM OF EGYPT.

1 KINGS 4:29-30

The most important word in these verses is easy to skate past. It's not "wisdom" or "understanding" but the little verb "gave." Solomon's world-renowned *chokmah* ("wisdom") did not come from burning his study candle at both ends or from soaking up the teachings of his rabbis (though study and teachers are both vital). His *chokmah* came gift-wrapped from the all-wise God. *Chokmah* is not merely IQ, bookish knowledge, or street smarts; it's all these and much more. Biblical wisdom is holistic: wise hands to engage in good; a wise mind in love with God's Word and world; a wise mouth to echo divine wisdom; a wise *lev shomea* ("listening heart") that heeds the divine voice. *Chokmah* is the gift to mirror—in speech, thought, will, and action—the wise God in whose image we are fashioned.

As a boy, Jesus "increased in wisdom and in stature and in favor with God and man" (Luke 2:52). Indeed, he became "to us wisdom from God" (1 Cor. 1:30), the very incarnation of *chokmah*, for he is the Father's gift to us.

"O Lord, how manifold are your works! In wisdom have you made them all; the earth is full of your creatures" (Ps. 104:24).

Weighing and Measuring God כוּל

[SOLOMON SAID], "BUT WILL GOD INDEED DWELL ON THE EARTH? BEHOLD, HEAVEN AND THE HIGHEST HEAVEN CANNOT CONTAIN YOU; HOW MUCH LESS THIS HOUSE THAT I HAVE BUILT!"

1 KINGS 8:27

The water that filled the vast Bronze Sea at the temple could be *kul* ("measured to see how much it contains"): "it held [*kul*] two thousand baths" (1 Kings 7:26). This giant vessel fully contained all that water. But Solomon exclaims to the Lord that "heaven and the highest heaven cannot contain [*kul*] you!" Our mysterious God cannot be boxed in. Yet he also locates himself in specific places like the temple. He is not like the liquid in the Bronze Sea, capable of being measured or walled in, but he also makes quite the splash when he moves into the temple (8:10–11). He's omnipresent, yes, but also omni-available specifically where he has promised to be for his people.

Solomon asks, "But will God indeed dwell on the earth?" This question receives a joyfully positive answer in the Messiah. Yes, God most certainly will "dwell on the earth"! The heaven of heavens might not be able to *kul* God in days of old, but "in [Jesus] the whole fullness of deity dwells bodily" (Col. 2:9). In him, the Lord is omnipresent and omni-available for us. Have Jesus step on the scales and you'll know exactly how much God weighs.

Lord Jesus, be with us, uphold us, and keep our eyes fixed on you.

Absolution: God's Wheelhouse סלח

"LISTEN TO THE PLEA OF YOUR SERVANT AND OF YOUR PEOPLE ISRAEL, WHEN THEY PRAY TOWARD THIS PLACE. AND LISTEN IN HEAVEN YOUR DWELLING PLACE, AND WHEN YOU HEAR, FORGIVE."

1 KINGS 8:30

God alone is the doer of a few Hebrew verbs, most notably *bara* ("create") and *salach* ("forgive"). In English, I can say, "She created a work of art," but not in Hebrew. To *bara* is God's exclusive wheelhouse. Likewise, to *salach* is the exclusive prerogative of heaven. *Salach* is repeatedly used in Leviticus for divine forgiveness through sacrifice. In his temple prayer, five times Solomon asks God to *salach* (1 Kings 8:30, 34, 36, 39, 50). In the new covenant, God promises through Jeremiah that he will "forgive [*salach*] their iniquity" (31:34). Just as every act of creating (*bara*) is an act of our powerful God, so every re-creative act of forgiving (*salach*) is an act of our merciful God.

When Jesus absolved the paralytic, the scribes accused him of blasphemy, asking, "Who can forgive sins but God alone?" (Mark 2:7). They were half right and half wrong—wrong about the blasphemy but right about the question. God alone can *salach*. And God alone did the forgiving, for Jesus is "my Lord and my God" (John 20:28). To hear "I forgive you," from God himself or through his spokesperson, is always to hear the lips of heaven speak.

"For your name's sake, O LORD, pardon my guilt, for it is great" (Ps. 25:11).

Bend Our Hearts Outward נטה

"THE LORD OUR GOD BE WITH US, AS HE WAS WITH OUR FATHERS. MAY HE NOT LEAVE US OR FORSAKE US, THAT HE MAY INCLINE OUR HEARTS TO HIM, TO WALK IN ALL HIS WAYS AND TO KEEP HIS COMMANDMENTS, HIS STATUTES, AND HIS RULES, WHICH HE COMMANDED OUR FATHERS."

1 KINGS 8:57–58

The verb *natah* is a common word, used to describe how something is stretched out (like a hand), spread (like a tent), or bent (like a bow). Joshua used it figuratively when he commanded Israel, "Put away the foreign gods that are among you, and *natah* ['incline'] your heart to the LORD, the God of Israel" (24:23). Solomon echoed Joshua when he prayed that God would "*natah* ['incline'] our hearts to him." Sadly, in his old age, idol-worshipping wives of this same king "turned away [*natah*] his heart after other gods" (1 Kings 11:4). Augustine describes the sinner as *incurvatus in se*, curved inward on oneself, navel-gazing, with hearts bent toward the god named Ego.

In Christ, God gives us what he promised through Ezekiel: hearts of flesh to replace our hearts of stone (36:26). Supple, bendable hearts that incline God-ward. In Jesus, "God's love has been poured into our hearts through the Holy Spirit who has been given to us" (Rom. 5:5)—the Spirit who inclines our hearts away from selfishness and toward God and his Word.

Lord Jesus, "incline my heart to your testimonies, and not to selfish gain!" (Ps. 119:36).

Israelite Navy אניה

KING SOLOMON BUILT A FLEET OF SHIPS AT EZION-
GEBER, WHICH IS NEAR ELOTH ON THE SHORE
OF THE RED SEA, IN THE LAND OF EDOM. AND
HIRAM SENT WITH THE FLEET HIS SERVANTS,
SEAMEN WHO WERE FAMILIAR WITH THE SEA,
TOGETHER WITH THE SERVANTS OF SOLOMON.

1 KINGS 9:26-27

Unlike many ancient peoples, such as the Phoenicians, the Israelites were not mariners. They preferred terra firma. In the Israelite imagination, voiced in her poetry, the sea is emblematic of restless evil, chaos, and death. The one major exception is during Solomon's cosmopolitan reign, when the *oniyyah* ("ship") made a brief appearance. When Jonah fled from the face of God, he boarded an *oniyyah* in Joppa, sailed by Gentiles (1:3). Isaiah prophesied that the *oniyyot* ("ships") of Tarshish would repatriate the exiled children of Israel (60:9). Almost every OT reference to ships and sailing entails Gentiles in some way.

How fitting, therefore, that when Jesus called his first Jewish disciples to be "fishers of men," he did so in "Galilee of the Gentiles," where they were casting their nets into the sea (Matt. 4:15-19). On a ship, the Messiah demonstrated his power over "the wind and the sea" (8:26). Into the vast Gentile sea, Jesus sent his followers "to make disciples of all nations" (28:19), casting the net of the Gospel to pull believers into the ship of the church.

May the breath of your Spirit, O Lord, fill the sails of your fishing church.

The Abomination of Desolation שִׁקּוּץ

SOLOMON WENT AFTER ASHTORETH THE GODDESS OF THE SIDONIANS, AND AFTER MILCOM THE ABOMINATION OF THE AMMONITES. SO SOLOMON DID WHAT WAS EVIL IN THE SIGHT OF THE LORD AND DID NOT WHOLLY FOLLOW THE LORD, AS DAVID HIS FATHER HAD DONE. THEN SOLOMON BUILT A HIGH PLACE FOR CHEMOSH THE ABOMINATION OF MOAB, AND FOR MOLECH THE ABOMINATION OF THE AMMONITES, ON THE MOUNTAIN EAST OF JERUSALEM.

1 KINGS 11:5-7

Centuries before Solomon, God had warned Israel to beware lest any of them bow down before the "*shiqqutzim* ['abominations'], their idols of wood and stone, of silver and gold" (Deut. 29:17). The word doesn't occur again until 1 Kings 11, when Solomon went whole hog into idolatry. Milcom the *shiqqutz* ("abomination")? Yes. Chemosh the *shiqqutz*? Yes. Even Molech, worshiped through child sacrifice? Sadly, yes. Abominations, like hazardous waste, seeped into the sacred soil of Judah, polluting the land. Later, Daniel prophesied the "abomination that makes desolation" (11:31), where the sacred altar would be profaned by an idolatrous sacrifice.

Jesus referenced this "abomination of desolation" as the time when his followers should flee from Judea into the mountains (Matt. 24:15). Paul says, "Flee from idolatry" (1 Cor. 10:14). Reject and repel every form of *shiqqutz*, bowing down before the one true God—Father, Son, and Holy Spirit, the Creator of heaven and earth—who alone can save us.

Rescue us, heavenly Father, from every abominable idol that would turn our hearts from you.

AUGUST 16

Tearing Clothes
and Kingdoms קרע

THE LORD SAID TO SOLOMON, "SINCE THIS HAS
BEEN YOUR PRACTICE AND YOU HAVE NOT KEPT
MY COVENANT AND MY STATUTES THAT I HAVE
COMMANDED YOU, I WILL SURELY TEAR THE KINGDOM
FROM YOU AND WILL GIVE IT TO YOUR SERVANT."

1 KINGS 11:11

Much of Israel's history is a "same song, second verse" kind of narrative. Two kings before Solomon was Saul, to whom the prophet said, "The LORD has *qara* ['torn'] the kingdom of Israel from you this day and has given it to a neighbor of yours" (1 Sam. 15:28). Now Solomon hears "the second verse" of this song: because he has glutted Zion with idols, God will "*qara* the kingdom" from him. And there's more. Because this verb, *qara*, is used predominantly to describe "tearing one's clothes" in grief, the whole sad scene with Solomon is full of melancholy. This wisest of men has shrunk into a gross and ungodly fool. After his death, his arrogant and hot-headed son would rip Israel in two—a breach that never would heal.

Isaiah prays, "Oh that you would rend [*qara*] the heavens and come down!" (64:1). So he does in his anointed Son, who came down from heaven to become one of us; to tear in two the temple veil; and to establish an unbreakable kingdom over which he, Wisdom, reigns as King of kings.

Lord Jesus, grant that we rend our hearts, not our garments, as we return to you, our merciful King.

228

Heavy and Light Yokes עֹל

JEROBOAM AND ALL THE ASSEMBLY OF ISRAEL CAME
AND SAID TO REHOBOAM, "YOUR FATHER [SOLOMON]
MADE OUR YOKE HEAVY. NOW THEREFORE LIGHTEN
THE HARD SERVICE OF YOUR FATHER AND HIS
HEAVY YOKE ON US, AND WE WILL SERVE YOU."

1 KINGS 12:3-4

Solomon's lavish lifestyle didn't pay for itself, nor did his massive building projects build themselves. Your average Joe did. So Israel demanded that his son lighten their heavy *ol* ("yoke"). An *ol*, a wooden crosspiece on the neck of oxen for pulling or plowing, is a common biblical metaphor for human bondage or hard labor. God broke Israel's yoke of slavery in Egypt (Lev. 26:13). Jeremiah acted out Judah's coming thralldom to Babylon by wearing a yoke (27:1-28:17). Early rabbis spoke of taking on "the yoke of the kingdom of heaven" by living according to the laws of the Torah.

The Messiah is a yoke-breaker and yoke-lightener. Isaiah says he will break "the yoke of [Israel's] burden" (9:4). To those who labor and are heavy laden, he says, "Take my yoke upon you, and learn from me, for I am gentle and lowly in heart, and you will find rest for your souls. For my yoke is easy and my burden is light" (Matt. 11:28-30). To wear the yoke of Jesus is to serve in freedom; in freedom to rest; and in rest to find peace under this gracious King.

Place on us, Lord Jesus, your light yoke of freedom that we may joyfully serve you.

Unwise Counsel יעץ

SO [JEROBOAM] TOOK COUNSEL AND MADE TWO
CALVES OF GOLD. AND HE SAID TO THE PEOPLE,
"YOU HAVE GONE UP TO JERUSALEM LONG ENOUGH.
BEHOLD YOUR GODS, O ISRAEL, WHO BROUGHT
YOU UP OUT OF THE LAND OF EGYPT." AND HE SET
ONE IN BETHEL, AND THE OTHER HE PUT IN DAN.

1 KINGS 12:28-29

King Jeroboam made two gross mistakes that spelled doom for the northern tribes. First, he listened to his heart. He said "in his heart" that, unless he initiated major worship alterations, his people would desert and kill him (12:26–27). Second, he *ya'atz* ("took counsel") with yes-men who only affirmed his wicked intentions. His internal and external counsels led to two replicas of the infamous golden calf at Sinai being erected in the northern (Dan) and southern (Bethel) cities of his kingdom, along with changes to the priesthood and festival calendar. Though the nation's funeral wouldn't happen for two hundred more years (722 BC), Jeroboam and his counselors had already signed Israel's death certificate.

Unlike this self-serving, idol-worshipping ruler, David's Son and Lord is called *Pele Yo'etz*, "Wonderful Counselor" (Isa. 9:6). In his heart the word of his Father reigns supreme. And to us he sends the Holy Spirit, who wisely counsels our hearts to worship the one true God who brought us up from the land of death into life again.

Blessed are you, O Lord, for you give us counsel and instruct us in the night (Ps. 16:7).

Dry Hand, Hard Face חלה

AND THE KING SAID TO THE MAN OF GOD, "ENTREAT NOW
THE FAVOR OF THE LORD YOUR GOD, AND PRAY FOR ME,
THAT MY HAND MAY BE RESTORED TO ME." AND THE MAN
OF GOD ENTREATED THE LORD, AND THE KING'S HAND
WAS RESTORED TO HIM AND BECAME AS IT WAS BEFORE.

1 KINGS 13:6

As God dried up (*yavesh*) the Red Sea and Jordan (Josh. 4:23), so he dried up
(*yavesh*) Jeroboam's hand to punish him (1 Kings 13:4). The king, seeing his
withered hand, asked the prophet "to soften [*chalah*] the face of the LORD
your God." The verb *chalah* is often used in the expression *chalah panim*
("soften the face"), meaning to appease. Indeed, just as Moses "softened
God's face" for Israel after their golden calf idolatry (Exod. 32:11), so now
idol-making Jeroboam asks this prophet to *chalah panim* for him. He does,
Jeroboam's hand is restored, but—as history goes on to show—his heart
remained as withered as his hand had been.

When we entreat the Lord's favor, we look to the face of the crucified one,
which is soft with mercy, smoothed with grace, for Christ looks on us as
those for whom he was willing to die. In him, the Father is fully and everlastingly appeased—and not our hands but all of who we are is restored by
his favor.

Heavenly Father, "I entreat your favor with all my heart; be gracious to me
according to your promise" (Ps. 119:58).

The Sidonian Widow אלמנה

THEN THE WORD OF THE LORD CAME TO [ELIJAH],
"ARISE, GO TO ZAREPHATH, WHICH BELONGS
TO SIDON, AND DWELL THERE. BEHOLD, I HAVE
COMMANDED A WIDOW THERE TO FEED YOU."

1 KINGS 17:8-9

In ancient Israel, an *almanah* ("widow") buried more than her husband; blanketed by that graveyard dirt was her provision and protection. She and her family were especially vulnerable to abuse, hunger, and injustice. For good reason, God ordained that "you shall not mistreat any *almanah* or fatherless child" (Exod. 22:22). There was no lack of widows in Israel in the days of Elijah, but God sent the prophet to Zarephath, to a Gentile widow, where she, her family, and Elijah were all miraculously fed by the Lord of Israel. Israel had so grossly despised God and his Word that the Lord pushed the prophet outside her borders, extending his mercy to a widow in the Gentile world.

In a sermon that nearly got him killed, Jesus referenced this incident to illustrate the maxim that "No prophet is acceptable in his hometown" (Luke 4:24). Often those closest to the Word despise it most—take it for granted, ignore it, treat it like an entitlement. So God pushes it outside the borders, to the "Zarephaths" of the world, where those who know the widow-like pain of loss and vulnerability eagerly hear and believe it.

Soften our hearts, O Lord, to treasure and trust in your Son, who has the words of eternal life.

The Fire of God אֵשׁ

[ELJAH SAID], "YOU CALL UPON THE NAME OF YOUR GOD, AND I WILL CALL UPON THE NAME OF THE LORD, AND THE GOD WHO ANSWERS BY FIRE, HE IS GOD." AND ALL THE PEOPLE ANSWERED, "IT IS WELL SPOKEN."

1 KINGS 18:24

For Baal to answer by *esh* ("fire") should have been like Poseidon answering by water. Since he was the sky god, casting down a lightning-like fire from heaven should have been child's play. But no matter how much the priests turned up the volume, raved, and gashed themselves, the heavens remained as cold as ice. But when Elijah's turn came, *esh* fell so violently that it decimated sacrifices, wood, stone, and dust. Its tongues of fire even licked up the water. This *esh* burned up any doubt that Baal was a delusion and Yahweh alone was God.

Since fire destroys, refines, enlightens, and warms, it is the ideal image for the Spirit's variety of works. The fiery Spirit of God incinerates idolatry, purges immoral dross from us, illumines our benighted lives, and thaws our icy hearts. When the Lord's fire falls on us, it hurts—but that pain is the portal to peace. "For the moment all discipline seems painful rather than pleasant, but later it yields the peaceful fruit of righteousness to those who have been trained by it" (Heb. 12:11).

O Holy Spirit, Fire of the Father, burn all evil from our lives and kindle faith, hope, and love within us.

A Still, Small Voice
קול דממה דקה

BEHOLD, THE LORD PASSED BY, AND A GREAT AND
STRONG WIND TORE THE MOUNTAINS AND BROKE
IN PIECES THE ROCKS BEFORE THE LORD, BUT THE
LORD WAS NOT IN THE WIND. AND AFTER THE WIND
AN EARTHQUAKE, BUT THE LORD WAS NOT IN THE
EARTHQUAKE. AND AFTER THE EARTHQUAKE A
FIRE, BUT THE LORD WAS NOT IN THE FIRE. AND
AFTER THE FIRE THE SOUND OF A LOW WHISPER.

1 KINGS 19:11-12

If we were to pick out the Almighty's clothes, we'd probably select some-thing flashy and grandiose, worthy of a deity. Several outfits are prome-naded before Elijah—a great wind, earthquake, fire—but none of these fit. All three were oversized. Then came the *qol d'mamah daqqah*: a voice (*qol*) that was still (*d'mamah*) and thin (*daqqah*)—the KJV's "still, small voice." However we translate it, this voice seems too miniscule for God's magnifi-cent frame.

And that's the point. Elijah is pining for God to do something big and showy. He's panicky, thinking he alone is left. In a barely audible whisper, God says, "I've got this. In fact, I have seven thousand more followers, just like you." Still today, the Lord hides in the little, the lowly, the quiet of his Word, his baptism, his meal. The great God still conceals himself in the "still, small voice" of Christ crucified and risen for you.

Lord Jesus, give us eyes to see your works, and ears to hear your Word, where we least expect it.

Dressed to Prophesy אדרת

SO [ELIJAH] DEPARTED FROM THERE AND FOUND
ELISHA THE SON OF SHAPHAT, WHO WAS PLOWING
WITH TWELVE YOKE OF OXEN IN FRONT OF HIM,
AND HE WAS WITH THE TWELFTH. ELIJAH PASSED
BY HIM AND CAST HIS CLOAK UPON HIM.

1 KINGS 19:19

When Matthew introduces us to John the Baptist, he says he "wore a garment of camel's hair and a leather belt around his waist" (3:4). That seems odd. Why bother to describe his attire? This is Matthew's indirect way of making us aware that John is the "Elijah" whom Malachi prophesied (4:5), for Elijah too "wore a garment of hair, with a belt of leather about his waist" (2 Kings 1:8). John was dressed to prophesy. Elijah also wore an *adderet* ("mantle" or "cloak"), which he threw over Elisha when he called him (1 Kings 19:19), with which Elijah parted the Jordan and which he dropped for Elisha when the chariot whisked him up to heaven (2 Kings 2:13). An *adderet* was evidently worn by other prophets as well (Zech. 13:4).

Elijah gave way to Elisha, John gave way to Jesus, but Jesus inherited no mantle from John. He inherited something better: the smooth way prepared for him by this forerunner. John, the voice crying in the wilderness, readied the nation for the Messiah, who, stripped bare on the cross, would clothe humanity with the raiment of life.

Deck us out in white garments, dear Lord, that we might appear pure and spotless before you.

Murder for a Vineyard כרם

AHAB SAID TO NABOTH, "GIVE ME YOUR VINEYARD,
THAT I MAY HAVE IT FOR A VEGETABLE GARDEN,
BECAUSE IT IS NEAR MY HOUSE, AND I WILL GIVE YOU
A BETTER VINEYARD FOR IT; OR, IF IT SEEMS GOOD
TO YOU, I WILL GIVE YOU ITS VALUE IN MONEY." BUT
NABOTH SAID TO AHAB, "THE LORD FORBID THAT I
SHOULD GIVE YOU THE INHERITANCE OF MY FATHERS."

1 KINGS 21:2-3

The story of Naboth, Ahab, and Jezebel is about much more than a single *kerem* ("vineyard"). It is the story, in brief, of the northern kingdom. Naboth is the faithful Israelite, honoring his *kerem* as an inheritance from the Lord. His land is a mini-Israel, "the *kerem* of the LORD of hosts" (Isa. 5:7). Just as Ahab and Jezebel—top candidates for the most dastardly duo in the OT—used lies and murder to steal the vineyard from Naboth, so by idolatry and bloodshed corrupt rulers have "stolen" Israel from her Lord.

Jesus' parable of the vineyard workers who beat the owner's servants and finally murdered his son is likely inspired by the story of Naboth's vineyard (Matt. 21:33-46). But in spite of Ahabs and Jezebels, the Lord will have his crop. "The kingdom of God will be . . . given to a people producing its fruits" (v. 43) of "love, joy, peace, patience, kindness, goodness, faithfulness, gentleness, [and] self-control" (Gal. 5:22-23).

Work in us, Holy Spirit, that we may work faithfully in the vineyard of the Lord of hosts.

The Divine Throne כסא

NOW THE KING OF ISRAEL AND JEHOSHAPHAT THE
KING OF JUDAH WERE SITTING ON THEIR THRONES . . .
AND ALL THE PROPHETS WERE PROPHESYING BEFORE
THEM . . . AND MICAIAH SAID, "THEREFORE HEAR THE
WORD OF THE LORD: I SAW THE LORD SITTING ON HIS
THRONE, AND ALL THE HOST OF HEAVEN STANDING
BESIDE HIM ON HIS RIGHT HAND AND ON HIS LEFT."

1 KINGS 22:10, 19

Though *kisse* can refer simply to a chair or seat of honor for a priest
(1 Sam. 1:9), most of the time it refers to a king's throne, or as a metaphor
for regal or divine power. First Kings 22 presents a vivid contrast between
earthly and heavenly thrones: two mortal kings each sit on a *kisse*, and the
one immortal King sits on his. The earthly kings are encompassed by lying
prophets (except Micaiah), while Yahweh has the heavenly host around him.
He is the true King of whom all earthly kings are a faint, flawed, and often
false image.

The archangel Gabriel told Mary that God would give her Son "the throne of
his father David" (Luke 1:32). In his ascension, as both king and high priest,
he sat down "at the right hand of the throne of the Majesty in heaven"
(Heb. 8:1). To that "throne of grace" we draw near with confidence, "that
we may receive mercy and find grace to help in time of need" (Heb. 4:16).

"Your throne, O God, is forever and ever. The scepter of your kingdom is a
scepter of uprightness" (Ps. 45:6).

Bears, Boys, and a Bald Prophet קרח

[ELISHA] WENT UP FROM THERE TO BETHEL, AND WHILE HE WAS GOING UP ON THE WAY, SOME SMALL BOYS CAME OUT OF THE CITY AND JEERED AT HIM, SAYING, "GO UP, YOU BALDHEAD! GO UP, YOU BALDHEAD!" AND HE TURNED AROUND, AND WHEN HE SAW THEM, HE CURSED THEM IN THE NAME OF THE LORD. AND TWO SHE-BEARS CAME OUT OF THE WOODS AND TORE FORTY-TWO OF THE BOYS.

2 KINGS 2:23-24

This "bear story" is easily misunderstood. The Hebrew for "small boys" could just as accurately be translated "young men." They were likely associated with the worship of Baal in Bethel. The word *qereach* ("baldhead") occurs only here and in Leviticus, in a section about skin disease (13:40). This suggests they were mocking him as unclean. They also say, "Go up!" meaning disappear, just like Elijah, his spiritual father, had just done. In short, this is a brief but fierce confrontation between the prophet of Yahweh and the worshipers of Baal.

Right before this, Elisha crossed the Jordan on dry ground, like Joshua had done. And like Joshua, Elisha now confronts and fights idolaters, who he curses and kills with bears. This is just one more episode in the age-old war between light and darkness, truth and lies—a war that will end when the King returns with a diadem crown adorning his brow (Rev. 1:14; 19:12).

Rescue us, O Lord, from lying lips and mocking tongues, that we may glorify you alone.

Naaman Reborn נער קטן

SO [NAAMAN] WENT DOWN AND DIPPED HIMSELF SEVEN
TIMES IN THE JORDAN, ACCORDING TO THE WORD OF
THE MAN OF GOD, AND HIS FLESH WAS RESTORED LIKE
THE FLESH OF A LITTLE CHILD, AND HE WAS CLEAN.

2 KINGS 5:14

We don't even know her name, but God used the bold confession a young girl (*na'arah q'tannah*) to forever alter the life of Naaman, the Aramean general. She told Naaman's wife, who relayed the message to her husband, that the prophet in Samaria could heal his skin disease. So the general undertook the journey to see Elisha. After an initial stubborn refusal, Naaman finally "dipped himself seven times in the Jordan." The result? "His flesh was restored like the flesh of a little child [*na'ar qaton*]." The Hebrew unveils a profound meaning. God used a *na'arah q'tannah* ("young girl/lady") to lead this powerful Gentile man to have skin like a *na'ar qaton* ("young boy/man"). The greatest becomes like the least in these cleansing waters.

Baptism, like the Jordan, is the great equalizer. No matter who we are as we enter those waters—powerful or vulnerable; rich or poor; famous or unknown—we all emerge the same: as children of God. The simple water and strong word wash away the disease of sin. We are clean, holy, and all part of the same family of our Father.

Thanks be to you, heavenly Father, for claiming us as your children in the Jordan of baptism.

From Shrine
to Toilet מחראה

THEY DEMOLISHED THE PILLAR OF BAAL,
AND DEMOLISHED THE HOUSE OF BAAL,
AND MADE IT A LATRINE TO THIS DAY.

2 KINGS 10:27

In 2016, archaeologists unearthed a shrine, probably to Baal, at Tel Lachish. Inside the room was a (damaged) four-horned altar, lamps, and bowls. In itself, this was hardly newsworthy, given the prevalence of illicit worship sites in ancient Israel. But it was another item in the shrine that made international headlines: a toilet. It seems that, at some point, faithful Yahweh-worshipping Israelites decided to give this idolatrous room the ultimate desecration. Jehu and his men did the exact same thing to another temple of Baal: they demolished it and made it a *machara'ah* ("latrine").

Transforming a pagan place of consecration into an everyday place of defecation is consistent with the Bible's view of false gods. Indeed, one of Ezekiel's favorite slang words for idols is *gillulim*, which likely means "things of dung" (e.g., 6:4–5). In no uncertain terms, God lets us know what he thinks of false gods. They are worthy of sewers, not sanctuaries. Instead, let us lift up our hearts to the one true God, who has made us, loved us, and given all of himself to us in Jesus Christ. He alone is worthy of our worship.

"Worthy are you, our Lord and God, to receive glory and honor and power, for you created all things, and by your will they existed and were created" (Rev. 4:11).

The Garb of Grief שַׂק

AS SOON AS KING HEZEKIAH HEARD IT, HE TORE HIS CLOTHES AND COVERED HIMSELF WITH SACKCLOTH AND WENT INTO THE HOUSE OF THE LORD.

2 KINGS 19:1

When we use the word "sack," Hebrew is on our lips. The English word is derived from the word *saq*, which can mean a sack/bag for food (Gen. 42:25), a makeshift blanket (2 Sam. 21:10), or—most commonly—sackcloth. Hezekiah and his officials donned *saq* when the Assyrians laid siege to Jerusalem. Jacob mourned Joseph by wearing *saq* as a loincloth (Gen. 37:34). The most bizarre use was in Nineveh, when even the animals were "covered with *saq*" (Jon. 3:8). Just as we might wear black clothing to a funeral as an outward sign of a saddened heart, Israelites put on *saq* as robes of repentance and the garb of grief.

Isaiah spoke of the heavens making "sackcloth their covering" (50:3), imagery picked up by John in Revelation when, at the opening of the sixth seal, "the sun became black as sackcloth" (6:12). This present time, so often awash with grief, pain, loss, evil, and shame, is an epoch of sackcloth. But in the twinkling of an eye, at the last trumpet, all will be changed when Jesus returns to vest us in the snow-white robes of joy, when all believers will shout in rapture:

"You have turned for me my mourning into dancing; you have loosed my sackcloth and clothed me with gladness" (Ps. 30:11).

The Third Day שְׁלִישִׁי

"THUS SAYS THE LORD, THE GOD OF DAVID YOUR
FATHER: I HAVE HEARD YOUR PRAYER; I HAVE SEEN
YOUR TEARS. BEHOLD, I WILL HEAL YOU. ON THE THIRD
DAY YOU SHALL GO UP TO THE HOUSE OF THE LORD."

2 KINGS 20:5

Paul writes that Christ "was raised on the third day in accordance with the Scriptures" (1 Cor. 15:4). This seems odd because there is no direct prophecy of a third-day resurrection of the Messiah. So what did Paul mean? The apostle was referring to the widespread pattern of events happening on the sh'lishi ("third") day. For example, all these events happened on the sh'lishi day: Abraham and Isaac saw Moriah, the place of sacrifice (Gen. 22:4); Yahweh dramatically descended onto Sinai to speak the law (Exod. 19:16); Hezekiah, healed by God, returned to the temple to worship (2 Kings 20:5); and, most significantly, Hosea prophesied that God would raise up Israel "on the third day" (6:2). In the Scriptures, the third day is the When-God-Does-Something-Big Day.

Just as on the sh'lishi day of creation, the Lord caused vegetation to spring from the earth (Gen. 1:11–12), so on the third day, the Creator himself, his body buried like a single grain of wheat in the soil of the tomb, sprang forth from the earth to bear the abundant fruit of giving us resurrection life in himself (John 12:24).

Lord Jesus, who heals the brokenhearted, bind up our wounds and sustain us (Ps. 147:3).

The Rolling Book ספר

AND HILKIAH THE HIGH PRIEST SAID TO SHAPHAN
THE SECRETARY, "I HAVE FOUND THE BOOK OF
THE LAW IN THE HOUSE OF THE LORD."

2 KINGS 22:8

At some point, part of the Torah (possibly Deuteronomy) was misplaced or stored away at the temple, then simply slipped through the cracks of Israel's memory. The high priest stumbled on it one day and gave it to King Josiah's secretary, who then read it to the king. Because this portion of the Torah pronounced an anathema on the idol-worshipping "new normal" in Judah, the humble and penitent Josiah immediately initiated a sweeping reformation.

Though most translations call this *sefer* a "book," the practice of binding pages into a book or codex wouldn't be invented for several more centuries. *Sefer* is the general word for "something written," usually in a letter or scroll. Such scrolls were ordinarily made of papyrus or leather, though archaeologists have discovered some formed from copper and even silver.

When Jesus was in the Nazareth synagogue, "the scroll of the prophet Isaiah was given to him. He unrolled the scroll" and read a portion of it (Luke 4:17). What a sight! The divine Word reading the written word to a congregation. Concerning this scroll of Isaiah—and concerning every biblical scroll—the Messiah could say, "It is written of me in the scroll of the book" (Heb. 10:7).

Jesus, fulfillment of the Law, Prophets, and Writings, may we meditate day and night on your sacred words.

Exile גלות

AND THE REST OF THE PEOPLE WHO WERE LEFT IN
THE CITY AND THE DESERTERS WHO HAD DESERTED
TO THE KING OF BABYLON, TOGETHER WITH THE
REST OF THE MULTITUDE, NEBUZARADAN THE
CAPTAIN OF THE GUARD CARRIED INTO EXILE.

2 KINGS 25:11

When Jews today describe the condition of being uprooted from their home-land of Israel, they often call it *Galut*. That noun refers to either a group of exiles (Isa. 20:4) or the exile itself (2 Kings 25:27). It's from the verb *galah*, which can mean uncover or go away, but commonly describes "being exiled," as when the Israelites were "carried into exile" by the Babylonians (v. 11). Not for years or even decades of provoking the Lord to anger by their idolatry, but for centuries of rebellion, dating all the way back to the exo-dus (21:15), Israel was finally dealt the most catastrophic blow they could receive: *galut* to Babylon.

The prophets foretold the Messiah who would not only bring back the exiled of Israel but be "a light for the nations" (Isa. 49:6). Jesus fulfilled this, but in an extraordinary, unexpected way. When he was "lifted up from the earth" atop the cross, he drew "all people" to himself (John 12:32), thus ending humanity's *galut* in his own exile to death and return to life again.

As we have sown our tears in exile, O Lord, may we come home with shouts of joy, bringing our sheaves with us (Ps. 126:5-6).

The Accuser שָׂטָן

THEN SATAN STOOD AGAINST ISRAEL AND
INCITED DAVID TO NUMBER ISRAEL.

1 CHRONICLES 21:1

In the NT, Satan is the name for the archenemy of Christ and his people. But in the OT, the Hebrew word *satan* is more fluid. It can be positive: when God's angel blocked Balaam's way, he acted "as his adversary [*satan*]" (Num. 22:22). It can also be negative: the psalmist complains of those who "accuse [*satan*]" him (Ps. 38:20). To *satan* (as a verb) or to be a *satan* (as a noun) thus means "to be an enemy" or "accuser." Just as we might say someone "bedeviled him," but not mean that person was the devil, so Israelites could say someone was a *satan*, without meaning Satan himself. There are a few OT examples, however, when Satan is a proper name of *the* enemy, *the* accuser, such as when he "incited David" or afflicted Job (cf. Zech. 3:1-2).

Jesus saw Satan "fall like lightning from heaven" (Luke 10:18). The "great dragon was thrown down, that ancient serpent, who is called the devil and Satan, the deceiver of the whole world—he was thrown down to the earth" (Rev. 12:9). "The accuser of our brothers has been thrown down, who accuses them day and night before our God" (v. 10). He was overcome "by the blood of the Lamb" (v. 11). In Christ, the Satan can no longer *satan* us.

All praise be to you, O Lamb of God, whose blood has silenced forever the Accuser.

Divine Love אהב

[THE QUEEN OF SHEBA SAID TO SOLOMON], "BLESSED BE THE LORD YOUR GOD, WHO HAS DELIGHTED IN YOU AND SET YOU ON HIS THRONE AS KING FOR THE LORD YOUR GOD! BECAUSE YOUR GOD LOVED ISRAEL AND WOULD ESTABLISH THEM FOREVER, HE HAS MADE YOU KING OVER THEM, THAT YOU MAY EXECUTE JUSTICE AND RIGHTEOUSNESS."

2 CHRONICLES 9:8

Two Gentile rulers who admired Solomon confessed that the Lord *ahav* ("loved") Israel. King Hiram of Tyre wrote to Solomon, "Because the LORD *ahav* his people, he has made you king over them" (2 Chron. 2:11). And the Queen of Sheba said, "Because your God *ahav* Israel and would establish them forever, he has made you king over them" (9:8). To love (*ahav*) and love itself (*ahavah*) describe the faithful commitment people have for others (Gen. 22:2), God has for his people (Deut. 7:8), and people have for God (6:5). For God, to love is to act: to save, redeem, protect, and be Israel's God. The patriarch Abraham, in particular, is called God's "friend," or, more literally, "beloved one" (Isa. 41:8; 2 Chron. 20:7).

Rather than "For God *so* loved the world . . . ," the Greek in John 3:16 might be better translated as "For God loved the world *in this way*." That captures the Hebrew essence of love: God embodies his love in this way, by the very act of giving his Son for us.

O Lover of humanity, gracious and magnanimous Lord, look on us with a heart of mercy.

Ezra: Student and Teacher of Torah דרש

EZRA WENT UP FROM BABYLONIA. HE WAS A SCRIBE SKILLED IN THE LAW OF MOSES THAT THE LORD, THE GOD OF ISRAEL, HAD GIVEN. . . . EZRA HAD SET HIS HEART TO STUDY THE LAW OF THE LORD, AND TO DO IT AND TO TEACH HIS STATUTES AND RULES IN ISRAEL.

EZRA 7:6, 10

When Israelites returned from exile in Babylon, they faced debilitating obstacles. Enemies were waxing and morale waning. Many of their leaders had married unbelievers. God raised up Ezra as a sort of neo-Moses to lead his wayward people. But how? He "set his heart to *darash*" the Torah of Yahweh. The verb *darash* means to care for, investigate, search out—thus the translation "study." As the psalmist says, "Great are the works of the LORD, *darash* ['studied'] by all who delight in them" (111:2). Ezra knew the "works of the LORD," inscribed in the Torah, would be a lamp to Israel's feet and a light to their path to guide them back to God (Ps. 119:105).

Jesus said, "You search the Scriptures because you think that in them you have eternal life; and it is they that bear witness about me" (John 5:39). All biblical searching, in one way or another, is about Christ. When we *darash* the Scriptures, we are seeking him in whom all God's promises are Yes (2 Cor. 1:20).

Lord Jesus, "I am yours; save me, for I have sought your precepts" (Ps. 119:94).

The Walls of Jerusalem חומה

AND AT THE DEDICATION OF THE WALL OF JERUSALEM
THEY SOUGHT THE LEVITES IN ALL THEIR PLACES,
TO BRING THEM TO JERUSALEM TO CELEBRATE THE
DEDICATION WITH GLADNESS, WITH THANKSGIVINGS
AND WITH SINGING, WITH CYMBALS, HARPS, AND LYRES.

NEHEMIAH 12:27

Proverbs says, "a man without self-control is like a city broken into and left without walls" (25:28). Such a man would be defenseless, vulnerable to any attack. So it was in fifth-century Jerusalem, when the city's *chomah* ("wall") was broken down and its gates destroyed by fire (Neh. 1:3). Just as God raised up Ezra to be a Torah teacher to his people at this time, so he raised up Nehemiah to be a wall builder. One provided *chokmah* ("wisdom"), the other a *chomah* ("wall"), the dedication of which was celebrated with holy fanfare. Through a variety of vocations, the Lord employs people to serve in his kingdom. For every biblical scholar, we also need architects, carpenters, and bricklayers.

The Messiah is both a wall destroyer and a wall builder. He has made Jew and Gentile "one and has broken down in his flesh the dividing wall of hostility" (Eph. 2:14). But he also has created the New Jerusalem, our resurrection home, a splendid city with "a great, high wall" (Rev. 21:12), inside of which shall reside forever those "who are written in the Lamb's book of life" (v. 27).

Heavenly Father, "do good to Zion in your good pleasure; build up the walls of Jerusalem" (Ps. 51:18).

Casting Lots פורים

HAMAN THE AGAGITE, THE SON OF HAMMEDATHA, THE
ENEMY OF ALL THE JEWS, HAD PLOTTED AGAINST
THE JEWS TO DESTROY THEM, AND HAD CAST PUR
(THAT IS, CAST LOTS), TO CRUSH AND TO DESTROY
THEM. BUT WHEN IT CAME BEFORE THE KING, HE GAVE
ORDERS IN WRITING THAT HIS EVIL PLAN THAT HE
HAD DEVISED AGAINST THE JEWS SHOULD RETURN ON
HIS OWN HEAD, AND THAT HE AND HIS SONS SHOULD
BE HANGED ON THE GALLOWS. THEREFORE THEY
CALLED THESE DAYS PURIM, AFTER THE TERM PUR.

ESTHER 9:24-26

J. R. R. Tolkien, of *The Lord of the Rings* fame, coined the word "eucatastrophe" to describe a sudden turn of events in which an impending catastrophe became something good (*eu* is Greek for "good"). In a Bible full of eucatastrophes, Esther's story ranks near the top.

Haman, "enemy of all the Jews," had cast *purim* (a Babylonian word for "lots") to determine when to initiate a pogrom against the Jews. God, however, in his providence, upended Haman's plan. He was hanged on the very gallows he had constructed for Mordecai, and the Jews were allowed to defend themselves from their adversaries. A eucatastrophe indeed!

This story forms the narrative of the Jewish festival of Purim. It is but one example in the long list of divine turnarounds, the greatest of which is the eucatastrophe of Easter.

All glory to you, Jesus our Lord, for causing all things to work together for the good for those who love you.

Fashion or Hurt?
Job's Painful Pun עצב

YOUR HANDS FASHIONED AND MADE ME, AND NOW YOU HAVE DESTROYED ME ALTOGETHER. REMEMBER THAT YOU HAVE MADE ME LIKE CLAY; AND WILL YOU RETURN ME TO THE DUST? DID YOU NOT POUR ME OUT LIKE MILK AND CURDLE ME LIKE CHEESE?

JOB 10:8-11

Puns are notoriously difficult to transfer from one language to another. Imagine trying to translate this sentence into another language: "The crows saw a murder." Did they witness another flock (murder) of crows or the killing (murder) of a man? Something similar occurs in the Hebrew when Job says to God, "Your hands *atzav* and made me." The verb *atzav* can be from two identical roots, but one means "fashion" and the other "cause pain." Did God's hands make Job or hurt him? The other two verbs in the verse, "made" and "destroyed," unpack the dual meaning of *atzav*. They explain the pun, as it were, in the two directions that *atzav* might go: one positive, one negative. Even in his suffering, Job remained a poet.

Indeed, God's hands do both, for he knows that we need to be not only made but remade. And remaking is never a painless process. Our Father's hands *atzav*—both fashion and pain—us that, just as we have borne the image of Adam, so we might bear the image of Christ, our crucified and resurrected Lord.

As you formed us in the womb, heavenly Father, reform us in Christ, to bear his image.

Miserable Comforters עָמָל

THEN JOB ANSWERED AND SAID: "I HAVE HEARD MANY
SUCH THINGS; MISERABLE COMFORTERS ARE YOU ALL."

JOB 16:1-2

Job's three friends, who came "to show him sympathy and comfort him," did well while they sat together with him in the brotherhood of silence (2:11-13). The more each of them spoke, however, the more it became painfully obvious that, with friends like that, who needs enemies? Job sums them up well: "*amal* ['miserable'] comforters are you all." *Amal* means "trouble, anxiety, need, harm." One friend, implying Job was being punished, told him those who "sow *amal* reap the same" (4:8). He added, "man is born to *amal*, as the sparks fly upward" (5:7). Another told Job that, if he would repent of his secret iniquity, he would soon forget his *amal* (11:6). Such "friends" only added more *amal* to Job's life—"miserable/troublesome comforters" indeed!

What a true friend we have in Jesus, for he has "borne our griefs and carried our sorrows" (Isa. 53:4). What's more, "out of the *amal* ['anguish'] of his soul he shall see and be satisfied; by his knowledge shall the righteous one, my servant, make many to be accounted righteous, and he shall bear their iniquities" (v. 11). He is the compassionate comforter we need!

O Lord, "you do see, for you note mischief and vexation, that you may take it into your hands; to you the helpless commits himself; you have been the helper of the fatherless" (Ps. 10:14).

Gnashing of Teeth חרק

HE HAS TORN ME IN HIS WRATH AND HATED ME; HE
HAS GNASHED HIS TEETH AT ME; MY ADVERSARY
SHARPENS HIS EYES AGAINST ME. MEN HAVE
GAPED AT ME WITH THEIR MOUTH; THEY HAVE
STRUCK ME INSOLENTLY ON THE CHEEK; THEY
MASS THEMSELVES TOGETHER AGAINST ME.

JOB 16:9-10

"Gnashing of teeth" does not mean what most people think it means. Five times in the OT, someone *charaq* ("gnashes") their teeth. Three are in the psalms: mockers and evil men gnash their teeth at David (Pss. 35:16; 37:12); and the wicked, angry at believers, gnash their teeth and melt away (112:10). Lamentations says Israel's enemies hiss and "gnash their teeth" (2:16). And Job, picturing God as his enemy, says he "gnashed his teeth against me." Every occurrence of *charaq* is not about pain but anger.

When Jesus speaks of people thrown into outer darkness or the fiery furnace, where there is "weeping and gnashing of teeth," the teeth-gnashing is all about their fury, hatred, and rage at God and his people, not necessarily their physical sufferings (e.g., Matt. 8:12; 13:42). Similarly, those who were enraged at Stephen "gnashed their teeth at him" (Acts 7:54 NIV). May God preserve us from such destructive hate, grant us unwavering faith, and fill our mouths not with gnashing teeth but with songs of praise to the one who delivers us from evil.

Smile on us, O Lord, with your mercy and favor that we may be saved from all our foes.

Seeing God in the Flesh בָּשָׂר

"FOR I KNOW THAT MY REDEEMER LIVES, AND AT THE LAST HE WILL STAND UPON THE EARTH. AND AFTER MY SKIN HAS BEEN THUS DESTROYED, YET IN MY FLESH I SHALL SEE GOD, WHOM I SHALL SEE FOR MYSELF, AND MY EYES SHALL BEHOLD, AND NOT ANOTHER. MY HEART FAINTS WITHIN ME!"

JOB 19:25-27

Souls forever floating in a celestial sphere, no longer trapped in the so-called prison of a body of flesh and blood, is not a biblical teaching. In fact, it is antithetical to Christianity. Job's confession is not "in my soul" but "in my *basar* ['flesh'] I shall God." When Adam first lays eyes on Eve, he says she is "bone of my bones and *basar* of my *basar*" (Gen. 2:23). Her flesh is part of her perfection. Though in the NT the Greek word for "flesh" often has a negative connotation, in Hebrew, human "flesh" primarily means "bodily existence." Job awaits a bodily resurrection, a raising of his *basar*, to see his divine Redeemer, who will "stand upon the earth" with him.

When believers die, we will go to be with Christ in paradise or heaven. But heaven is not our home; it is a lovely waiting place. We await the resurrection of the flesh at Christ's return, the raising of our bodies, and life forever with our Redeemer in the new heavens and new earth.

Jesus our Redeemer, sustain us through life's trials with hope in the resurrection of the body.

Feasting on Leviathan לוית‍ן

"CAN YOU DRAW OUT LEVIATHAN WITH A FISHHOOK OR
PRESS DOWN HIS TONGUE WITH A CORD? CAN YOU PUT
A ROPE IN HIS NOSE OR PIERCE HIS JAW WITH A HOOK?"

JOB 41:1-2

Just as preachers today might reference mythological creatures from *The Lion, the Witch and the Wardrobe* to illustrate a truth, so biblical prophets sometimes drew on cultural myths popular in their day. *Livyatan* ("Leviathan"), known in ancient literature as a mythological sea creature, is an obvious example. This monster pops up twice in Job, as a crocodile-like creature (41:1-34) and in his opening lament (3:8). Psalm 104 has him playfully swimming by ships (v. 26). God's defeat of Pharaoh at the Red Sea is pictured as the Lord taking a sword to *Livyatan*, "the twisting serpent . . . the dragon that is in the sea" (Isa. 27:1). And in a psalm with overtones of creation and the exodus, God crushes *Livyatan*'s heads and makes him a meal for wilderness travelers (74:14). Oddly, this verse was the basis for later Jewish traditions about believers feasting on Leviathan in heaven!

The dragon in Revelation 12, symbolic of both the devil and the evil kingdom that oppress Christ's church, is based on this creature. Just as God crushed Pharaoh, symbolized as Leviathan, so he will destroy every foe, human or hellish, that seeks to harm his chosen people, for the Lamb triumphs over them all (12:11).

Blessed are you, O Lord, King of creation, for you will mercifully save your people.

Blessed Is the Man אשרי

BLESSED IS THE MAN WHO WALKS NOT IN THE
COUNSEL OF THE WICKED, NOR STANDS IN THE WAY
OF SINNERS, NOR SITS IN THE SEAT OF SCOFFERS;
BUT HIS DELIGHT IS IN THE LAW OF THE LORD, AND
ON HIS LAW HE MEDITATES DAY AND NIGHT.

PSALM 1:1-2

The opening two psalms are a poetic unit about the Messiah and his people. Psalm 1 begins by describing an individual, "the man," who is *ashrey* ("blessed"), and Psalm 2 concludes by describing a group, the *ashrey* who take refuge in God's Son (2:12). Christ is this blessed man who does not walk, stand, or sit with the wicked, but delights in constant meditation on his Father's word (1:1-2). He is the tree who yields ongoing fruit (1:3). In Psalm 2 this same man is the Lord's Anointed (2:2), the Son begotten of the Father (2:7), who rules over all kings and kingdoms with a rod of iron (2:8-11). "*Ashrey* are all who take refuge in him," for he will make them part of the righteous, whose way the Lord knows and who will not perish (1:6).

The Beatitudes, with their repeated "Blessed are . . ." phrases, encapsulate the message of all 150 psalms. Especially on the cross, Jesus embodies both the beatitudes and the psalms. Blessed is that man, God's Son, our Messiah. And blessed are we who live and trust in him.

"O Lord of hosts, blessed is the one who trusts in you!" (Ps. 84:12).

God's Beloved Ones חסיד

O MEN, HOW LONG SHALL MY HONOR BE TURNED
INTO SHAME? HOW LONG WILL YOU LOVE VAIN
WORDS AND SEEK AFTER LIES? *SELAH* BUT KNOW
THAT THE LORD HAS SET APART THE GODLY FOR
HIMSELF; THE LORD HEARS WHEN I CALL TO HIM.

PSALM 4:2-3

When we read, "the LORD has set apart the godly," we might assume the Hebrew adjective for "godly" is from the word for "God." That would make sense. But actually, "godly" is *chasid*, derived from *chesed*, that almost untranslatable word for divine love, fidelity, mercy. The *chasidim* (plural) are thus the objects of *chesed*, those upon whom the Lord showers his love. Rather than "godly," we might translate it "beloved." The Lord sets apart his beloved ones. "Precious in the sight of the LORD is the death of his *chasidim*" (Ps. 116:15). In the psalms, the *chasidim* "sing praises" (30:4), "love the LORD" (31:23), "offer prayer" (32:6). Their Lord will not forsake them (37:28), speaks peace to them (85:8), preserves their life (86:2). Are the *chasidim* godly, faithful, and loving? Yes, but only because they are the recipients of the *chesed* of the Father.

When the Messiah is crucified and buried, God will not abandon his soul to Sheol, or let his *chasid* see corruption (Ps. 16:10; Acts 2:25-32). In Christ, the Beloved one, we too are the Beloved of the Father.

"All your works shall give thanks to you, O Lord, and all your *chasidim* shall bless you!" (Ps. 145:10).

Be Gracious to Me חנן

O LORD, REBUKE ME NOT IN YOUR ANGER, NOR
DISCIPLINE ME IN YOUR WRATH. BE GRACIOUS TO ME,
O LORD, FOR I AM LANGUISHING; HEAL ME, O LORD,
FOR MY BONES ARE TROUBLED. MY SOUL ALSO IS
GREATLY TROUBLED. BUT YOU, O LORD—HOW LONG?

PSALM 6:1-3

When the Lord passed by Moses, he identified himself as "merciful and gracious [*channun*]" (Exod. 34:6). The adjective *channun* is part of a cluster of grace-words, interconnected by the verb *chanan*, "to be gracious" or "to favor." The prayer "*chanan* to me, O LORD" in Hebrew is like *Kyrie eleison* in Greek: it is the cry of those who realize there is one and only one true hope in this world—a God of grace and mercy.

Justice will only get us so far. We can't bootstrap ourselves up to a new lease on life. Blood, sweat, and tears have their limits. But a Father of grace? The Lord Jesus who makes his face shine on us and is *chanan* to us (Num. 6:25)? The forgiving Spirit who, in his grace, blots out our transgressions (Ps. 51:1)? He is our life. He is our light. He is our all-sufficient "salvation in the time of trouble" (Isa. 33:2). We "are justified by his grace as a gift, through the redemption that is in Christ Jesus" (Rom. 3:24).

"Be gracious to me, O God, according to Your lovingkindness; According to the greatness of Your compassion blot out my transgressions" (Ps. 51:1 NASB)

The Majestic Name שֵׁם

O LORD, OUR LORD, HOW MAJESTIC IS YOUR
NAME IN ALL THE EARTH! YOU HAVE SET
YOUR GLORY ABOVE THE HEAVENS.

PSALM 8:1

In the Harry Potter series, evil Voldemort is "He-Who-Must-Not-Be-Named." In the Bible, God's *shem* ("name") is the exact opposite—he must be named! We call on his *shem*, praise it, preach it, trust in it. Names, especially the divine name, are not a mere string of letters but the person himself. To misuse God's name (Exod. 20:7) is to misuse God himself. The name equals the person. For God to "put [his] name" at the sanctuary (Deut. 12:5) so that his "name might be there" (1 Kings 8:16) is to put himself there. Psalm 8:1 puts God's name and glory in parallel, for they are both stand-ins for the Lord. With this background, one can easily understand why, in Jewish tradition, God is often referred to as HaShem, "the name."

"The name that is above every name" that is given to Jesus is not "Jesus" but the divine name, Yahweh (Phil. 2:9–10). Already in Exodus, this was clear, for the Father said of the messenger who would lead Israel, "my *shem* is in him" (23:21), meaning, he is a divine agent, my Son, who shares my essence and power. At the name that Jesus possesses, Yahweh, every knee will bow.

"Those who know your name put their trust in you, for you, O LORD, have not forsaken those who seek you" (Ps. 9:10).

The Cup of the Lord כוס

THE LORD TESTS THE RIGHTEOUS, BUT HIS
SOUL HATES THE WICKED AND THE ONE WHO
LOVES VIOLENCE. LET HIM RAIN COALS ON THE
WICKED; FIRE AND SULFUR AND A SCORCHING
WIND SHALL BE THE PORTION OF THEIR CUP.

PSALM 11:5-6

In the psalms, the Lord's *kos* ("cup") shimmers with salvation or boils with destruction. Positively, "the LORD is . . . my *kos*" (16:5); our "*kos* overflows" (23:5); and we lift "the *kos* of salvation" (116:13). But negatively, the Lord holds a *kos* that the wicked must drain down to the dregs (75:8)—a chalice brimming with "fire and sulfur and a scorching wind" (11:6). The prophetic trio—Isaiah, Jeremiah, and Ezekiel—warn of the Lord's cup of wrath (Isa. 51:17; Jer. 25:15) and "a cup of horror and desolation" (Ezek. 23:33).

In Gethsemane, the crucifixion looming, Jesus prays, "My Father, if it be possible, let this cup pass from me; nevertheless, not as I will, but as you will" (Matt. 26:39). The Lord's will was done when Christ tilted back his head on the cross and drank, down to the dregs, the liquid judgment of fire, sulfur, and scorching wind. It was finished. Then having drained that cup of woe, he refilled it with the blood of his own divine life to pour his salvation on our sin-parched lips.

"Thou preparest a table before me in the presence of mine enemies: thou anointest my head with oil; my cup runneth over" (Ps. 23:5 KJV).

A Hope-Trust בטח

BUT I HAVE TRUSTED IN YOUR STEADFAST
LOVE; MY HEART SHALL REJOICE IN YOUR
SALVATION. I WILL SING TO THE LORD, BECAUSE
HE HAS DEALT BOUNTIFULLY WITH ME.

PSALM 13:5-6

In Hebrew, trust and hope are theological twin brothers. In fact, the Greek translation of the OT ordinarily rendered the Hebrew verb *batach* ("to trust") as the Greek verb *elpizein* ("to hope"). When we *batach*, we place a "hope-trust" in someone or something. Of course, that hope-trust is often misguided. The OT is rife with warnings against trusting in everything from princes (Ps. 146:3) to riches (Ps. 49:6) to one's own righteousness (Ezek. 33:13). Strikingly, the only human relationship where *batach* is wholly commended is when the husband of a noble wife trusts in her (Prov. 31:11). To place one's hope and trust in the Lord is to find peace and security based completely on his "steadfast love [*chesed*]" (Ps. 13:5).

In Psalm 22, the Messiah cries out in excruciating pain, "My God, my God, why have you forsaken me?" (v. 1), yet he also cries out in faith, "You made me trust [*batach*] you at my mother's breasts" (v. 9). Perhaps even on the cross, Jesus cast his eyes toward his mother, Mary, as he prayed these words. He had hope. He had trust. He *batach* in his Father who would raise him—and all of us in him—from the grave.

"O Lord of hosts, blessed is the one who trusts in you!" (Ps. 84:12).

The Apple of God's Eye אִישׁוֹן

KEEP ME AS THE APPLE OF YOUR EYE; HIDE ME IN THE SHADOW OF YOUR WINGS, FROM THE WICKED WHO DO ME VIOLENCE, MY DEADLY ENEMIES WHO SURROUND ME.

PSALM 17:8–9

"You are the apple of my eye" has that Valentine's Day feel, a romantic sentiment one whispers to a lover on a twilight walk in the park. That might work on Hallmark cards, but not in the Hebrew Bible. In fact, this is an odd case where the English metaphor is not reflected in the Hebrew. The *ishon* of the eye is simply the pupil, not an apple. Some think *ishon* means "little man," a diminutive form of *ish* ("man")—thus "the little man (in the eye)." In any case, to ask God, "Keep [or guard] me as the pupil of your eye" is to ask for his intimate, ongoing protection from "the wicked" and "the deadly enemies." Just as we shield our eyes from being harmed, so we ask the Lord to shield us, to treat us as if we are as near and dear to him as his very pupils.

The embodiment of God's Son is the Father's answer to our prayer. He becomes one of us and we become part of him: bone of his bone, flesh of his flesh, pupil of his pupil. In Jesus, we are in the very eye of God.

Lord Jesus, grant us your Spirit, to keep your teachings as the apple of our eye (Prov. 7:2).

Horn of Salvation קֶרֶן

I LOVE YOU, O LORD, MY STRENGTH. THE LORD IS MY
ROCK AND MY FORTRESS AND MY DELIVERER, MY GOD,
MY ROCK, IN WHOM I TAKE REFUGE, MY SHIELD, AND
THE HORN OF MY SALVATION, MY STRONGHOLD.

PSALM 18:1-2

David heaps up images of God: rock, fortress, deliverer, refuge, shield, stronghold, and horn. The last, *qeren* ("horn"), is intriguing. How is God the horn of salvation? A *qeren* can refer to actual animal horns, altar corners, musical instruments, or receptacles for anointing oil. To "raise someone's horn" is to strengthen them (Ps. 112:9). On the cross, the Messiah is threatened by "the horns of the wild oxen" (22:21). These last two examples illustrate how the *qeren* symbolizes power and might, like the four horns in Zechariah stand for worldly power (1:18-19) or the ten horns in Revelation represent ten kings (17:12).

The father of John the Baptist sang thanksgiving to the God who "has visited and redeemed his people and has raised up a horn of salvation for us in the house of his servant David" (Luke 1:68-69). This Davidic "horn of salvation" is the Messiah, of whom Hannah sang long before: the Lord "will give strength to his king and exalt the horn [*qeren*] of his anointed" (1 Sam. 2:10). Christ is the King of David, Hannah, Zechariah, and all of us. He is our horn of salvation.

Blessed are you, O Christ, our strength and the horn that saves us from sin and death.

Pleasing Words and Meditation רָצוֹן

LET THE WORDS OF MY MOUTH AND THE MEDITATION
OF MY HEART BE ACCEPTABLE IN YOUR SIGHT,
O LORD, MY ROCK AND MY REDEEMER.

PSALM 19:14

Psalm 19 is rich in speech. Celestial lips recount God's glory. Day to day pours forth speech. Not only is creation loquacious, so is the Lord's Word. The Torah, testimony, and commandments revive souls, rejoice hearts, and enlighten eyes. From the solar system to the sacred scroll, words of God and about God reverberate. David concludes this psalm by asking that his mouth-words and heart-meditations be *ratzon* in the Lord's eyes. To be *ratzon* is to be pleasing, favorable, acceptable, like the sacrifices on the altar were the means by which the worshiper was "*ratzon* [accepted] before the LORD" (Lev. 1:3). As elsewhere David prays that his prayer be counted as incense before God (Ps. 141:2), so here he asks that his words and meditations be reckoned as an acceptable sacrifice to the Lord.

That not just our words and meditations, but all of who we are, be acceptable to the Father, his Son came to "proclaim the year of the LORD's *ratzon*" (Isa. 61:2; Luke 4:19). "Now is the favorable time; behold, now is the day of salvation" (2 Cor. 6:2), for now and forever, in Jesus, we are fully acceptable to the Father.

"Remember me, O LORD, in Your favor toward Your people; Visit me with Your salvation" (Ps. 106:4 NASB)

Why Have You Exiled Me? עזב

MY GOD, MY GOD, WHY HAVE YOU FORSAKEN
ME? WHY ARE YOU SO FAR FROM SAVING ME,
FROM THE WORDS OF MY GROANING?

PSALM 22:1

The Messiah laments his separation from God atop the cross. Three times, he complains that God is "so far" (v. 1), "far from me" (v. 11), and "far off" (v. 19). God has *azav* ("forsaken") him, a verb freighted with exile connotations. In Deuteronomy, God threatened that if his people *azav* him, he will *azav* them (31:16-17). The same verbal form used in Psalm 22:1 is used in Deuteronomy 28:20 when God says he will send curses (including exile) on Israel because "you have forsaken me [*azavtani*]." The Lord says through Jeremiah that he has "*azav* his house" and will send the people into exile in Babylon (12:7). In his crucifixion, Jesus is recapitulating—doing over again in himself—what Israel did. Just as they had the Babylonian exile, the cross is his Roman exile.

He undergoes this exile to bring us home to the Father in his resurrection. The effect is cosmic, for "all the ends of the earth shall remember and turn to the Lord" (Ps. 22:27). His crucifixion exile and resurrection return will mean Easter for the world. Because Jesus prayed, "Do not forsake me," we know that God will hear us when we pray:

"Do not forsake me, O Lord! O my God, be not far from me!" (Ps. 38:21).

Pursued by Mercy רדף

SURELY GOODNESS AND MERCY SHALL FOLLOW
ME ALL THE DAYS OF MY LIFE, AND I SHALL
DWELL IN THE HOUSE OF THE LORD FOREVER.

PSALM 23:6

In the Hebrew of Psalm 23, "goodness and mercy" do not "follow" us all the days of our lives. That translation is far too bloodless for the verb *radaf*. It means to chase after, like Abram in armed pursuit of his enemies (Gen. 14:14-15), Pharaoh hounding Israel even into the sea (Exod. 14:23), or Barak breathing down Sisera's neck (Judg. 4:22). When you *radaf* someone, you don't lollygag behind them at a safe distance. You go hard and heavy until you reach them—or die trying. Obstacles don't matter. No effort is too great. *Radaf* is a verb that packs a punch. It's full of energy, sweat, and an unswerving commitment to reach your goal.

The goodness and mercy of God do not follow us like a good little puppy dog, letting us lead the way. They chase us down labyrinthine paths like Francis Thompson's "Hound of Heaven." They gallop after us like a celestial stallion. They stay hot on our heels. The goodness and mercy of Jesus Christ *radaf* us all the way to heaven's gate and into the arms of our waiting and smiling heavenly Father.

Praise and glory be to you, Jesus Christ, for seeking us, pursuing us, and chasing us by grace and mercy back to our Father.

The Way דרך

GOOD AND UPRIGHT IS THE LORD; THEREFORE HE INSTRUCTS SINNERS IN THE WAY. HE LEADS THE HUMBLE IN WHAT IS RIGHT, AND TEACHES THE HUMBLE HIS WAY.

PSALM 25:8-9

Christians were first called those who belonged to the Way (Acts 9:2). In Hebrew, we would say they belonged to the *Derek*. This noun refers to a way, road, custom, journey, or behavior. Thus it can refer to where your feet travel, what your hands do, or where your heart leads. It is a good name for following Jesus because it is a broad word that encompasses "deeds and creeds," believing and doing, faith and love. Psalm 25 could be named the Derek Psalm since that noun or its verbal form (*darak*) occur six times. Verse 9 is especially striking because the opening verb ("he leads") and the closing noun ("way") are *darak* and *derek*, bookending the verse.

When Thomas told Jesus, "Lord, we do not know where you are going. How can we know the way?" Jesus replied, "I am the way, and the truth, and the life" (John 14:6). Were Jesus speaking Hebrew, he would have said, "I am the *derek*." He is the path to the Father. He "instructs sinners in the way" (Ps. 25:8). He is the *derek* that both embodies and leads to life in the communion of the Holy Spirit and the Father.

"Make me to know your ways, O LORD; teach me your paths" (Ps. 25:4).

God's Hiding Place סתר

HE WILL HIDE ME IN HIS SHELTER IN THE DAY OF
TROUBLE; HE WILL CONCEAL ME UNDER THE COVER
OF HIS TENT; HE WILL LIFT ME HIGH UPON A ROCK.

PSALM 27:5

David is in dire straits. His pursuers are like cannibalistic men, ready "to eat up [his] flesh" (Ps. 27:2). The lying lips of false witnesses "breathe out violence" (v. 12). Rather than running for the hills, however, the poet wants to plant his feet in one place and one place only: "the house of the LORD" (v. 4). Close to his God, he is safe, for "he will conceal me under the cover of his tent" (v. 5)—literally, "he will hide me in the hiding place" or "secret me in the secret place." To *satar* is to hide something, to keep it secret. David's confidence rests not on his military prowess or political wits but entirely on sheltering with God. Even though David could not physically enter the Holy of Holies, that secret, sacrosanct place was where he found courage and hope.

As our forerunner, Jesus has entered "into the inner place behind the curtain," into the Father's heavenly Holy of Holies, that we might have "a sure and steadfast anchor of the soul" (Heb. 6:19). Our life, "hidden with Christ in God" (Col. 3:3), is secret and secure in him who anchors us to the Father.

Lord Jesus, "hide me in the shadow of your wings" (Ps. 17:8).

Divine Silence חרשׁ

FOR WHEN I KEPT SILENT, MY BONES WASTED AWAY
THROUGH MY GROANING ALL DAY LONG. FOR DAY
AND NIGHT YOUR HAND WAS HEAVY UPON ME; MY
STRENGTH WAS DRIED UP AS BY THE HEAT OF SUMMER.

PSALM 32:3-4

A closed mouth is usually preferable to an open one. "Even a fool who keeps silent is considered wise" (Prov. 17:28). There is "a time to keep silence, and a time to speak" (Eccles. 3:7). But David did himself no good when he *charash* ("kept silent" or "held back"), when he did not acknowledge his sin to the Lord (Ps. 32:5). Unconfessed evildoing was a devouring cancer: "my bones wasted away through my groaning all day long." Another Hebrew word, spelled exactly the same as *charash*, means "to plow." Perhaps a play on words is used here, as if David plowed his sin beneath the soil. Corked wine may grow better with age, but sin that is all bottled up grows nothing but death and decay within us.

To confess is not to tell God anything he doesn't already know. Nor is it to barter for forgiveness, as if the Lord "sells" absolutions, like shoes or hamburgers, for the cash of confession. To not keep silence, but to confess, is simply to speak the truth. And our loving Father responds with a greater, stronger truth: "I have already forgiven you, forgive you now, and always will."

"I said, 'I will confess my transgressions to the LORD,' and you forgave the iniquity of my sin" (Ps. 32:5).

Lord, Be Big and High גדל

OH, MAGNIFY THE LORD WITH ME, AND
LET US EXALT HIS NAME TOGETHER!

PSALM 34:3

In this verse, the words "magnify" and "exalt," while correct translations, take concrete Hebrew images and flatten them into abstractions. The verb *gadal*, translated as "magnify," means "to make big or great." While "make the Lord big with me" is a strange sentence to our ears, it communicates the idea. The verb *rum*, translated as "exalt," means "to make high" or "raise up." Paraphrasing this verse, we might say, "Let's all together make the Lord and his name big and high!"

After prophesying the birthplace of the Messiah, Micah goes on to say that this Son of David shall shepherd his people, and "he shall be great [*gadal*] to the ends of the earth" (5:4). This tiny baby boy, swaddled in a feed trough, later transfixed to a cross, then raised high in his resurrection and ascension, would be big. Bigger than Bethlehem. Bigger than Israel. Bigger than the world. So big and so high that heaven and earth cannot contain him but are contained by him. "You are great, O LORD God," for "great are the works of the LORD" who is "great in lovingkindness" (2 Sam. 7:22; Ps. 111:2; 145:8 NASB). Jesus, be big! Jesus, be high!

"May all who seek you rejoice and be glad in you! May those who love your salvation say evermore, 'God is great!'" (Ps. 70:4).

Blessed Are the God-Dependent עָנָו

IN JUST A LITTLE WHILE, THE WICKED WILL BE NO MORE; THOUGH YOU LOOK CAREFULLY AT HIS PLACE, HE WILL NOT BE THERE. BUT THE MEEK SHALL INHERIT THE LAND AND DELIGHT THEMSELVES IN ABUNDANT PEACE.

PSALM 37:10-11

When Jesus said, "Blessed are the meek, for they shall inherit the earth" (Matt. 5:5), he was speaking with an OT accent. A millennium before, David had written, "The *anav* ['meek'] shall inherit the land." The *anav* are the polar opposite of the arrogant. We might call them the God-dependent. In the psalms, God feeds them (22:26), leads them (25:9), and adorns them with salvation (149:4). They cry to him (9:12), are glad in the Lord (34:2), and seek God (69:32). They are not doormats, mousy men, or pushovers. Moses, a man of strength and courage, is described as "very *anav*, more than all people who were on the face of the earth" (Num. 12:3). Like him, the *anav* are bold, faithful, stronghearted believers who submit themselves to the ways and will of the Lord—and are ready to suffer the world's mistreatment, even martyrdom, because of his name.

Their inheritance is the land, the new earth that the Lord will fashion when he comes again. "The wicked will be no more" (Ps. 37:10), but the righteous, the *anav*, will flourish in the abundance of peace that pervades the kingdom of God.

"Arise, O LORD; O God, lift up your hand; forget not the afflicted" (Ps. 10:12).

Hurry up, God! חוש

DO NOT FORSAKE ME, O LORD! O MY GOD,
BE NOT FAR FROM ME! MAKE HASTE TO
HELP ME, O LORD, MY SALVATION!

PSALM 38:21-22

When our hopes are in shreds, our lives are a dumpster fire, or we're racked by stress or grief, we pound our fists on heaven's door. We want God to intervene—and we mean now! In these situations, well-meaning believers might caution us, "Now be patient and don't subject God to your timetable." Or, "Don't tell the Lord when to do something." Against such pious-sounding sentiments, seven times in the psalms, the cry rises from God's people, *Chush*! (22:19; 38:22; 40:13; 70:1, 5; 71:12; 141:1). The verb means to hasten something, to speed things along. The Israelites had no qualms about crying out to the Lord, "Hurry up! Answer me quickly! Act now!"

Yes, we live by faith and hope. Yes, we pray, "Thy will be done." But we pray honestly and earnestly and boldly. That means, very often, telling God we want and need him to wake up, get up, and do something now. *Chush*! Remember the pertinacious widow whom Jesus commended for giving the earthly judge no rest until he heard her case (Luke 18:1–8)? Jesus adds that our heavenly Judge will give justice to us "speedily" (v. 8). As beloved children, we are free and invited to pray, "Dear Father, hurry!"

"Make haste, O God, to deliver me! O LORD, make haste to help me!" (Ps. 70:1).

Merciful "Revenge" שׁלם

EVEN MY CLOSE FRIEND IN WHOM I TRUSTED, WHO
ATE MY BREAD, HAS LIFTED HIS HEEL AGAINST
ME. BUT YOU, O LORD, BE GRACIOUS TO ME,
AND RAISE ME UP, THAT I MAY REPAY THEM!

PSALM 41:9-10

There is a surprise Hebrew gift waiting to be unwrapped in these verses. "My close friend" is more literally "a man in shalom [at peace] with me." In the phrase "that I may repay them," the word "repay" is a form of the verb *shalam*. It can mean make complete, reward, or take revenge. These two Hebrew words, *shalam* and *shalom*, are from the same root. Jesus applies these verses to himself, where the "man in shalom with him" is Judas, who is about to lift up his heel against him (John 13:18). The end result will be the Messiah's death.

In verse 10, Jesus prays, "Raise me up, that I may *shalam* them!" Since this is Jesus speaking, how do we translate this word? When he was raised up from the dead, did Jesus seek retribution? Revenge? No! How did he *shalam* all those shalom-friends who ran away from him? "Jesus came and stood among them and said to them, 'Peace be with you'" (John 20:19). This is the way of our Lord: rather than looking for a pound of flesh, he gives us a ton of forgiveness.

"In peace I will both lie down and sleep; for you alone, O LORD, make me dwell in safety" (Ps. 4:8).

God's River of Joy נהר

THERE IS A RIVER WHOSE STREAMS MAKE GLAD THE
CITY OF GOD, THE HOLY HABITATION OF THE MOST
HIGH. GOD IS IN THE MIDST OF HER; SHE SHALL NOT BE
MOVED; GOD WILL HELP HER WHEN MORNING DAWNS.

PSALM 46:4-5

Psalm 46 is interwoven with cataclysmic imagery: the earth melts, mountains faceplant into the sea, waters roar and foam, nations rage and totter. In this cosmic shakeup, the last thing we expect is joy. But there it is, in the "river whose streams make glad the city of God." The first appearance of a *nahar* ("river") in Scripture is the river that flowed from Eden and spilled into four tributaries, on which rippled, as it were, Eden's blessings to the world (Gen. 2:10-14). In imitation of this river, vivifying water flowed from God's temple in Ezekiel's vision, deepening as it streamed southward to the Dead Sea, desalinating those waters (47:1-12). Zion's joy-giving river mixes with the rivers of Eden and the temple to be one and the same brook of blessing.

This same river reappears in Revelation as "the river of the water of life, bright as crystal, flowing from the throne of God and of the Lamb," down the street of the New Jerusalem (22:1-2). Jesus dips us into these life-giving, sin-removing, joy-bestowing waters already in baptism. There our hope resides, no matter how violently the world may shake.

O God, our refuge and strength, be always our very present help in trouble (Ps. 46:1).

Cutting a Covenant כרת

HE CALLS TO THE HEAVENS ABOVE AND TO
THE EARTH, THAT HE MAY JUDGE HIS PEOPLE:
"GATHER TO ME MY FAITHFUL ONES, WHO MADE
A COVENANT WITH ME BY SACRIFICE!"

PSALM 50:4-5

It's helpful, when reading the OT in English, to do instant word changes in your head when you encounter certain terminology. For instance, when you read "law," think Torah, which means "teaching." Or, when you see "obey," think "listen to the voice of." Likewise, when you encounter the common phrase "make a covenant," substitute "cut" for "make." A covenant is *karat* ("cut") because it is made "by sacrifice" (Ps. 50:5), by animals *karat* into pieces. When God cut a covenant with Abraham (Gen. 15:18), the patriarch cut animals in two. Then God in the form of "a smoking fire pot and a flaming torch passed between the pieces" (Gen. 15:17). What was God indicating by this action? That should he break this covenant, his fate should rightfully be the same as those animals. It was an audacious, binding pledge of divine loyalty to Abraham and his heirs.

When the Father cut the new covenant with us, the Lamb of God was *karat*. Cut by whips. Cut by thorns. Cut by spikes and the tip of a spear. By his body broken and blood outpoured, we have the highest pledge of divine loyalty and love the human mind can fathom.

Blessed are you, Lord Jesus, for cutting the new covenant with us.

Purging Hyssop אֵזוֹב

PURGE ME WITH HYSSOP, AND I SHALL BE CLEAN;
WASH ME, AND I SHALL BE WHITER THAN SNOW.

PSALM 51:7

It's easy to skim over David's words, "purge me with *ezov* ['hyssop']," and completely miss the Holy Spirit tapping us on the shoulder. Hyssop is a plant with a Gospel history. *Ezov* was used to paint the blood of the Passover lamb over the Israelites' doors in Egypt (Exod. 12:22), to sprinkle a cleansing concoction over a leper (Lev. 14), and to purify a person who had come into contact with a corpse (Num. 19). Captivity, leprosy, and death—all three summarize what David did with his life. He impregnated the wife of one of his trusted warriors and then murdered him in a perfect storm of depravity, abuse, and egotism. He needed God to take hyssop in hand and sprinkle him with atoning blood. His soiled soul, black as midnight, needed to be made white as wool.

While God's Son was hanging between heaven and earth, his lips were touched by "a sponge full of the sour wine on a hyssop branch" (John 19:29). Immediately after, he said, "It is finished" (v. 30). Hyssop finally touched the divine Passover Lamb himself. He bore our captivity, our leprosy, our death. In him, we and David and all the world are purged, cleansed, washed, and made white as wool.

Though our sins are like crimson, O Lord, make them white as wool in Jesus' blood (Isa. 1:18).

Skin or Scroll of Tears? נאד

YOU HAVE KEPT COUNT OF MY TOSSINGS; PUT MY TEARS
IN YOUR BOTTLE. ARE THEY NOT IN YOUR BOOK?

PSALM 56:8

In this verse, "kept count" (*safar*) and "book" (*sefer*) are from the same root. A scribe would *safar* in a *sefer*—that is, "write down in a writing down object." God is imaged as a celestial scribe, making marks in his scroll of compassion, tallying up tears. The middle phrase has been translated as "put my tears in your bottle" (ESV) but also as "list my tears on your scroll" (NIV). Why? A *nod* is a leather bottle or skin, used to hold liquids such as wine (Josh. 9:4) or milk (Judg. 4:19). But since leather was also used for scrolls, and the rest of the verse refers to scrolls and writing, perhaps David meant, "List my tears on your leather [scroll]." Whether our Lord inks our tears onto his scroll or (more likely) bottles them in a skin, the message is consistent: his compassion toward us is so precise that not one miniscule drop of our liquidized pain passes by him unnoticed.

"Even the hairs of your head are all numbered," Jesus adds (Matt. 10:30). And we shouldn't be surprised. With God, we are never mere objects or numbers; each of us is minutely known and individually loved, with whole books in heaven written about us.

We praise you, dear Father, for you knitted us together in our mothers' wombs (Ps. 139:13).

Man's Best Friend? כלב

EACH EVENING THEY COME BACK, HOWLING LIKE DOGS
AND PROWLING ABOUT THE CITY. THERE THEY ARE,
BELLOWING WITH THEIR MOUTHS WITH SWORDS IN
THEIR LIPS—FOR "WHO," THEY THINK, "WILL HEAR US?"

PSALM 59:6-7

Dog lovers (like me) might be disappointed to learn that, overall, the Bible doesn't portray canines as man's best friend. The *kelev* ("dog") is known for eating corpses (1 Kings 14:11) and was a slang term for male prostitutes (Deut. 23:18). Fools repeating their folly are likened to dogs returning to their vomit (Prov. 26:11; 2 Pet. 2:22). When Saul sent bloodthirsty braggarts to ambush David, he said they were "howling like dogs and prowling about the city" (Ps. 59:6, 14). In Psalm 22, those who encircled the crucified Messiah are called "dogs" (v. 16). The NT mainly echoes the OT, calling evildoers "dogs" (Phil. 3:2; Rev. 22:15). Perhaps the dogs that licked Lazarus' sores were friendly, though it's not clear (Luke 16:21).

The one glowing example, however, is the Syrophoenician mother whose daughter was demon possessed. When Jesus initially rebuffed the woman because she was a Gentile, then labeled her a dog, she said, "Yes, Lord, yet even the dogs eat the crumbs that fall from their masters' table" (Matt. 15:27). Her faithful, dogged persistence paid off. And Jesus fed her with a gift that indicated she too sat as a daughter at the Master's table.

Lord Jesus, friend of sinners, though we are unworthy, grant us also a place at your feast.

The Goyim גוים

MAY GOD BE GRACIOUS TO US AND BLESS US AND
MAKE HIS FACE TO SHINE UPON US, *SELAH* THAT YOUR
WAY MAY BE KNOWN ON EARTH, YOUR SAVING POWER
AMONG ALL NATIONS. LET THE PEOPLES PRAISE
YOU, O GOD; LET ALL THE PEOPLES PRAISE YOU!

PSALM 67:1-3

When the Lord gave the so-called Aaronic Benediction, he specified the audience: "Thus you shall bless the people of Israel" (Num. 6:23). Notice what happens, however, when the words of this blessing are echoed in Psalm 67. Not just Israel but "all nations," "the peoples," and "all the peoples" benefit and respond in praise. God's blessings, with centrifugal grace, ripple outward to the *goyim* ("nations"). Though there are exceptions, as a rule *goyim* refers to non-Israelites, the Gentiles. In the Israelite mind, there were seventy nations of the world. This psalm confesses and celebrates that the Lord of Israel is the Lord of all seventy, God of "all the ends of the earth" (v. 7).

At Pentecost, "devout men from every nation under heaven" were there in Jerusalem (Acts 2:5). Not just Jews but *goyim* who were believers in the God of Israel. All received the same Spirit. All partook of his saving power. God was gracious to all of them, blessed them, and made his face shine upon them. As he'd promised Abram long before, in his Seed "all the *goyim* of the earth" were blessed (Gen. 22:18).

"Praise the LORD, all nations! Extol him, all peoples!" (Ps. 117:1).

A Long Time Ago
and Ahead עוֹלָם

I CONSIDER THE DAYS OF OLD, THE YEARS LONG
AGO. I SAID, "LET ME REMEMBER MY SONG IN
THE NIGHT; LET ME MEDITATE IN MY HEART."

PSALM 77:5-6

Though often translated "forever," the Hebrew temporal word *olam* does not refer to endlessness or eternity. In fact, it can designate the future *or the past*. For instance, in Psalm 77, when Asaph says he will consider the "years long ago," he uses the plural of *olam* for "long ago." Basically, *olam* means "a long time ago" or "a long time ahead," like a distant temporal horizon we can't quite see behind us or in front of us. *Olam* is a time hidden from present sight. When Hebrew wants to communicate something like eternity or endlessness, it will sometimes double the *olam*, such as in 1 Chronicles 29:10, where David says, "Blessed are you, O LORD, the God of Israel our father, forever [*olam*] and ever [*olam*]." Every time we pray the Lord's Prayer, we end up speaking like a Hebrew: "For Thine is the kingdom and the power and the glory forever and ever. Amen."

Though written in Aramaic, not Hebrew, Daniel 7:18 piles up similar time words when describing the kingdom we, the saints, will inherit in the Messiah, the Son of Man (7:13). We will "possess the kingdom forever, forever and ever." Therefore, we pray:

"Give thanks to the LORD, for he is good, for his steadfast love endures forever" (Ps. 136:1).

The Kiss נָשַׁק

STEADFAST LOVE AND FAITHFULNESS MEET;
RIGHTEOUSNESS AND PEACE KISS EACH OTHER.

PSALM 85:10

When Aaron reunited with Moses, he met (*pagash*) him and kissed (*nashaq*) him (Exod. 4:27). These same two Hebrew verbs are used in Psalm 85, where "steadfast love and faithfulness meet [*pagash*]; righteousness and peace kiss [*nashaq*] each other." As the two brothers embraced and kissed before heading to Egypt to announce the Lord's liberation of his people, so the "four brothers" named Love, Faithfulness, Righteousness, and Peace unite to bring us salvation and liberation. To *nashaq* is to kiss those whom we love, especially family, but also those we worship—as we "kiss the Son" (Ps. 2:12) or Baal worshipers kissed his idol (1 Kings 19:18). The Song of Songs, the poem between Christ and his bride, opens with the church proclaiming, "Let him kiss me with the kisses of his mouth!" (1:2).

Of course, not every kiss is to be trusted, for "deceitful are the kisses of an enemy" (Prov. 27:6 NASB). Judas Iscariot told the mob with him, "The one I will kiss is the man; seize him" (Matt. 26:48). And so it was. The Son of Man was betrayed by a kiss (Luke 22:48). But in Jesus, righteousness and peace had already kissed each other. He united them both in himself, along with love and faithfulness. The kiss of Christ is peace and liberation.

Lord of the church, embrace us as your own and kiss us as your beloved people.

Prayer תפלה

O LORD, GOD OF MY SALVATION, I CRY OUT DAY
AND NIGHT BEFORE YOU. LET MY PRAYER COME
BEFORE YOU; INCLINE YOUR EAR TO MY CRY!

PSALM 88:1-2

Psalm 88 is the darkest of the dark psalms. The poet is as good as dead. He languishes in a grave-like existence, in "regions dark and deep" (v. 6). He is a nightmare to his friends, who turn their backs on him (v. 8). Divine wrath has swept over him and hemmed him in (vv. 15-17). His "companions have become darkness" (v. 18). Indeed, the closing Hebrew word of the psalm, "darkness," encapsulates its contents. And yet even in this dreadful state, his *t'fillah* ("prayer") rises to God (v. 2). From the verb *palal* ("to pray"), *t'fillah* is the most common of the dozen or so Hebrew words used for prayer or intercession. A few of the psalms are even entitled *t'fillah*, such as Psalm 17, "A *T'fillah* of David."

St. Augustine sees in Psalm 88 a prophecy of Christ's passion. Every word speaks with a crucifixion accent. On that cruel tree, Jesus still prayed, as the poet of Psalm 88 does. He prays for himself, for us, for the world, even for those who hammered the nails. And his *t'fillah* was heard, for after his days in darkness, he walked into the sunrise of a resurrection morning so that we too may live and pray to him.

"Hear my prayer, O LORD; let my cry come to you!" (Ps. 102:1).

Abba, Father אב

HE SHALL CRY TO ME, "YOU ARE MY FATHER,
MY GOD, AND THE ROCK OF MY SALVATION."
AND I WILL MAKE HIM THE FIRSTBORN, THE
HIGHEST OF THE KINGS OF THE EARTH.

PSALM 89:26-27

In the first century, Jewish children called their father Abba. This Aramaic word is very similar to the Hebrew word for father, *Ab* (pronounced *Av*). It's in the first two letters of the names Abraham ("father of a multitude") and Abimelech ("my father is king"). Just as in English, "father" can refer to a dad, a priest, or the founder of something, so an *Ab* can designate a literal father, master, prophet, or protector. David cries out to God, "You are my *Ab*," and God declares David his firstborn (Ps. 89:26-27). The Lord is the "Father of the fatherless" (Ps. 68:5). God's people call him "our Father" (Isa. 63:16) even as he calls Israel "my son" (Hosea 11:1).

In Psalm 2, the Father said to the Messiah, "You are my Son; today I have begotten you" (v. 7). Jesus prayed to "Abba, Father" (Mark 14:36). We too who "have received the Spirit of adoption as sons . . . cry, 'Abba! Father!'" (Rom. 8:15; Gal. 4:6). The Son of the Father has made us children of the Father in baptism. We are adopted into the family of God, with Christ as our brother. He teaches us to pray as beloved children to a dear Father:

Our Abba, who art in heaven, hallowed be Thy name . . .

The Discipline of the Lord יסר

BLESSED IS THE MAN WHOM YOU DISCIPLINE,
O LORD, AND WHOM YOU TEACH OUT OF YOUR
LAW, TO GIVE HIM REST FROM DAYS OF TROUBLE,
UNTIL A PIT IS DUG FOR THE WICKED.

PSALM 94:12-13

"No discipline seems pleasant at the time, but painful" (Heb. 12:11 NIV). That's one verse I think almost everyone agrees with. Discipline hurts. Discipline humbles. So how can the psalmist pronounce a blessing on the one whom God *yasar* ("discipline, chastise, rebuke")? Because it is proof that the Lord loves us. "The LORD disciplines those he loves, as a father the son he delights in" (Prov. 3:12 NIV). Any father who lets his child get away with wrongdoing, who never disciplines him, does not love that child. Love corrects. Love teaches. Love seeks to improve another. So discipline is one facet of love in action. In the wilderness, God *yasar* Israel "as a man disciplines his son" (Deut. 8:5). He taught them the Torah. He rebuked their idolatry. He sought their reformation.

Our Father wants us to "share his holiness," to have the "peaceful fruit of righteousness," so he disciplines us "for our good" (Heb. 12:10-11). All this he does because he has made us his sons and daughters in Christ, on whom fell "the chastisement ['discipline'] that brought us peace, and with his wounds we are healed" (Isa. 53:5).

Rebuke us not in your wrath, heavenly Father, but discipline us in your love.

Orienting Ourselves מזרח

FOR AS HIGH AS THE HEAVENS ARE ABOVE THE EARTH, SO GREAT IS HIS STEADFAST LOVE TOWARD THOSE WHO FEAR HIM; AS FAR AS THE EAST IS FROM THE WEST, SO FAR DOES HE REMOVE OUR TRANSGRESSIONS FROM US.

PSALM 103:11-12

Our English verb "orient" is from the Latin for "the rising sun." Thus if we were literally "to orient ourselves," we would face eastward. In so doing we would be much like the Israelites, for one of their words for "east," *qedem*, also means "in front of." Another Hebrew word for "east," *mizrach*, occurs in Psalm 103. *Mizrach* refers to "sunrise," thus "east." Now put this together: to truly orient ourselves, we face eastward, to the rising of the sun. And what does that rising tell us? It orients us toward the God who removes our transgressions "as far as the east is from the west." There are poles for north and south; we can measure the distance from the north pole to the south pole. But it is impossible to measure the distance from the east to the west, from sunrise to sunset.

That is how far God's love stretches. How far his forgiveness extends. How far our sins have been removed in Christ. When we orient ourselves to that joyous reality and bathe in its rising light of grace, we will never be lost.

From the rising of the sun to its setting, we praise your name, O Lord! (Ps. 113:3).

God's Land ארץ

O LORD, HOW MANIFOLD ARE YOUR WORKS!
IN WISDOM HAVE YOU MADE THEM ALL; THE
EARTH IS FULL OF YOUR CREATURES.

PSALM 104:24

"In the beginning God created the heavens and the earth." These opening words of the Bible declare that all creation hangs on God's Word. Nothing has an independent existence, from atoms to humans to planets. Psalm 104 translates this truth in soaring poetry. "The *eretz* ['earth'] is full of your creatures." Not brimming with autonomous entities, but creatures. That is why, as Jewish scholar Abraham Heschel puts it, "Psalm 104 is a hymn to God rather than an ode to the cosmos." Not "mother nature" but the Father is worthy of blessing, for he "set the earth upon its foundations, so that it should never be moved" (v. 5).

The word *eretz* can mean "land," as in *Eretz Yisrael* ("the land of Israel"), but also the "world" or "earth." And fittingly so, for from Israel were to flow the blessings that irrigated the whole earth. When Jesus sent his followers to "make disciples of all nations" (Matt. 28:19), he sent them with pockets full of promises and lips full of praise, for "all authority in heaven and on earth" had been given to him. He, the Word who hung on the tree, sent them to proclaim that all creation hangs on his word of grace and power.

"Be exalted, O God, above the heavens! Let your glory be over all the earth!" (Ps. 108:5).

In the Wilderness מדבר

HE TURNS RIVERS INTO A DESERT, SPRINGS OF WATER
INTO THIRSTY GROUND, A FRUITFUL LAND INTO A SALTY
WASTE, BECAUSE OF THE EVIL OF ITS INHABITANTS. HE
TURNS A DESERT INTO POOLS OF WATER, A PARCHED
LAND INTO SPRINGS OF WATER. AND THERE HE LETS THE
HUNGRY DWELL, AND THEY ESTABLISH A CITY TO LIVE IN.

PSALM 107:33-36

The Lord of Israel is a turning-everything-topsy-turvy kind of God. Uglifying beauty and beautifying ugly, making the dead alive and the alive dead—well, that's just another day at the office. Psalm 107 poeticizes these actions with the vision of croplands transmogrified into salt wastes, deserts transformed into watered gardens. The *midbar*, often translated "desert" or "wilderness," is the general name for vast, arid regions, such as where Israel languished for forty years. The *midbar* evokes multiple images—death, suffering, godforsakenness—but certainly not water. But simply by his will and word, God "turns a *midbar* into pools of water" (v. 35).

This is how God always operates: he wrenches life out of death, hope out of despair, creation out of nothing, his Son out of the grave—and us with him. As Martin Luther once said, "God breaks what is whole and makes whole what is broken." No souls are too broken, or too desert-dry, that our Father can't water them and heal them in Christ.

We give thanks to you, O Lord, for you are good, and your steadfast love endures forever (Ps. 107:1).

To What Shall I Compare It? מָשַׁל

THE PROVERBS OF SOLOMON, SON OF DAVID, KING
OF ISRAEL: TO KNOW WISDOM AND INSTRUCTION,
TO UNDERSTAND WORDS OF INSIGHT, TO RECEIVE
INSTRUCTION IN WISE DEALING, IN RIGHTEOUSNESS,
JUSTICE, AND EQUITY; TO GIVE PRUDENCE TO THE
SIMPLE, KNOWLEDGE AND DISCRETION TO THE YOUTH.

PROVERBS 1:1-4

When Jesus says, "To what shall I compare the kingdom of God?" he is speaking the language of *mashal* (Luke 13:20). As a verb, *mashal* means "to speak a parable" or "to compare this to that." As a noun, *mashal* means "parable, proverb, wisdom saying." The Hebrew name of Proverbs is from the book's opening word, *Mishley* ("the proverbs of"). Jesus was a *mashal* rabbi, a teacher of parables. He likened God's kingdom to everything from a miniscule mustard seed to a net fat with fish. When he did so, he was taking a page from the playbook of Proverbs and the prophets. For centuries, Israelite sages had been painting the highest and holiest truths in the hues and tones of earthen simplicity.

But the Messiah's *mashal* was also unique, for in his topsy-turvy tales, a hated Samaritan is the good guy, dishonest stewards are commended, and latecomers to work pocket the same paycheck as early birds. His parables, then, are also illustrations of the cross and cross-shaped life, where the dead live, the last are first, and weakness is strength.

Blessed are you, O Lord Jesus, for you have hidden your saving truth in scandalous stories of grace.

The Architect of the World אמון

"WHEN [GOD] ASSIGNED TO THE SEA ITS LIMIT, SO THAT THE WATERS MIGHT NOT TRANSGRESS HIS COMMAND, WHEN HE MARKED OUT THE FOUNDATIONS OF THE EARTH, THEN I WAS BESIDE HIM, LIKE A MASTER WORKMAN, AND I WAS DAILY HIS DELIGHT, REJOICING BEFORE HIM ALWAYS, REJOICING IN HIS INHABITED WORLD AND DELIGHTING IN THE CHILDREN OF MAN."

PROVERBS 8:29-31

Wisdom (*chokmah*) is speaking—the Wisdom that is of God, with God, begotten by God. At the beginning, Wisdom says, I was with the Creator (8:22). Indeed, Wisdom is *the* Beginning, by which God created the heavens and the earth. Before the mountains were shaped, when no seas yet roared, "when he established the heavens, I was there" (v. 27). "I was beside him, like an *amon*" (v. 30). This rare Hebrew word probably means "master workman, craftsman, or artisan." The Father's Wisdom, Word, Son is the world's architect, rejoicing before the Creator, "rejoicing in his inhabited world and delighting in the children of man" (v. 31).

What a picture! Humanity's *amon*, the architect of the world, dances with joy over us! He quiets us by his love and exults over us with singing (Zeph. 3:17). That singing reached its crescendo when, for the joy set before him, he endured the cross, scorning its shame, that he might delight even more in the children of man whom he had saved.

All praise, glory, and thanksgiving be to you, Jesus our Wisdom, for making us as your own.

Covering Sins כסה

THE MOUTH OF THE RIGHTEOUS IS A FOUNTAIN
OF LIFE, BUT THE MOUTH OF THE WICKED
CONCEALS VIOLENCE. HATRED STIRS UP
STRIFE, BUT LOVE COVERS ALL OFFENSES.

PROVERBS 10:11-12

You wouldn't know it from this translation, but "conceals" and "covers" are the same word in Hebrew—*kasah*. This verb is used to describe how Shem and Japheth *kasah* the nakedness of Noah (9:23). In Proverbs 10, the emphasis is on the mouth as a kind of veil, for good or for evil. The mouth of the wicked *kasah* violence—that is, it veils evil with lies. As the psalmist says, "His speech was smooth as butter, yet war was in his heart; his words were softer than oil, yet they were drawn swords" (55:21). The mouth of the righteous, on the other hand, *kasah* all offenses in love—that is, it veils the words that would speak evil, lies, or rumors of another.

Love hides or covers the sins of our neighbor; hatred unveils them. Both James 5:20 and 1 Peter 4:8 quote a version of this proverb. Indeed, James must have considered it so important that he saves it for the final, climactic verse of his epistle: "Whoever brings back a sinner from his wandering will save his soul from death and will cover a multitude of sins." Restoration of the sinner, not gossiping about his offenses, is Christ's vocation for us.

Jesus Christ, "you forgave the iniquity of your people; you covered all their sin" (Ps. 85:2).

Souls and Throats נפש

WHOEVER GUARDS HIS MOUTH PRESERVES HIS LIFE;
HE WHO OPENS WIDE HIS LIPS COMES TO RUIN.

PROVERBS 13:3

Proverbs is full of admonitions to *natzar* ("guard or keep") wisdom, commandments, and knowledge. In 13:3, a wise son uses a mouthguard, as it were, to keep or preserve his life. He stations a language soldier on his mouth to keep those two lip-gates shut. But there's a hidden Hebrew wordplay here as well. The word translated as "life," *nefesh*, can also mean soul or personality or the physical throat. Since this verse highlights the mouth as well as the lips, the pun on *nefesh* as throat/soul/life gives us a taste of artistic writing. Like so much of Proverbs—not to mention the rest of the Bible—the mouth is highlighted as the portal out of which evil loves to launch its besmirching crusades.

Any dental hygienist will tell you that our mouths are the window to the rest of our body's health. All varieties of diseases have oral manifestations. What is true physically is far truer spiritually. "But what comes out of the mouth proceeds from the heart, and this defiles a person" (Matt. 15:18). So we pray to listen more and speak less. And we ask the Lord to make our hearts the lexicon of his love, that out of our hearts may come verbs of truth and nouns of mercy.

"O Lord, open my lips, and my mouth will declare your praise" (Ps. 51:15).

Train up or Dedicate? חנך

TRAIN UP A CHILD IN THE WAY HE SHOULD GO; EVEN
WHEN HE IS OLD HE WILL NOT DEPART FROM IT.

PROVERBS 22:6

This well-known verse may not be known as well as we assume. The verb rendered "train up" is *chanak*, which occurs only five times in the Bible. In four of these, what is *chanak* is a house, either a domestic dwelling (Deut. 20:5 [twice]) or the Lord's temple (1 Kings 8:63; 2 Chron. 7:5). To *chanak* a building is to "dedicate" it, to say, "This place belongs to so-and-so. It's his and no one else's." *Chanak* is behind the word Hanukkah, the Jewish festival at which the temple's "rededication" is celebrated. Bearing in mind the other four occurrences of *chanak*, we get this: "Dedicate a child in the way he should go [literally, 'according to his way']; even when he is old he will not depart from it."

We *chanak* our children in baptism. In that liquid exchange, they pass from us to the arms of our Father. They become his house, his little temple, where his Son and Spirit "make [their] home with him" (John 14:23). He says, "This child belongs to me. I am his or her Father." Parenting is hard. As moms and dads, we fail in many ways. But in one way, we cannot fail: when we hand our children over to their dear heavenly Father.

Bless our sons and daughters, heavenly Father, with your grace and paternal compassion.

Mega-Vanity! הבל

THE WORDS OF THE PREACHER, THE SON OF DAVID,
KING IN JERUSALEM. VANITY OF VANITIES, SAYS THE
PREACHER, VANITY OF VANITIES! ALL IS VANITY.

ECCLESIASTES 1:1–2

Havel havalim, vanity of vanities. So begins one of the most bizarre—and philosophical—books of the Bible. Its English title is Ecclesiastes; in Hebrew it's Qoheleth; but Vanity might have been a more fitting title, considering that the word populates eleven of the twelve chapters. *Hevel* means "breath," and, by extension, "vanity" (something as insubstantial as breath) and "idols" (things without essence). "Vanity of vanities" is a Hebrew superlative like "servant of servants" ("abject slave" Gen. 9:25) or "forever and ever" ("everlastingly" Isa. 34:10). It means something like "utter futility" or "mega-vanity." What is utter futility? Life "under the sun" (v. 3). It's all as vain as "chasing after the wind" (v. 14 NIV).

This book drops an atomic bomb onto every one of our private towers of Babel. We are so easily bloated with self-importance and our delusions of grandeur. Vanity of vanities! Foolishness! Rather, during our time under the sun, let us lose ourselves in the life of Christ—and thus find true life, true meaning in the King of kings and Lord of lords. In him, we receive a treasure to which nothing in this world can compare.

Breathe in us, Holy Spirit, your life-giving and hope-bestowing grace, that we might serve you all our days.

The Fool כְּסִיל

THEN I SAW THAT THERE IS MORE GAIN IN WISDOM
THAN IN FOLLY, AS THERE IS MORE GAIN IN LIGHT
THAN IN DARKNESS. THE WISE PERSON HAS
HIS EYES IN HIS HEAD, BUT THE FOOL WALKS
IN DARKNESS. AND YET I PERCEIVED THAT THE
SAME EVENT HAPPENS TO ALL OF THEM.

ECCLESIASTES 2:13-14

One might expect that Solomon, renowned for his wisdom, would have much to say about fools—and he does. Though there is more than one Hebrew word for "fool," *k'sil* (pronounced "ka-SEEL"), which he uses eighteen times in Ecclesiastes, seems to be his favorite. Being a *k'sil* has nothing to do with IQ; someone with three PhDs can be the biggest fool in the room. "The fool walks in darkness" (v. 14). He is stupid regarding daily life and insolent regarding religion. He hates knowledge (Prov. 1:22). The fool is a cancer to the lives of friends and family and community. Perhaps worst of all, a fool does not even believe himself to a fool. He is intoxicated on the rotgut of his own faux wisdom.

Unlike the fool, the wise acknowledge one truth above all: "Christ the power of God and the wisdom of God" (1 Cor. 1:24). Conformed to him, they are transformed by the Father into bearers of his wisdom to others. Wise in Christ, they walk in the light of truth.

Dear Father, rescue us from folly and teach us the wisdom that comes from on high.

Cistern and Grave בּוֹר

[REMEMBER YOUR CREATOR] BEFORE THE SILVER
CORD IS SNAPPED, OR THE GOLDEN BOWL IS BROKEN,
OR THE PITCHER IS SHATTERED AT THE FOUNTAIN, OR
THE WHEEL BROKEN AT THE CISTERN, AND THE DUST
RETURNS TO THE EARTH AS IT WAS, AND THE SPIRIT
RETURNS TO GOD WHO GAVE IT.

ECCLESIASTES 12:6-7

Janus was a Roman god with two faces: one looking forward, one looking back. In Hebrew, there is a literary device named after him, called Janus parallelism, where a word points back with one of its meanings and forward with another of its meanings. We see an example of this in Ecclesiastes 12:6. The verse ends with the word *bor*, which means both "cistern" and "grave." As "cistern," *bor* points back to the fountain imagery that precedes it. As "grave," *bor* points forward to the imagery of dust and death. This "two-faced" word thus bridges the gap between a fountain full of life and a grave full of death.

The very same Creator whom Solomon urges us to remember in the days of our youth, before we age and eventually enter that grave, knows a thing or two about getting out of the grave. And when this world is done, he'll get our bodies out of the grave as well. In the meantime, we rejoice that we have already passed from death to life in the revivifying fountain of mercy.

"O LORD . . . you restored me to life from among those who go down to the pit" (Ps. 30:3).

This Is the All of Humanity כל

THE END OF THE MATTER; ALL HAS BEEN HEARD. FEAR GOD AND KEEP HIS COMMANDMENTS, FOR THIS IS THE WHOLE DUTY OF MAN. FOR GOD WILL BRING EVERY DEED INTO JUDGMENT, WITH EVERY SECRET THING, WHETHER GOOD OR EVIL.

ECCLESIASTES 12:13–14

Ecclesiastes starts off with "vanity of vanities" but closes the book—more positively—with "the whole duty of man." The little word *kol* is translated as "whole." It means "all, everything, totality." The great Shema tells us to love the Lord with "*kol* your heart and with *kol* your soul and with *kol* your might" (Deut. 6:5). That last word, "might," might better be rendered "very-ness." The totality of who we are. So too in Ecclesiastes, to "fear God and keep his commandments," in other words, to love him, is "the whole duty of man." Or, more literally, "the all of humanity." Our all, our everything, our very-ness as humans is to fear and love God, to guard (*shamar*) his commandments, for he "will bring every deed into judgment."

"All the commandments of God are kept, when what is not kept is forgiven" (Augustine). This is the way of God, who is *kol* of love. Love is his everything-ness, his essence. If the all of humanity is to love him, the all of God is to love us, forgive us, and make us right in Christ.

"O LORD, our Lord, how majestic is your name in all the earth!" (Ps. 8:9).

Dark but Lovely שׁחר

"I AM VERY DARK, BUT LOVELY, O DAUGHTERS OF JERUSALEM, LIKE THE TENTS OF KEDAR, LIKE THE CURTAINS OF SOLOMON. DO NOT GAZE AT ME BECAUSE I AM DARK, BECAUSE THE SUN HAS LOOKED UPON ME."

SONG OF SONGS 1:5-6

Hannah sang of how the Lord "makes poor and makes rich; he brings low and he exalts" (1 Sam. 2:7). In her canticle, Mary too sings of how God "looked upon the humble estate of his servant . . . brought down the mighty from their thrones and exalted those of humble estate" (Luke 1:48, 52). This theme of "great reversal" is touched on in the opening lines of the Song of Songs. The lover of Solomon—iconic of Israel and the church—is "very *shachor*, but lovely." *Shachor* is "swarthy, sunbaked, dark." Although sun-kissed bodies have sex appeal today, in this ancient culture there was a stigma attached to this look. Sun-darkened skin signaled that you worked outside, were of a lower class, and were certainly not royalty.

Yet this is the woman whom wise, powerful, internationally famous Solomon loved. He chose her. He looked upon the humble estate of this servant, exalted her, kissed her, and wrapped her in his royal arms. He beautified her with his love, as Christ does his church, his resplendent bride. She may not look like much to the world, but in the eyes of King Messiah, she is lovely beyond reckoning.

Exalt your church, Lord Jesus, that we may partake of the glory that is yours.

When Christ Knocks דָּפַק

I SLEPT, BUT MY HEART WAS AWAKE. A SOUND! MY
BELOVED IS KNOCKING. "OPEN TO ME, MY SISTER, MY
LOVE, MY DOVE, MY PERFECT ONE, FOR MY HEAD IS WET
WITH DEW, MY LOCKS WITH THE DROPS OF THE NIGHT."
I HAD PUT OFF MY GARMENT; HOW COULD I PUT IT ON?
I HAD BATHED MY FEET; HOW COULD I SOIL THEM?

SONG OF SONGS 5:2-3

The church of Laodicea said to herself, "I am rich, I have prospered, and I need nothing," but they didn't realize they were "wretched, pitiable, poor, blind, and naked" (Rev. 3:17). Much like the woman in Song of Songs, who was naked in bed, had washed her feet, and was initially unwilling to open the door to her beloved, so the Laodicean church was spiritually lazy, lukewarm, unwilling to act. Yet the Lover *dafaq* ("knocks"). Based on the other two occurrences of this verb (Gen. 33:13; Judg. 19:22), this is not light tapping but vigorous pounding. The knuckles rap with vehement desire. In the Song, she hesitates, then finally gets up, but by then her "beloved had turned and gone" (5:6).

Jesus stood "at the door and knock[ed]" at Laodicea (Rev. 3:20). He calls us, not like a door-to-door salesman, but a zealous lover, battering our hearts, seeking entrance, seeking us. Repent and believe. The Lord of grace and forgiveness desires us as his own.

Holy Spirit, who calls us by the Gospel, give us open and contrite hearts that rejoice at your entrance.

Love and Mandrakes דודאים

COME, MY BELOVED, LET US GO OUT INTO THE FIELDS
AND LODGE IN THE VILLAGES; LET US GO OUT EARLY TO
THE VINEYARDS . . . THERE I WILL GIVE YOU MY LOVE.
THE MANDRAKES GIVE FORTH FRAGRANCE, AND BESIDE
OUR DOORS ARE ALL CHOICE FRUITS, NEW AS WELL AS
OLD, WHICH I HAVE LAID UP FOR YOU, O MY BELOVED.

SONG OF SONGS 7:11-13

Dudaim ("mandrakes") are "love fruits," plants that, as the Song says, "give forth fragrance"—a fragrance often linked with intimacy in other ancient texts and iconography. We might compare them to our romantic perfumes and colognes, perhaps even an aphrodisiac. In Genesis, they are mentioned in a barter between the sister-wives, Rachel and Leah, for who will have Jacob in her bed that night (30:14–16). In the Song, their scent wafts through the air where the Shulammite, Solomon's wife, says, "There I will give you my love." There is even a play on words, because "my love" (*dodai*) and "my beloved" (*dodi*) sound like mandrakes (*dudaim*).

This earthy, romantic scene, scented with mandrakes, where husband and wife embrace, is one of the many ways the Bible pictures the intimate bond between God and his people, Christ and his church, who are no longer two but one flesh, joined as a head to a body in love.

Christ our Bridegroom, who gave your life as a ransom for the church, make us one with you, even as you are one with the Father and Spirit.

Rebellious Rulers סרר

HOW THE FAITHFUL CITY HAS BECOME A WHORE, SHE
WHO WAS FULL OF JUSTICE! RIGHTEOUSNESS LODGED IN
HER, BUT NOW MURDERERS. YOUR SILVER HAS BECOME
DROSS, YOUR BEST WINE MIXED WITH WATER. YOUR
PRINCES ARE REBELS AND COMPANIONS OF THIEVES.

ISAIAH 1:21-23

Isaiah is the king of Hebrew wordsmithing. He weaves in puns, tinkers with names, winks with linguistic sarcasm. He's cooked up a rhyme in this law-heavy sermon against his people and their leaders. The four-word phrase "Your princes are rebels" is but two words in Hebrew: *sarayik sor'rim* (Say it slowly aloud: saw-rah-yik sow-re-reem). The simple form of the two Hebrew nouns, *sar* ("ruler") and *sarar* ("rebel"), is just begging for them to be paired. But that's not all. The word *sarar* carries baggage; it describes the rebellious son who earned the death penalty (Deut. 21:18-21) and rebellious Israel who earned forty years of wilderness wanderings (Ps. 78:8). Isaiah pulls no punches: the whore-like nation (v. 21), full of murderers (v. 21), has the lowlife leaders they deserve.

Like Isaiah, Jesus sugarcoated nothing. When he verbally whipped the religious leadership of his day, he drew on images of graves, snakes, and dirty dishes to characterize their hypocrisy. What Israel needed—and what we need—is a ruler who is true, gentle, just, merciful, and righteous. And that's precisely what we have in our Lord, the truth-telling, anointed King.

Holy Father, break our stubborn hearts and rebuild them in the shape and texture of your own.

Torah Not Law תורה

"COME, LET US GO UP TO THE MOUNTAIN OF THE LORD, TO THE HOUSE OF THE GOD OF JACOB, THAT HE MAY TEACH US HIS WAYS AND THAT WE MAY WALK IN HIS PATHS." FOR OUT OF ZION SHALL GO FORTH THE LAW, AND THE WORD OF THE LORD FROM JERUSALEM.

ISAIAH 2:3

Isaiah sees God's mountain inflated, towering above all peaks. People from across the globe, like a human river in reverse, flow upward to it. Here is the prophetic image of the church, making disciples of all nations, washing them into Christ's temple. What will precipitate this? From Zion the Torah shall march forth, ushering people in. Torah does not mean law. It derives from *yarah* ("teach")—the same verb on the mouths of the Gentiles when they say, "that he may teach [*yarah*] us his ways." The Messiah's teaching, his Torah, the message of his kingdom and grace and life, will bring Jews and Gentiles to the church's mountain sanctuary.

Isaiah 2 is the OT cousin of Matthew 28, the "Great Commission." The effects of the discipling in Matthew 28 are graphically described by the prophet. Believers worldwide will ascend Zion as they are baptized in the name of the Father, Son, and Holy Spirit, and as they are "torah-ed" in everything Christ has instructed. Having received this priceless gift, we rejoice to say:

O Lord, the Torah of your mouth "is better to me than thousands of gold and silver pieces" (Ps. 119:72).

Mishpat and Murder מִשְׁפָּט

FOR THE VINEYARD OF THE LORD OF HOSTS IS
THE HOUSE OF ISRAEL, AND THE MEN OF JUDAH
ARE HIS PLEASANT PLANTING; AND HE LOOKED
FOR JUSTICE, BUT BEHOLD, BLOODSHED; FOR
RIGHTEOUSNESS, BUT BEHOLD, AN OUTCRY!

ISAIAH 5:7

There must have been an audible gasp from the Jerusalem crowd. There stood Isaiah, preaching. He'd reeled in his listeners by singing a song of a vineyard, the Lord's vineyard. God worked his fingers to the bone for this vineyard. Cleared away the stones. Planted choice vines. Then he waited. Finally, harvest time arrived. And this vineyard, for which the Lord had gone above and beyond, what was its fruit? What did God harvest?

> He looked for *mishpat*, but behold, *mispach*!
> He looked for *tzedaqah*, but behold, *tzeʿaqah*!

No translation can do justice to this masterful pairing of rhymes. He looked for the correcting of wrongs (*mishpat* [justice]) and found only wrongdoing (*mispach* [bloodshed]). He looked for what was right (*tzedaqah* [righteousness]) and found only the cries of those who had been wronged (*tzeʿaqah* [outcry]).

The vineyard parables of Jesus grow from the literary soil of this one—only Christ adds a postscript. Rather than destroying his vineyard, he hands it over to those who will produce its fruit (Matt. 21:43). By the Gospel, he calls and gathers servants through whom the Spirit works faith, hope, love, justice, and righteousness in the world.

Defend your vineyard, O Lord, from all enemies, and produce in us fruits in keeping with repentance.

Woe upon Woe! הוֹי

WOE TO THOSE WHO CALL EVIL GOOD AND
GOOD EVIL, WHO PUT DARKNESS FOR LIGHT
AND LIGHT FOR DARKNESS, WHO PUT BITTER
FOR SWEET AND SWEET FOR BITTER!

ISAIAH 5:20

Hoy can be used to lament ("Alas!"), but almost every instance is the verbal equivalent of taking someone's face in your hands and preparing to inform them of a cold, hard, unwelcome truth. With six occurrences of *hoy* in it, Isaiah 5 has this word more than any other OT chapter. Woe to those who hog land (v. 8), guzzle wine (v. 11), rope themselves to sin (v. 18), lie and twist truth (v. 20), are know-it-alls (v. 21), and are gold-medal winners at inebriation (v. 22). The only other portions of Scripture awash with this many woes is when Jesus unleashes a string of them upon the scribes and Pharisees (Matt. 23). "Woe" may be an old-fashioned, churchy sounding word, but it's one we would do well to recycle. Calling good evil and evil good is as stylish and mainstream today as millennia ago.

Hoy is the call of repentance, which is not an occasional emotion but an ongoing motion. We move out of ourselves, out of sin, into contrition, faith, and forgiveness in Christ. To heed the woe is to speed into the blessing, to pass from death in sin to life in the Son of God.

Give us broken and contrite hearts, O Lord, to repent, believe, and rejoice in your forgiving love.

The Choir of Fire שְׂרָפִים

IN THE YEAR THAT KING UZZIAH DIED I SAW THE LORD
SITTING UPON A THRONE, HIGH AND LIFTED UP; AND
THE TRAIN OF HIS ROBE FILLED THE TEMPLE. ABOVE HIM
STOOD THE SERAPHIM. EACH HAD SIX WINGS: WITH TWO
HE COVERED HIS FACE, AND WITH TWO HE COVERED
HIS FEET, AND WITH TWO HE FLEW. AND ONE CALLED
TO ANOTHER AND SAID: "HOLY, HOLY, HOLY IS THE LORD
OF HOSTS; THE WHOLE EARTH IS FULL OF HIS GLORY!"

ISAIAH 6:1–3

Seraphim are mentioned only here in the Bible. They derive their name from *saraf* ("to burn"), like the burning or "fiery serpents" in the wilderness (Num. 21:6). These six-winged, burning angels form a choir of fire. With eyes blindfolded by wings and feet covered, their mouths chant the Trisagion, the triple-holy to the Lord of hosts. Perhaps Isaiah named them seraphim because one of them touched his lips with a live coal (v. 6). Or perhaps they resembled flying flames. Either way, these celestial beings sing the Lord's praise, do his bidding, and serve sinners with a purifying touch.

Isaiah was privileged to see with the naked eye the active sphere all around us, hidden from view. Angels watch over us. Angels sing God's praises. And we, with them, worship the Christ, the Lord upon the throne, to whose glory Isaiah bore witness (John 12:41).

"O LORD, I love the habitation of your house and the place where your glory dwells" (Ps. 26:8).

Stand or Stumble אָמַן

"IF YOU ARE NOT FIRM IN FAITH, YOU
WILL NOT BE FIRM AT ALL."

ISAIAH 7:9

In the lengthy list of Judah's deadbeat kings, Ahaz was notoriously atrocious. He sold his soul to the Assyrians; built a pagan altar for the temple; sacrificed children. There was bad, then there was Ahaz bad. His legacy could have been radically different. When two rival powers threatened Judah, the Lord sent Isaiah to place before Ahaz life and death, good and evil. He offered to move heaven and earth to give Ahaz a sign to bolster his faith. But the king refused.

In stunning poetry, the Lord summarized Ahaz's situation. Transliterated so as to catch the sound in English, we read: "If you will not *tah-ah-me-nu*, you will certainly not *tay-ah-mey-nu*." The two words are different forms of the same verb, *aman*, but the first means "believe, trust, have faith" and the second means "endure, last, be permanent." Raise your faith or razed you will be. Firm in faith or not firm at all.

Ahaz was religious, hyperreligious even, but only in idolatry. To this day, he stands as a warning as well as a beckoning—a beckoning by the Lord to believe, to stand fast in faith, to entrust our hearts, souls, minds, and bodies to the one true God in Christ, whose love for us is as firm as firm can be.

"Lord, I believe; help thou mine unbelief" (Mark 9:24 KJV).

Shadow of Death צַלְמָוֶת

THE PEOPLE WHO WALKED IN DARKNESS HAVE SEEN
A GREAT LIGHT; THOSE WHO DWELT IN A LAND OF
DEEP DARKNESS, ON THEM HAS LIGHT SHONE.

ISAIAH 9:2

A midnight walk in the park may be dark, but it's not *tzalmavet* dark. Spelunk into the bowels of a cave, extinguish every source of illumination, and experience being blanketed by black. That's *tzalmavet*. Though traditionally translated "shadow of death," "deep darkness" or "impenetrable gloom" are more accurate. *Tzalmavet* is dark on steroids. But of course, the darker the dark, the more blindingly beautiful the light becomes when it shines. Isaiah foresaw the age when the northern tribes, bruised and benighted by one foreign power after another, would spy the radiance of hope. "Those who dwelt in a land of *tzalmavet*, on them a light has shone."

That light, Matthew tells us, had two legs, two hands, and a mouth that preached, "Repent, for the kingdom of heaven is at hand" (4:17). Jesus kicked off his ministry in Galilee, just as Isaiah had prophesied. He did not stand aloof from our sin-darkened world but dove headfirst and lovefirst into the bowels of our cosmic cave to be the light of the world, to lead us blinded sinners into the rays of grace, where we might behold a world illumined by divine and enlivening mercy.

"Yea, though I walk through the valley of the shadow of death, I will fear no evil: for thou art with me" (Ps. 23:4 KJV).

Root of Jesse שֹׁרֶשׁ

THERE SHALL COME FORTH A SHOOT FROM THE
STUMP OF JESSE, AND A BRANCH FROM HIS ROOTS
SHALL BEAR FRUIT. . . . IN THAT DAY THE ROOT OF
JESSE, WHO SHALL STAND AS A SIGNAL FOR THE
PEOPLES—OF HIM SHALL THE NATIONS INQUIRE,
AND HIS RESTING PLACE SHALL BE GLORIOUS.

ISAIAH 11:1, 10

From December 17 to 23, the church has traditionally sung the "O Antiphons," the third of which is *O Radix Jesse* ("O Root of Jesse")—or, in Hebrew, *Shoresh Yishai*. This stanza is based on Isaiah 11:1, 10. The prophet employs three images from nature to describe the Messiah: shoot, branch, and root. Now it is one thing to call God's anointed "a shoot from the stump of Jesse" or "a branch from his roots." That is surely glorious, for it means he is the promised Son of David, who sprouts from Jesse's line. It is far more radical to call him "the *shoresh* of Jesse," for this means he is the root, source, and foundation for Jesse himself!

How is this possible? How can Christ spring from Jesse *and* Jesse spring from him? In one way and one way only: by being both God and man, divine and human. Jesus is the Son of Mary and the Son of God, of one nature with us and of one nature with the Father. In him we see God and in him God sees us.

O Root of Jesse, standing as a sign before the people, come and deliver us.

The Key of David מפתח

IN THAT DAY I WILL CALL MY SERVANT ELIAKIM THE
SON OF HILKIAH, AND I WILL CLOTHE HIM WITH
YOUR ROBE, AND WILL BIND YOUR SASH ON HIM,
AND WILL COMMIT YOUR AUTHORITY TO HIS HAND.
AND HE SHALL BE A FATHER TO THE INHABITANTS
OF JERUSALEM AND TO THE HOUSE OF JUDAH. AND
I WILL PLACE ON HIS SHOULDER THE KEY OF THE
HOUSE OF DAVID. HE SHALL OPEN, AND NONE SHALL
SHUT; AND HE SHALL SHUT, AND NONE SHALL OPEN.

ISAIAH 22:20-22

To *patach* is "to open," so an opening device—a key—is a *mafteach*. Eliakim, the king's chief steward, was promoted to great authority. He dressed the part with robe, sash, and headgear. On his shoulder, perhaps as some official insignia, was the *mafteach* of David's house. He was given "the key to the city," we might say, but not in a merely symbolic way. He had authority. He was the man in charge. What he shut stayed shut. What he opened stayed open.

Christ is the reality of which Eliakim was the shadow. He tells the church in Philadelphia that he "has the key of David, who opens and no one will shut, who shuts and no one opens" (Rev. 3:7). And he stands ready to turn the key that locks his kingdom's doors to all who reject him, and to open them to all who trust in his name.

Open to us the gates of righteousness, Lord Jesus, that we may enter through them and give thanks to you (Ps. 118:19).

Death-Eater מות

ON THIS MOUNTAIN THE LORD OF HOSTS WILL MAKE
FOR ALL PEOPLES A FEAST OF RICH FOOD, A FEAST OF
WELL-AGED WINE, OF RICH FOOD FULL OF MARROW,
OF AGED WINE WELL REFINED. AND HE WILL SWALLOW
UP ON THIS MOUNTAIN THE COVERING THAT IS CAST
OVER ALL PEOPLES, THE VEIL THAT IS SPREAD OVER
ALL NATIONS. HE WILL SWALLOW UP DEATH FOREVER.

ISAIAH 25:6–8

The loom on which the veil of *mavet* ("death") is woven sits deep in the caverns of human existence. Weaving, weaving, evermore weaving. *Mavet* is "the covering that is cast over all peoples." Faces wintered by wrinkles and faces in the spring of life are shrouded by its fabric of mortality and woe. *Mavet* moves mercilessly, sparing none, taking all. Ashes to ashes, dust to dust. Yet the prophet's eye, peering down the corridors of time, spies the Lord of resurrection, standing on a festive mountain, holding something in his hand. What is it? It's a hammer, raised high, coming down, down, down on that veil-making loom. Again and again, until it is but a mass of splinters.

Then in his hand he takes the veil, opens his mouth, and swallows it. The "veil that is spread over all the nations" goes down the gullet of God, gone for good. He is the Death-Eater. And we feast! We, alive in the living Christ, swallow the wine of heaven at the feast without end.

Resurrected Savior, eater of death, fill our cups with the wine of life.

Controversial Cornerstone פנה

THEREFORE THUS SAYS THE LORD GOD, "BEHOLD,
I AM THE ONE WHO HAS LAID AS A FOUNDATION
IN ZION, A STONE, A TESTED STONE, A PRECIOUS
CORNERSTONE, OF A SURE FOUNDATION:
'WHOEVER BELIEVES WILL NOT BE IN HASTE.'"

ISAIAH 28:16

When the Lord twisted a whirlwind into a megaphone to interrogate Job, he asked, "Who laid [the earth's] cornerstone?" (38:4, 6). That's a rhetorical question, of course. God didn't convene a committee of human consultants and angelic advisors to garner their architectural wisdom when he made the world. He knew what he was doing. As with creation, so with redemptive re-creation: he chose the perfect *pinnah* ("cornerstone") for the job. But people, intoxicated by their own wisdom, stumble like blind drunks on this stone of salvation. They reject him, toss him into the disposal pit like a chunk of cracked concrete. But "the stone that the builders rejected has become the cornerstone [*pinnah*]" (Ps. 118:22). One man's trash is the one God's treasure.

We "come to him, a living stone rejected by men but in the sight of God chosen and precious" (1 Pet. 2:4). And we, human stones palpitating with the life of Jesus, are cemented by the Spirit into a spiritual house, to be his priests, to offer to him sacrifices with shouts of joy.

Blessed are you, Jesus, the Rock of our redemption, in whom we are found and on whom we are founded as the church of the living God.

John the Highway-Builder מסלה

A VOICE CRIES: "IN THE WILDERNESS PREPARE THE
WAY OF THE LORD; MAKE STRAIGHT IN THE DESERT
A HIGHWAY FOR OUR GOD. EVERY VALLEY SHALL
BE LIFTED UP, AND EVERY MOUNTAIN AND HILL BE
MADE LOW; THE UNEVEN GROUND SHALL BECOME
LEVEL, AND THE ROUGH PLACES A PLAIN."

ISAIAH 40:3-4

They plied John with questions: "Who are you? The Christ? Elijah? Spit it out. Who are you?" He gave them only one answer: "I am a voice. A hill-leveling, valley-filling, way-straightening voice. I'm a highway-maker. That's who I am" (cf. John 1:19–23). Inside John's mouth roared God's motor grader, excavator, and asphalt paver. He built the Messiah's *m'sillah*, his "highway." The ancient peoples had their roads, like the King's Highway that ran from Egypt to Damascus, on which the Israelites once traveled (Num. 20:17, 19). John's road was shoveled with nouns and paved with verbs. His preaching of baptism and repentance constructed a *m'sillah* from the Jordan to Jesus.

Elsewhere Isaiah calls it "the Way of Holiness" (35:8). On it the weary feet of those exiled in the land of sin and death make their way home. "The redeemed shall walk there," "the ransomed of the LORD" who return "to Zion with singing" (vv. 9–10). By faith we walk this road as baptized pilgrims, pointing our feet toward the New Jerusalem, to our great God and King, Jesus the Christ.

"Blessed are those whose strength is in you, in whose heart are the highways to Zion" (Ps. 84:5).

Mishpat מִשְׁפָּט

BEHOLD MY SERVANT, WHOM I UPHOLD, MY CHOSEN, IN
WHOM MY SOUL DELIGHTS; I HAVE PUT MY SPIRIT UPON
HIM; HE WILL BRING FORTH JUSTICE TO THE NATIONS.

ISAIAH 42:1

We have encountered a few words, such as *chesed*, that encompass so much that they defy translation. It's like trying to compress a whole Hebrew essay into an English soundbite. Meet one more: *mishpat*. Usually translated "justice" or "judgment," it also means customs, divine laws, authority, and more. In Isaiah 42, the Servant, the Messiah, brings "forth *mishpat* to the nations." He doesn't trot all over the globe arguing legal cases. Nor is he the Messianic Supreme Court. Rather, he brings *mishpat* by speaking the Word of his Father into a fractured world that he might establish shalom. He is not a pushy loudmouth, for "he will not cry aloud or lift up his voice" (v. 2). He deals gently with the downtrodden and weak, for "a bruised reed he will not break, and a faintly burning wick he will not quench" (v. 3).

Nor will the Servant "grow faint or be discouraged till he has established *mishpat* in the earth; and the coastlands wait for his law" (v. 4). When Matthew quotes these verses to describe Jesus' ministry, we find Christ healing, teaching, and casting out demons (12:18–21). The Messiah's *mishpat* is the restoration and salvation of sinners.

"I will sing of steadfast love and justice; to you, O LORD, I will make music" (Ps. 101:1).

Tattooed by Wounds חקק

"CAN A WOMAN FORGET HER NURSING CHILD, THAT SHE SHOULD HAVE NO COMPASSION ON THE SON OF HER WOMB? EVEN THESE MAY FORGET, YET I WILL NOT FORGET YOU. BEHOLD, I HAVE ENGRAVED YOU ON THE PALMS OF MY HANDS; YOUR WALLS ARE CONTINUALLY BEFORE ME."

ISAIAH 49:15–16

The psalmist's broken heart cries, "Has God forgotten to be gracious?" (77:9). Has his mind become so preoccupied with governing galaxies that I've slipped his memory? Are his hands so busy shuffling planets and stirring oceans that he hasn't the time to hold me? Am I nothing to him anymore? To such questions that rise like smoke from a life in ashes, God replies: "Can a woman forget the babe at her breast, suckling life from her body? Yes, it can happen. Her mind can wander. Yet, dear child, I will never forget you."

How do we know? We, like Zion, have been *chaqaq* onto the palms of God. Job uses this verb when he wishes his words were "inscribed in a book" (19:23). God tells Ezekiel to engrave (*chaqaq*) a picture of Jerusalem on a brick (4:1). When the Lord looks at his palms, he sees skin that's been cut by nails, chiseled by pain, and tattooed by wounds into a portrait of his beloved people. Into the very flesh of our God has been engraved the faces of those whom he will never forget.

See us, Lord Jesus, in the nail-pierced hands that betoken your undying mercy.

Wounded Intercessor פָּגַע

ALL WE LIKE SHEEP HAVE GONE ASTRAY; WE
HAVE TURNED—EVERY ONE—TO HIS OWN WAY;
AND THE LORD HAS LAID ON HIM THE INIQUITY OF
US ALL. . . . YET HE BORE THE SIN OF MANY, AND
MAKES INTERCESSION FOR THE TRANSGRESSORS.

ISAIAH 53:6, 12

Consider these two phrases: "He hit upon an idea" and "He hit at him." The same verb ("hit") joined to different prepositions ("upon" and "at") conveys two very different meanings. We see something similar in Isaiah's masterful words. The same Hebrew verb, *paga*, is used for "laid on him" and "makes intercession," but two different prepositions are joined to it. *Paga* basically suggests touching or making contact. Sometimes this is generic ("meeting or making contact with someone" 1 Sam. 10:5) and sometimes it is violent ("falling upon someone to kill them" Judg. 8:21). But *paga* can also mean making contact in the sense of "pressuring, entreating, interceding."

The double-*paga* of the Messiah is this: God "touches him" or "makes fall upon him" our iniquity (v. 6). He becomes the world's sin-bearer. But he also "touches" or "makes contact" with the Father "for the transgressors" (v. 12). On him our iniquity is laid, and he laid his petitions for us before God. He is thus both sacrifice (bearer of sin) and priest (intercessor for sinners) so that in him the many are "accounted righteous" (v. 11).

Holy Jesus, our atoning sacrifice and great high priest, forgive us and pray for us poor sinners.

Watching Almonds שָׁקֵד

AND THE WORD OF THE LORD CAME TO ME, SAYING,
"JEREMIAH, WHAT DO YOU SEE?" AND I SAID,
"I SEE AN ALMOND BRANCH." THEN THE LORD
SAID TO ME, "YOU HAVE SEEN WELL, FOR I AM
WATCHING OVER MY WORD TO PERFORM IT."

JEREMIAH 1:11–12

Because the almond is the first tree to blossom in Israel, to watch for its blooms is to watch for spring's arrival. Hebrew playfully expresses this connection because "almond tree" is *shaqed* and "watch, stay awake, guard" is *shaqad*. To *shaqad* the *shaqed* is to watch the almond. Thus God points to an almond tree (*shaqed*) to impress on Jeremiah that he is "watching over [*shaqad*] his word to perform it." This also explains the almond-like bulbs atop the branches of the menorah (Exod. 25:31–40). Just as nature is renewed by the arrival of spring, so life itself was renewed and sustained by the light of God that burned within his tabernacle.

Jesus used the fig tree as a parallel illustration. Just as the fig signals the approach of summer, so the world's unraveling means the kingdom of God is near (Luke 21:29–31). Until that happens, we watch God's Word, live in his light, and watch for the second coming of Christ, when the Lamb shall be our light, our Menorah, in an earth that is the holy place of God (Rev. 21:23).

O Lord, keep our eyes on your Word, illumine us with your light, and keep us steadfast in the faith.

Turn, Return, Repent שׁוּב

A VOICE ON THE BARE HEIGHTS IS HEARD, THE WEEPING
AND PLEADING OF ISRAEL'S SONS BECAUSE THEY
HAVE PERVERTED THEIR WAY; THEY HAVE FORGOTTEN
THE LORD THEIR GOD. "RETURN, O FAITHLESS SONS;
I WILL HEAL YOUR FAITHLESSNESS." "BEHOLD, WE
COME TO YOU, FOR YOU ARE THE LORD OUR GOD."

JEREMIAH 3:21-22

As chefs have their signature dish and musicians their trademark sound, so authors have words or themes that serve as their verbal fingerprint. For Jeremiah, that word is *shuv*. A diamond of a word is *shuv*, multifaceted, capable of meaning "turn, turn back, turn around, abandon, apostatize, bring back, pay back, restore, repent." Jeremiah's poetic dexterity is shown in 3:22, where he uses *shuv* three times with three different nuances: "Return, O faithless sons; I will heal your faithlessness." The words "return," "faithless," and "faithlessness" are all renderings of *shuv*. We might translate the Hebrew in this way to catch the original wordplay: "Turn, you sons of back-turning, and I will heal your turning away."

Jews call repentance *Teshuvah* (note the *shuv* in the middle). This *Teshuvah* is not an occasional pit stop on the Christian journey, but the journey itself. God's kindness is constantly turning us back to himself, repenting us, *"shuving"* us, that we might, like the prodigal son, return home to his ongoing feast of healing love (Rom. 2:4; Luke 15:11-32).

"Restore us, O God; let your face shine, that we may be saved!" (Ps. 80:3).

Temple or Cave of Thugs? מערה

"WILL YOU STEAL, MURDER, COMMIT ADULTERY, SWEAR
FALSELY, MAKE OFFERINGS TO BAAL, AND GO AFTER
OTHER GODS THAT YOU HAVE NOT KNOWN, AND THEN
COME AND STAND BEFORE ME IN THIS HOUSE, WHICH IS
CALLED BY MY NAME, AND SAY, 'WE ARE DELIVERED!'—
ONLY TO GO ON DOING ALL THESE ABOMINATIONS?
HAS THIS HOUSE, WHICH IS CALLED BY MY NAME,
BECOME A DEN OF ROBBERS IN YOUR EYES?"

JEREMIAH 7:9–11

Need a place to hole up after God has scorched your city? A place to bury your dead? Hide from the enemy? A *m'arah* ("cave") served all these needs in Israel. In Jeremiah's day, however, unrepentant sinners transformed God's temple into a *m'arah*—a cave of thugs or den of robbers. They were trying to mug God and snatch forgiveness by claiming, "We are delivered!" even as their hands were streaked with the blood of the innocent. But God would not be mocked. Soon thereafter, their temple-cave became their temple-tomb as it lay in rubble beneath Babylon's feet.

Jesus quoted Jeremiah when he drove out those who were buying and selling in the temple, overturning their tables (Matt. 21:13). This was a prophetic sign: the temple itself would soon by overturned by the Romans. And the only temple needed would be the one who is Jesus, hanging between two thieves, delivering us all from sin, and vacating his own *m'arah* on Easter.

Glory to you, Jesus Christ, our temple, our holiness, our salvation.

Violent Fishers of Men דיג

"BEHOLD, I AM SENDING FOR MANY FISHERS, DECLARES THE LORD, AND THEY SHALL CATCH THEM. AND AFTERWARD I WILL SEND FOR MANY HUNTERS, AND THEY SHALL HUNT THEM FROM EVERY MOUNTAIN AND EVERY HILL, AND OUT OF THE CLEFTS OF THE ROCKS."

JEREMIAH 16:16

We have wrongly romanticized what it means to be a "fisher of men" (Matt. 4:19). In its Hebrew context, fishing for men is a savage affair. In Jeremiah, fishermen are God's instruments of judgment (16:16–18). In Ezekiel, God spreads his net to catch the runaway prince to ship him into exile (12:13). In Amos, he wields fishhooks to drag people away (4:2). In Habakkuk, Babylonians net Israel like fish (1:14–16). Every OT instance of men fishing for a "human catch" involves violence. So in Hebrew, for someone to *dig* ("fish") for you, to hook or net you, means that your life, as you once knew it, is now over.

So when Jesus calls his disciples to be "fishers of men," he is not sending them on a quaint mission. He's sending them to make sure that those sinners they hook or net by God's Word will know that their lives, as they once knew them, are now over. They must die, ironically, in water. We, human fish, die in the baptismal river and are raised in that same river to a new life in Jesus Christ.

Praise to you, heavenly Father, for killing us and making us a new creation in your Son.

The Heart's Rough Terrain עקב

THE HEART IS DECEITFUL ABOVE ALL THINGS, AND
DESPERATELY SICK; WHO CAN UNDERSTAND IT?

JEREMIAH 17:9

In Hebrew, "heart" (*lev*) rarely refers to our blood-pumping organ but to the core of our being, the epicenter of our thoughts and desires. The heart is humanity's innermost headquarters. And what kind of shape are those headquarters in? Not good. Not good at all. Jeremiah uses two graphic words to describe the heart: *aqov* and *anush*. *Aqov* can mean "deceitful" (it's related to the name Jacob [*Ya'aqov*], that deceitful trickster), but its nuances include "uneven, bumpy, rough terrain" (see Isa. 40:4). The psalmist says, "For the inward mind and heart of a man are deep" (64:6). The heart is tortuous to explore—deep, dark, uneven, rough, deadly, deceitful. It's also *anush*, a medical term meaning "incurable and disastrous." We might say "inoperable." Don't even attempt surgery. The *lev* is too far gone.

That is bad news, to be sure. What hope then do we have? None in our own hearts! Our hope, rather, is in the heart of another—a heart that is smooth with mercy, true to the core, healthy beyond words. It is the heart pulsating within the babe in Mary's arms, the man on the cross, the king on his throne. The heart of Jesus is love above all things. Who can praise it enough?

Lord Jesus, "I have trusted in your steadfast love; my heart shall rejoice in your salvation" (Ps. 13:5).

Gehenna גיא הנם

THUS SAYS THE LORD, "GO, BUY A POTTER'S
EARTHENWARE FLASK, AND TAKE SOME OF THE ELDERS
OF THE PEOPLE AND SOME OF THE ELDERS OF THE
PRIESTS, AND GO OUT TO THE VALLEY OF THE SON OF
HINNOM AT THE ENTRY OF THE POTSHERD GATE, AND
PROCLAIM THERE THE WORDS THAT I TELL YOU."

JEREMIAH 19:1–2

Often in the Bible, locations begin to betoken bigger realities. For instance, Armageddon in Revelation 16:16 comes from the Hebrew *Har Megiddo* ("Mount Megiddo"), the site of ancient Israelite battles. Similarly, Gehenna, translated as "hell" in the NT, gets its name from an actual place: the *gey hinnom*, "the valley of Hinnom" or "the Valley of the Son of Hinnom." This gorge outside Jerusalem was infamous as a place of idolatry, including child sacrifice (2 Kings 23:10). Jeremiah prophesied that it would be the disgraceful burial place of the people of Jerusalem when the Babylonians flattened the city, transforming it into "the Valley of Slaughter" (19:6).

Just as idolaters chose to sacrifice to false gods in Hinnom's valley, so unbelievers, who reject Christ and worship the gods of this world, choose Gehenna. "Hell's doors are locked on the inside," as C. S. Lewis observed. Be wise, not a fool. Believe in the God of love, truth, and mercy, who chooses you as his beloved child.

"Be gracious to me, O LORD! See my affliction from those who hate me, O you who lift me up from the gates of death" (Ps. 9:13).

The Man Named Branch צמח

> "BEHOLD, THE DAYS ARE COMING, DECLARES
> THE LORD, WHEN I WILL RAISE UP FOR DAVID A
> RIGHTEOUS BRANCH, AND HE SHALL REIGN AS KING
> AND DEAL WISELY, AND SHALL EXECUTE JUSTICE
> AND RIGHTEOUSNESS IN THE LAND. IN HIS DAYS
> JUDAH WILL BE SAVED, AND ISRAEL WILL DWELL
> SECURELY. AND THIS IS THE NAME BY WHICH HE WILL
> BE CALLED: 'THE LORD IS OUR RIGHTEOUSNESS.'"

JEREMIAH 23:5-6

Humanity's problems originated at a tree, when man utterly botched his vocation as the king of God's world. It is apt, therefore, that the second Adam is painted with the colors of a king and tree. He is a righteous *tzemach* ("branch") who springs from the stump of David's family tree (Isa. 11:1). Unlike the long lineup of fools and scoundrels who besmirched Judah's throne, this one, the Messiah, will "deal wisely, and shall execute justice and righteousness in the land."

Jeremiah's description of this king as a *tzemach* became so popular that later prophets used it as a name for the Messiah. Zechariah calls him "the man whose name is the Branch" (6:12; cf. 3:8). Jesus is "the branch of the LORD" (Isa. 4:2), but he is also named "the LORD is our righteousness" (Jer. 23:6). King Adam botched his vocation, but King Jesus' "one act of righteousness leads to justification and life for all men" (Rom. 5:18).

"In you, O LORD, do I take refuge; let me never be put to shame; in your righteousness deliver me!" (Ps. 31:1).

Cryptic Name אתבש

THEN I TOOK THE CUP FROM THE LORD'S HAND
AND MADE ALL THE NATIONS TO WHOM THE LORD
SENT ME DRINK IT . . . ALL THE KINGS . . . AND
ALL THE KINGDOMS OF THE EARTH WHICH ARE
UPON THE FACE OF THE GROUND, AND THE KING
OF SHESHACH SHALL DRINK AFTER THEM.

JEREMIAH 25:17, 26 (NASB)

Pore over every ancient map in the world and you'll never locate Sheshach—not because it didn't exist but because, for some unknown reason, Jeremiah goes all CIA on us here. Sheshach is a cryptic name for Babylon, formed by a cipher called Athbash. Here's how Athbash works: The first letter of the Hebrew alphabet is replaced by the last letter, the second letter by the next-to-last letter, and so forth. In English, *A* would be replaced by *Z*, *B* by *Y*, and so on. So, for example, "low" in Athbash becomes "old" and "zoo" becomes "all." In Hebrew, through this clever alphabetic trick, Babylon becomes Sheshach. Some translations—rather boringly, in my opinion—shelve Jeremiah's trick altogether by rendering Sheshach as Babylon.

Why the secrecy? We don't know. Elsewhere Jeremiah is quite willing to mention Babylon by name. What we do know is that Sheshach would be drinking the Lord's cup soon. And we also know that at the world's end, Babylon—symbol of all evil power—will be defeated by the returning King of kings (Rev. 18:2). There's nothing cryptic about that.

To you, King Messiah, we lift the cup of salvation and call on your redeeming name.

I Have Plans for You מחשבה

"FOR THUS SAYS THE LORD: WHEN SEVENTY YEARS ARE COMPLETED FOR BABYLON, I WILL VISIT YOU, AND I WILL FULFILL TO YOU MY PROMISE AND BRING YOU BACK TO THIS PLACE. FOR I KNOW THE PLANS I HAVE FOR YOU, DECLARES THE LORD, PLANS FOR WELFARE AND NOT FOR EVIL, TO GIVE YOU A FUTURE AND A HOPE."

JEREMIAH 29:10-11

God sometimes pulls out the big guns on hardhearted sinners. For Judah that "big gun" was a seventy-year exile. Away from their homes. Away from their land. It was a season for his people to sit with their sin. To repent, pray, and remember who and whose they were. It was God's tough love toward children strung out on the meth of idolatry. But it wasn't forever. The Lord had a *machashavah* for them—a word that can mean "thought, intention, plan, or invention." God uses *machashavah* when he says, "For my thoughts are not your thoughts" (Isa. 55:8). And the divine thought toward his people was to carry them back home. He had plans for his people's shalom and hope.

As he did for Israel, God has a wonderful plan for our life as well: to crucify and resurrect us with Christ. To fill us with his peace. In Jesus, to fill us with hope for a future of joy with no end.

"You have multiplied, O LORD my God, your wondrous deeds and your thoughts toward us; none can compare with you!" (Ps. 40:5).

A Fresh Covenant חדש

"BEHOLD, THE DAYS ARE COMING, DECLARES THE
LORD, WHEN I WILL MAKE A NEW COVENANT WITH
THE HOUSE OF ISRAEL AND THE HOUSE OF JUDAH."

JEREMIAH 31:31

The covenant that the Lord cut with Israel at Sinai was temporary and inadequate. Temporary, because it would stick around only until God made good on his promise to send the Seed by whom all nations would be blessed. Inadequate, because its sanctuary, priests, and sacrifices could never deliver a *tetelestai* ("It is finished!") atonement. His people pulverized the old covenant, trampled on it, time and again. So God promised something *chadash* ("new or fresh"). Like the *chadash* song of the psalmist, this *chadash* covenant would be about the "marvelous things" of the Lord, who works salvation (98:1). A covenant penned on the heart. A covenant in which to know God is to know the God who forgives iniquity and forgets sins. In this new or fresh covenant, God would do a "new [*chadash*] thing," as Isaiah says (43:19), including the promise of "new [*chadash*] heavens and a new [*chadash*] earth" (65:17).

Hebrews quotes Jeremiah 31:31–34 in its entirety (8:8–12). In fact, it is the longest quotation of any OT text in the NT—and with good reason. This new covenant is given to us by the perfect priest, perfect sanctuary, perfect sacrifice who makes us a "new creation" (2 Cor. 5:17).

"Oh sing to the LORD a new song, for he has done marvelous things!" (Ps. 98:1).

How! איכה

HOW LONELY SITS THE CITY THAT WAS FULL OF PEOPLE!
HOW LIKE A WIDOW HAS SHE BECOME, SHE WHO WAS
GREAT AMONG THE NATIONS! SHE WHO WAS A PRINCESS
AMONG THE PROVINCES HAS BECOME A SLAVE.

LAMENTATIONS 1:1

The Hebrew name for Lamentations is *Eykah*, its opening word (also in 2:1; 4:1-2). But our ears should probably hear this word elongated into Eykaaaah! It's a gut-wrenching wail stretched on the rack of ruin. Tears become ink in this book, penned with cruciform calligraphy. Translating *Eykah* as "How" just seems too bland. The word needs to burn the mouth as it's spoken, baptizing the tongue with ashes, for it erupts from a heart torched by grief. Alas, Jerusalem, Jerusalem, the princess now slave, the wife now widow, the living now coffined city of God. Every ninth of Ab (*Tisha B'Av*), Jews around the world sing the words of this book to remember Jerusalem's past destructions. The poetry of this ancient song limps on and on.

This book is just as important for what it says as for what its very existence shows: that God's ears and heart are open to lament. We are given permission—indeed, the blessing—to weep, wail, and moan our way toward healing. Faith necessitates no stiff upper lip. Jesus wept. So do we. While we grieve, our Lord of love will never walk away.

"Restore us to yourself, O LORD, that we may be restored! Renew our days as of old" (Lam. 5:21).

Throne-Bearers חיות

AS I LOOKED, BEHOLD, A STORMY WIND CAME OUT OF
THE NORTH, AND A GREAT CLOUD, WITH BRIGHTNESS
AROUND IT, AND FIRE FLASHING FORTH CONTINUALLY,
AND IN THE MIDST OF THE FIRE, AS IT WERE GLEAMING
METAL. AND FROM THE MIDST OF IT CAME THE LIKENESS
OF FOUR LIVING CREATURES. AND THIS WAS THEIR
APPEARANCE: THEY HAD A HUMAN LIKENESS, BUT EACH
HAD FOUR FACES, AND EACH OF THEM HAD FOUR WINGS.

EZEKIEL 1:4-6

Ezekiel opens with a vision of *chayyot* ("living creatures"), which he later
identifies as cherubim (10:15). *Chayyot* is not a fancy, esoteric word; it's just
the plural form of *chayah* ("animal"). Four, a favorite number of Ezekiel,
symbolizes totality, so these four probably represent all other living things.
The *chayyot* are a strange amalgamation of human and animal, with wings;
bovine hooves; human hands; and the faces of a man, lion, ox, and eagle.
They were the throne-bearers, for over their heads was a crystal expanse on
which was a throne, on which sat a man with a rainbow round about him
(vv. 26–28).

The *chayyot* Ezekiel saw, John saw as well, including the throne, rainbow,
and man (Rev. 4:1-11). Who is this man who is also God? John tells us. He
is the Lion of Judah's tribe, the Root of David, and the Lamb (5:5-6). The
chayyot carry the Christ, to whom we pray:

Son of Man, "all the earth worships you and sings praises to you; they sing
praises to your name" (Ps. 66:4).

Barking Watchmen צפה

"SON OF MAN, I HAVE MADE YOU A WATCHMAN FOR THE
HOUSE OF ISRAEL. WHENEVER YOU HEAR A WORD FROM
MY MOUTH, YOU SHALL GIVE THEM WARNING FROM ME."

EZEKIEL 3:17

One whose job is to *tzafah* ("watch") is a *tzofeh* ("watchman"). A *tzofeh* was to keep his eyes peeled and ears pricked. People's lives were in his hands. Ezekiel was "a watchman for the house of Israel," but of a different variety. He warned them of the enemy, to be sure, but it turned out the enemy was already within the walls of the city. Israel's enemy was Israel. Ezekiel was to stand on Zion's walls and, unlike the blind watchmen of Isaiah's day, those "silent dogs" (56:10), Ezekiel was to bark. Whatever word fell from God's mouth into his ear was to exit the prophet's mouth into the ears of Israel. Some would repent and believe; others would not. But both parties would "know that a prophet [had] been among them" (2:5).

The Lord still plants watchmen on Zion's walls—our pastors. Like a good *tzofeh*, they "keep a close watch on [themselves] and on the teaching," for by persisting in this, they will save both themselves and their hearers (1 Tim. 4:16) as they preach "Christ Jesus [who] came into the world to save sinners" (1:15).

"But as for me, I will watch expectantly for the LORD; I will wait for the God of my salvation. My God will hear me" (Mic. 7:7 NASB).

Sealed on the Forehead וַת

[GOD] CALLED TO THE MAN CLOTHED IN LINEN, WHO
HAD THE WRITING CASE AT HIS WAIST. AND THE LORD
SAID TO HIM, "PASS THROUGH THE CITY, THROUGH
JERUSALEM, AND PUT A MARK ON THE FOREHEADS
OF THE MEN WHO SIGH AND GROAN OVER ALL THE
ABOMINATIONS THAT ARE COMMITTED IN IT."

EZEKIEL 9:3–4

The Bible is punctuated with narratives of God sealing people to protect them. The Lord "put a mark [*oth*] on Cain" to shield him from attack
(Gen. 4:15). The lamb's blood on Israelite homes was a "sign [*oth*]" to protect
them from the Destroyer (Exod. 12:13). In Ezekiel's vision, a scribe writes
on the foreheads of the faithful "a mark," literally, a *tav* (also written as
taw), the final letter of the Hebrew alphabet. We know from archaeological
finds that, in Ezekiel's day, the *tav* was written in the shape of a cross. While
everyone else in Jerusalem was slain, those marked with this cross-shaped
letter were saved.

Finally, in Revelation, the servants of God are "sealed . . . on their foreheads" (7:3). What is this seal? It is the name of the Lamb "and his Father's
name" (14:1). "His name will be on their foreheads" (22:4), the holiest name,
Yahweh, which was also written on the headband of the OT high priest. We
are sealed in baptism, marked by the cross, claimed as God's priests by his
holy name inscribed on us.

With your finger of grace, holy Jesus, trace on our brows the name that is
above every name.

Eastern Departure, Eastern Return קדם

THEN THE CHERUBIM LIFTED UP THEIR WINGS, WITH THE WHEELS BESIDE THEM, AND THE GLORY OF THE GOD OF ISRAEL WAS OVER THEM. AND THE GLORY OF THE LORD WENT UP FROM THE MIDST OF THE CITY AND STOOD ON THE MOUNTAIN THAT IS ON THE EAST SIDE OF THE CITY.

EZEKIEL 11:22–23

Israel had befouled the Lord's temple, transmogrifying it into a swamp of idolatry. So God packed his bags and left, trailing east. From the threshold (10:18), to the east gate (10:19), and finally to the "mountain that is on the east side of the city" (11:23), his glory departed, shaking the dust from his feet. With his prophetic eye, however, Ezekiel saw an end-time temple, and "the glory of the LORD entered the temple by the gate facing east" (43:4). Various "east" words are used by Ezekiel—*qedem, qadim, qadmon*—all formed from the root q-d-m. From his temple, the Lord had an eastern departure and would have an eastern return.

And there he is, at the beginning of Passover week, approaching Jerusalem from "Bethphage and Bethany, at the Mount of Olives," on the eastern side of the city (Mark 11:1). God's glory left Jerusalem, riding eastward on cherubim. That same glory returns, riding from the east on a donkey. He comes to build and inhabit a new temple of living stones, his church (1 Pet. 2:5).

Stir up our hearts, O Lord, to be ever watchful for your return in power and glory.

Israel's Idolatrous Nymphomania זנה

"ADULTEROUS WIFE, WHO RECEIVES STRANGERS INSTEAD OF HER HUSBAND! MEN GIVE GIFTS TO ALL PROSTITUTES, BUT YOU GAVE YOUR GIFTS TO ALL YOUR LOVERS, BRIBING THEM TO COME TO YOU FROM EVERY SIDE WITH YOUR WHORINGS."

EZEKIEL 16:32-33

No prophet uses more R-rated, sexually charged language than Ezekiel does to castigate Israel for her idolatry. In one sermon, he says Israel prostituted herself in idolatry in Egypt, going after gods "whose genitals were like those of donkeys and whose emission was like that of horses" (23:20 NIV). Ezekiel 16 is one long attack on Israel for being a nymphomaniac when it comes to idolatry. Over and over, he refers to how God's people *zanah* ("fornicate," "play the harlot," "whore"). "You spread your legs to every passer-by to multiply your harlotry" (16:25 NASB). Only Israel is a bizarre prostitute: she pays people to sleep with her! She was giving gifts to her lovers, "bribing them" into her bed. Ezekiel's goal is to show how shameful, idiotic, and defiling is the worship of false gods.

Nothing has changed. Our world, with its panoply of pleasures, powers, and possessions, will ceaselessly attempt to woo us away from Christ. "Flee from idolatry," Paul says (1 Cor. 10:14). Run to Jesus. Cling to him, the only true God, our Savior and the ever-faithful, ever-merciful Bridegroom of the church.

Keep us awake and alert, O Lord Jesus, to flee from falsehood and to hold fast to you.

God Is No Sadist חפץ

"HAVE I ANY PLEASURE IN THE DEATH OF THE WICKED,
DECLARES THE LORD GOD, AND NOT RATHER THAT
HE SHOULD TURN FROM HIS WAY AND LIVE?"

EZEKIEL 18:23

Critics of the Bible often use the moth-eaten cliché that the God of the OT is a sadist. He gets off on hurting people. He finds great pleasure in human slaughter. Anyone who's taken the time to read the Scriptures discovers this supposed "sadistic God" is nothing but a strawman. He doesn't exist. What we do find, however, is a God who is "merciful and gracious, slow to anger, and abounding in steadfast love and faithfulness" (Exod. 34:6). He takes absolutely no "*chafatz* ['pleasure'] in the death of the wicked" (cf. 18:32; 33:11). He wants them to repent and believe! The Lord "does not retain his anger forever, because he"—in this lyrical phrase—"*chafatz* in *chesed*," he "delights in steadfast love," as Micah says (7:18).

The Messiah, in the psalms, says to his Father, "I *chafatz* ['delight'] to do your will, O my God" (40:8; Heb. 10:7). What is the will of the Father? That all people might be reconciled to him, all iniquity atoned for, all humanity justified, "the LORD was pleased [*chafatz*] to crush" his Son and raise him back to life (Isa. 53:10 NASB). God's pleasure is always to save, enliven, forgive.

Grants us hearts that delight in you, heavenly Father, even as you delight in us.

No Mourning ספד

"SON OF MAN, BEHOLD, I AM ABOUT TO TAKE THE
DELIGHT OF YOUR EYES AWAY FROM YOU AT A
STROKE; YET YOU SHALL NOT MOURN OR WEEP,
NOR SHALL YOUR TEARS RUN DOWN. SIGH, BUT
NOT ALOUD; MAKE NO MOURNING FOR THE DEAD.
BIND ON YOUR TURBAN, AND PUT YOUR SHOES ON
YOUR FEET; DO NOT COVER YOUR LIPS, NOR EAT
THE BREAD OF MEN." SO I SPOKE TO THE PEOPLE IN
THE MORNING, AND AT EVENING MY WIFE DIED.

EZEKIEL 24:16-18

Being a prophet was not a nine-to-five job, but an entire existence. It defined you. And sometimes it killed you—or, in Ezekiel's case, one you loved. His wife would suddenly die, God said, just as Jerusalem and her temple were about to die. The prophet was to model what his people's reaction to the news must be. Nothing. Business as usual. They are not to *safad* ("mourn, lament, wail"). We have our grieving rituals; in the ancient world, they had theirs: loud lamentation, cutting hair, going shoeless, and so on. Ezekiel and his people were to say no to *safad*.

The harsh acceptance of God's decree is one facet of the life of faith. There are times to weep and wail, just there are times to say Amen and move on. Ezekiel exemplifies the latter. He knew, as do we, that whatever pains the past holds, the future is always God's storehouse of hope.

Increase our faith, O Lord, as we pray, "Thy will be done."

Sprinkling זרק

I WILL TAKE YOU FROM THE NATIONS AND GATHER YOU FROM ALL THE COUNTRIES AND BRING YOU INTO YOUR OWN LAND. I WILL SPRINKLE CLEAN WATER ON YOU, AND YOU SHALL BE CLEAN FROM ALL YOUR UNCLEANNESSES, AND FROM ALL YOUR IDOLS I WILL CLEANSE YOU.

EZEKIEL 36:24-25

Israelites who helped prepare the body of a loved one for burial would become ritually unclean through physical contact with death. Like a contagion, you "caught" uncleanness. To remove it, God ordained that a special mixture of blood, water, and other ingredients be *zaraq* ("sprinkled") on the unclean person (Num. 19). Ezekiel is riffing off this ancient practice to describe what will happen in the messianic age. God will repatriate believers "from all the countries" where they've been exiled. In those far-off places, they were defiled by corpse-like idols, so he will "*zaraq* clean water" on them. Central to the Messiah's mission, therefore, is removing the stain of death by means of cleansing water.

The writer of Hebrews picks up on this when he says that, by the blood of Jesus, we enter God's presence "with our hearts sprinkled clean from an evil conscience and our bodies washed with pure water" (10:22). Not only does Jesus bring us home from exile; he sprinkles his blood of atonement and water of baptism on us, to remove the stain of death and bedew us with his life.

Blessed are you, holy Father, for bathing and beautifying us with the waters of life.

Resurrection and the Richter Scale רעש

THE HAND OF THE LORD WAS UPON ME, AND HE
BROUGHT ME OUT IN THE SPIRIT OF THE LORD AND
SET ME DOWN IN THE MIDDLE OF THE VALLEY; IT
WAS FULL OF BONES . . . AS I PROPHESIED, THERE
WAS A SOUND, AND BEHOLD, A RATTLING, AND THE
BONES CAME TOGETHER, BONE TO ITS BONE.

EZEKIEL 37:1, 7

In Matthew, two earthquakes are recorded. The first coincides with the death of Christ, when "the earth shook, and the rocks were split," tombs opened, and the bodies of saints rose (27:51–54). The second is when Jesus is raised: "And behold, there was a great earthquake" when the angel descended and rolled the stone from the tomb (28:2). This connection between earthquakes and resurrection originates in Ezekiel 37. When he was preaching in the valley of dry bones, "there was a sound, and behold, a *ra'ash*." Though most translations render this word as "rattling," *ra'ash* is also the word for "earthquake" (1 Kings 19:11; Isa. 29:6; Amos 1:1).

The Richter scale thus measures preresurrection quivers. The earth, as it were, is trembling like a woman in labor, "groaning together in the pains of childbirth until now" (Rom. 8:22). She is ready to open up her womb to give birth in resurrection to the bodies of the children of God within her. Earthquakes are scary, to be sure, but they also betoken coming hope.

Holy Spirit, teach us to discern your mysterious ways written on the scroll of creation.

Hiding and
Healing Leaves עלה

"AND ON THE BANKS, ON BOTH SIDES OF THE RIVER,
THERE WILL GROW ALL KINDS OF TREES FOR FOOD.
THEIR LEAVES WILL NOT WITHER, NOR THEIR FRUIT
FAIL, BUT THEY WILL BEAR FRESH FRUIT EVERY
MONTH, BECAUSE THE WATER FOR THEM FLOWS
FROM THE SANCTUARY. THEIR FRUIT WILL BE FOR
FOOD, AND THEIR LEAVES FOR HEALING."

EZEKIEL 47:12

When biblical authors portray the end of all things, they often dip their brush in the colors of Genesis. End-time resembles beginning-time (*Endzeit gleicht Urzeit*, as the German phrase goes). So when Ezekiel and John (Rev. 22:1–2) describe vivifying waters flowing from God, they borrow the imagery of Eden's river watering the world (Gen. 2:10–14). But they also both mention the *aleh* ("leaf or foliage"). In Eden, Adam and Eve used the *aleh* of fig trees to hide their naked shame (3:7), but at the end of all things, leaves will serve an entirely opposite purpose: they will be "for healing" (Ezek. 47:12) or "for the healing of the nations" (Rev. 22:2).

The Hebrew verb *alah* means "go up," so the green "goings up" or "sprouts" on a tree—its leaves—are called *aleh*. There's a lovely image there: these "goings up," these leaves, will in turn lift us up, heal us, stand us on our feet as we rise into the joy of the resurrection.

All glory to you, Lord Jesus Christ, for reversing our sickness and death, to fill us with healing and life in your resurrection.

Eat Your Vegetables זרעֹנים

[DANIEL SAID,] "TEST YOUR SERVANTS FOR TEN
DAYS; LET US BE GIVEN VEGETABLES TO EAT AND
WATER TO DRINK. THEN LET OUR APPEARANCE AND
THE APPEARANCE OF THE YOUTHS WHO EAT THE
KING'S FOOD BE OBSERVED BY YOU, AND DEAL WITH
YOUR SERVANTS ACCORDING TO WHAT YOU SEE."

DANIEL 1:12-13

Daniel's dietary scruples in Babylon had nothing to do with him wanting to lead a healthy lifestyle. He wasn't writing a cookbook or working on a beach bod. Daniel was an exile. Living on unholy soil. Far from Jerusalem. Things were bad enough. He wasn't about to make them worse by defiling himself with food that God had prohibited (1:8). As a compromise, he asked for a simple test: let him and his friends eat only *zere'onim* ("vegetables," a word formed from *zera* ["seed"]). Afterward, it was found that "they were better in appearance and fatter in flesh" than their counterparts (1:15). As happens repeatedly in the Scriptures, God blessed his children by means of food.

The spokes of human life have always revolved around the table. There is hardly a more fundamental human activity than eating. From the tree of life, to Passover, to the Lord's Supper, God has sanctified the table. He feeds, we eat, and thereby we partake of his blessings in this life, even as we await the wedding feast of the Lamb in his new creation.

Jesus, Bread of Life from heaven, fill our mouths with the food of salvation.

No Handmade Kingdom ‏יד‎

"AS YOU LOOKED, A STONE WAS CUT OUT BY NO
HUMAN HAND, AND IT STRUCK THE IMAGE ON ITS FEET
OF IRON AND CLAY, AND BROKE THEM IN PIECES. . . .
BUT THE STONE THAT STRUCK THE IMAGE BECAME A
GREAT MOUNTAIN AND FILLED THE WHOLE EARTH."

DANIEL 2:34–35

These verses are from a section of Daniel (2:4b–7:28) written in Aramaic, a language in the same family as Hebrew. In both languages, the word for "hand" is *yad*. In Nebuchadnezzar's dream, which Daniel interprets, a stone "cut out by no human hand" destroyed earthly kingdoms and "became a great mountain and filled the whole earth." In the Bible, the human *yad* corrupts. Something "made with [human] hands" is flawed, of the old order of fallen creation (e.g., 2 Cor. 5:1; Acts 7:48). Unlike legendary Midas, everything that sinners touch doesn't turn to gold but to dust, mud, gravel, or worse. The worldly kingdoms of iron, clay, bronze, silver, and gold were "handmade," sinner-made kingdoms, destined not to last.

This nonhandmade stone, "the stone that the builders rejected" (Ps. 118:22), grows into a worldwide mountain. It is the kingdom of the Messiah. A God-made kingdom. Not the hand of fallen humanity, but the Son at the Father's right hand formed this realm of mercy. Against this kingdom, the gates of hell don't stand a chance (Matt. 16:18).

"As your name, O God, so your praise reaches to the ends of the earth. Your right hand is filled with righteousness" (Ps. 48:10).

The Fiery Furnace אַתּוּן

THESE THREE MEN, SHADRACH, MESHACH,
AND ABEDNEGO, FELL BOUND INTO
THE BURNING FIERY FURNACE.

DANIEL 3:23

This well-known account is about far more than a mean old king, three faithful Israelites, and a fiery furnace from which God delivered them. No Israelite, whose mind was steeped in the stories of old, could hear the Aramaic word *attun* ("furnace") without thinking of its equivalent in Hebrew—the *kur*. And where is the *kur*? Egypt. This place of Israel's ancient exile is the "iron furnace [*kur*]" (Deut. 4:20; 1 Kings 8:51; Jer. 11:4). How did the Lord get Israel out of Egypt's "iron furnace"? He sent his "angel" or messenger to lead them to freedom. Out of the Egyptian furnace, Israel emerged unharmed because the Lord their God delivered them by the hand of his messenger.

Likewise, Shadrach, Meshach, and Abednego embody Israel, cast into the new "Egyptian" furnace that is Babylon, ruled over by Nebuchadnezzar, who plays the part of Pharaoh. The Lord "sent his angel and delivered his servants" from the furnace (Dan. 3:28), just as he did in Exodus. This story, therefore, is a sort of acted-out promise of the future exodus of Israel out of Babylon and back to the promised land. And as with every biblical exile/return, it foreshadows the final, perfect exodus of salvation accomplished by the Son of God for us.

Holy Father, as we walk through fires of suffering in this world, deliver us by your merciful might.

The Handwriting on the Wall מנא

IMMEDIATELY THE FINGERS OF A HUMAN HAND
APPEARED AND WROTE ON THE PLASTER OF THE
WALL OF THE KING'S PALACE, OPPOSITE THE
LAMPSTAND . . . AND THIS IS THE WRITING THAT WAS
INSCRIBED: MENE, MENE, TEKEL, AND PARSIN.

DANIEL 5:5, 25

Belshazzar had no excuse. He'd seen firsthand what happened to Nebuchadnezzar when his head bloated with pride and God hammered him into humility (5:18–22). Belshazzar knew better but did no better. He and his fellow partiers guzzled wine from sacred vessels taken as spoils from Jerusalem's temple. As if that were not enough, he also "praised the gods of gold and silver, bronze, iron, wood, and stone" (5:4). This was spitting-in-the-face-of-God blasphemy. When the handwriting on the wall appeared, and four Aramaic words were inscribed by divine fingers, his doom was sealed.

Mene: his days were *manah* ("counted" or "numbered"). Tekel: in the balances, he had been *taqal* ("weighed") and found deficient. Peres or Parsin: a double meaning, for his kingdom would be *paras* ("divided") and given to the *paras* ("Persians"). This story, which has become proverbial in our language, remains a dire warning that God will not be mocked. Let us take heed. Let us repent. And let us ever throw ourselves on the mercy of the one who "wiped out the handwriting of requirements that was against us . . . , having nailed it to the cross" (Col. 2:14 NKJV).

Write on our hearts, O Lord, your words of truth, that we may bear witness to your holy name.

Ancient of Days עַתִּיק

"AS I LOOKED, THRONES WERE PLACED, AND THE ANCIENT OF DAYS TOOK HIS SEAT; HIS CLOTHING WAS WHITE AS SNOW, AND THE HAIR OF HIS HEAD LIKE PURE WOOL; HIS THRONE WAS FIERY FLAMES; ITS WHEELS WERE BURNING FIRE."

DANIEL 7:9

"Ancient of Days" is a cool, mysterious title. That being said, the Aramaic behind it—*attiq yomin*—is fairly mundane; it simply means "aged one" or "old of days." Hebrew shares this word with Aramaic, for when it describes "ancient records," it uses *attiq* (1 Chron. 4:22). The Almighty's white, wool-like hair accentuates his antiquity. This minimal depiction of our Father is about as close as the Scriptures ever get to giving us a picture of him.

This should not surprise us, however, for the Father wants to reveal himself to us in his Son. We see this in Daniel, for the Old One gives dominion, glory, and a kingdom to the Son of Man (7:13-14). The Messiah represents the Old One. Jesus himself says, "Whoever has seen me has seen the Father" (John 14:9). This is made crystal clear in Revelation 1, when John describes Christ as the Old One was described: "The hairs of his head were white, like white wool, like snow" (1:14). To see the Son of Man is also to see the Ancient of Days, the *attiq yomin*.

Our Father, the Ancient of Days, keep the eyes of our hearts ever fixed on your Son.

The Holy Christian Jezreel יזרעאל

AND THE LORD SAID TO [HOSEA], "CALL HIS NAME JEZREEL, FOR IN JUST A LITTLE WHILE I WILL PUNISH THE HOUSE OF JEHU FOR THE BLOOD OF JEZREEL, AND I WILL PUT AN END TO THE KINGDOM OF THE HOUSE OF ISRAEL."

HOSEA 1:4

Hosea and Gomer had three children: Jezreel, No-Mercy, and Not-My-People. Each of their names prophesied both punishment and promise. The latter two are obvious: the Lord would reject and show no mercy to Israel (1:6, 9), but later he would have mercy and reclaim them as his people (2:23). But what is the symbolism of Jezreel? The Hebrew name *Yizre'el* means "God [*El*] sows [*zara*]." Jezreel was the site of idolatry and bloodshed in the northern kingdom. For these sins God would punish Israel. However, God promises that later he will bless the desolate valley of Jezreel, for he says, "I will sow [*zara*] her for myself in the land" (2:23). Jezreel ("God sows"), which he destroyed, would, by divine grace, later live up to the meaning of its name.

Peter, referencing Hosea, says to the church, "Once you were not a people, but now you are God's people; once you had not received mercy, but now you have received mercy" (1 Pet. 2:10). He could have added: Once you were not Jezreel, but now you are Jezreel, for God has sown within you the salvation and life of Christ, his Seed.

Thanks be to you, Almighty God, for making your church the new Jezreel.

Hosea and Flannery O'Connor פתה

"THEREFORE, BEHOLD, I WILL ALLURE HER, AND BRING HER INTO THE WILDERNESS, AND SPEAK TENDERLY TO HER."

HOSEA 2:14

To explain the startling language she often employed in her writings, Flannery O'Connor once said, "To the hard of hearing you shout, and for the almost blind you draw large and startling figures." Hosea and O'Connor would have been literary pals. Hosea says that Israel, like a lustful fool, had stepped out on her husband (Yahweh) to chase down her lovers (the Baals). So the Lord "will *patah* her, and bring her into the wilderness, and speak tenderly to her [literally, 'to her heart']." *Patah*, usually translated "allure," carries dicey overtones of "entice" (Judg. 14:15) or "seduce" (Exod. 22:16; Judg. 16:5), especially when men and women are concerned. *Patah* is a risqué word. Hosea pictures God like a husband, desperate and daring, who will try every romantic ploy to win back his cheating bride. He will entice her into the wild, speak to her heart, seduce her with his love—whatever it takes to recapture her wayward heart.

This over-the-top romantic imagery is a prophetic way of depicting the lengths to which God will go to retrieve his beloved people—even if it means becoming one of them, being spit in the face, spiked to wood, and treated like a dog. For the love of us, God will push every boundary.

O Lover of humanity, Christ our Lord, all praise to you for sacrificing everything to get us back.

Out of Egypt
I Call My Son בֵּן

WHEN ISRAEL WAS A CHILD, I LOVED HIM, AND OUT OF
EGYPT I CALLED MY SON. THE MORE THEY WERE CALLED,
THE MORE THEY WENT AWAY; THEY KEPT SACRIFICING
TO THE BAALS AND BURNING OFFERINGS TO IDOLS.

HOSEA 11:1–2

When Matthew narrates how Joseph, Mary, and Jesus fled from Herod into Egypt, remained there until his death, then returned to Israel, he says, "This was to fulfill what the Lord had spoken by the prophet, 'Out of Egypt I called my son'" (2:15). When we read this verse from Hosea, however, the prophet is describing how God called his son, Israel, out of Egypt, yet Israel went after other gods. How then could Jesus "fulfill" this verse from Hosea when it's describing a past action, not a future messianic event?

God calls Israel "my firstborn *ben* [son]" (Exod. 4:22). The Father did everything for his *ben*—chose him, called him, redeemed him. But this rebellious son dishonored and disavowed his Father repeatedly. Jesus, the divine *ben* of the Father and human *ben* of Mary, comes to fulfill—"fill to the full"—Israel's history. By repeating that history, including his own exodus from Egypt, and perfecting that history, Jesus the Son makes Israel the son right with the Father. He fills Israel's history (and all human history!) with the fullness of his perfect righteousness for us.

Call us home, heavenly Father, through the righteousness found only in your Son.

Blood Moon ירח

"AND I WILL SHOW WONDERS IN THE HEAVENS AND ON THE
EARTH, BLOOD AND FIRE AND COLUMNS OF SMOKE. THE
SUN SHALL BE TURNED TO DARKNESS, AND THE MOON TO
BLOOD, BEFORE THE GREAT AND AWESOME DAY OF THE
LORD COMES. AND IT SHALL COME TO PASS THAT EVERYONE
WHO CALLS ON THE NAME OF THE LORD SHALL BE SAVED."

JOEL 2:30-32

In Revelation, when John sees the sixth seal opened, creation comes unraveled (6:12–17). The earth quakes. The sun blackens. Stars fall. The sky scrolls. And the moon turns to blood. He sees what the prophets saw, for Haggai foretold the shaking of heaven and earth (2:6), and Joel the *yare'ach* ("moon") becoming like blood. Why blood? Because, as Isaiah says, the Lord's sword "has drunk its fill in the heavens" (34:5). The *yare'ach* is sprayed with the blood of judgment, the "wrath of the Lamb" (Rev. 6:16), that befalls the unbelieving world. A "blood moon" is not some sign that the end is near; it means the end is here.

What follows is the "great and awesome day of the Lord," when those who "call upon the name of the Lord" will be saved. Their home will be the New Zion, "the city [that] has no need of sun or moon to shine on it, for the glory of God gives it light, and its lamp is the Lamb" (Rev. 21:23).

Lamb of God, "give us life, and we will call upon your name!" (Ps. 80:18).

Kibbutz of Judgment קבץ

"I WILL GATHER ALL THE NATIONS AND BRING THEM
DOWN TO THE VALLEY OF JEHOSHAPHAT. AND I
WILL ENTER INTO JUDGMENT WITH THEM THERE, ON
BEHALF OF MY PEOPLE AND MY HERITAGE ISRAEL."

JOEL 3:2

A kibbutz is a collective community in modern Israel. The name is derived from the verb *kabatz* (also written *qavatz*), which means "collect, gather, assemble." Joel foresees, however, a very different kind of kibbutz: God will "*qavatz* all the nations" for judgment. Making a pun, he says this judging will happen in a valley called "Jehoshaphat," a name that means "the Lord [*Jeho*] judges [*shaphat*]." The prophecy of a final, decisive "day of the Lord" is common in the OT. There will be a kibbutz where all humanity will be present for the Lord to judge.

This day has already happened; and it has not already happened. In Christ, God has already *qavatz* all humanity and judged them. Jesus was all people in one person. His resurrection was the Father's declaration of "not guilty" for the world. But another day is also coming. All those who refused to believe in this verdict will be judged of their own guilt. But for those in Jesus, this final judgment will be joyful, for "there is therefore now no condemnation for those who are in Christ Jesus" (Rom. 8:1).

"Save us, O LORD our God, and gather us from among the nations, that we may give thanks to your holy name and glory in your praise" (Ps. 106:47).

The Lion Has Roared שָׁאַג

"THE LION HAS ROARED; WHO WILL NOT FEAR? THE LORD GOD HAS SPOKEN; WHO CAN BUT PROPHESY?"

AMOS 3:8

At the beginning of MGM's films is the face of a lion, filling the screen with his roar. It's a trademark noise. "Pay attention," it says. A lion's roar cannot *not* be heard. In the days of Amos, the Asiatic lion still roamed the hills and woods of Israel. Since Amos had been a herdsman, he would often have heard the lion's roar shake the night (7:14). Perhaps for that reason, he begins his book, "The LORD *sha'ag* ['roars'] from Zion" (1:2). Cover your ears, bury your head in the sand, act deaf—it matters not. The roar of this Lion will be heard. He *sha'ag* through the mouths of prophets like Amos. He roars still yet today. Who will not fear?

In the Chronicles of Narnia, Beaver famously says of Aslan, "He isn't safe. But he's good. He's the King, I tell you . . . He's wild, you know. Not like a tame lion." God is not safe. He is not our pet deity to whom we throw bones. He's wild. His roar will pierce our benighted soul. His roar will remind us who is King. His roar from the altar of his death and our atonement echoes now and ever that he is good.

O Lion of the tribe of Judah, may we hear, fear, believe, and live by the roar of your voice.

A Fruity Pun קץ

THIS IS WHAT THE LORD GOD SHOWED ME: BEHOLD, A
BASKET OF SUMMER FRUIT. AND HE SAID, "AMOS, WHAT
DO YOU SEE?" AND I SAID, "A BASKET OF SUMMER FRUIT."
THEN THE LORD SAID TO ME, "THE END HAS COME UPON
MY PEOPLE ISRAEL; I WILL NEVER AGAIN PASS BY THEM."

AMOS 8:1-2

Just as the Lord used the "almond tree" (*shaqed*) to show Jeremiah that he
would "watch" (*shaqad*) over his word (1:11-12), so he used a fruity pun
with Amos. The word *qayitz* means "summer" or "summer fruit," and *qetz*
is "end." The *qayitz* visualizes the *qetz*, the fruit symbolizes the end. It's one
of several agricultural images that this man, who once was "a dresser of
sycamore figs," uses (7:14). He speaks of fruits destroyed (2:9), famines
of the word (8:11), swindling in grain markets (8:5). Creation itself is called
by the prophetic prosecution as a witness against people's infidelity, perver-
sity, and impending doom.

Creation is awry because her king and queen—and we their children—have
tossed their crowns in the mud. Sin has seeped into every aspect of existence. Creation therefore groans, as Paul says (Rom. 8:22). We await the
qetz, the end, when destruction will come, yes, but on its heels a new heaven
and a new earth, where fruits of love and peace will flourish in a summer
that has no end.

"O LORD, make me to know my end and what is the measure of my days"
(Ps. 39:4).

Casting Lots גורל

ON THE DAY THAT YOU STOOD ALOOF, ON THE DAY
THAT STRANGERS CARRIED OFF HIS WEALTH AND
FOREIGNERS ENTERED HIS GATES AND CAST LOTS
FOR JERUSALEM, YOU WERE LIKE ONE OF THEM.

OBADIAH 11

Goral were small stones that were cast to make decisions. Drawing straws or flipping a coin are modern equivalents. *Goral* were used to decide between goats (Lev. 16:8), to pinpoint the guilty (Jon. 1:7), to divvy up Israel's land among the tribes (Num. 26:55). When Obadiah says that strangers (probably Babylonians) "cast *goral* for Jerusalem," he likely means not the city itself but the city's inhabitants, the POWs. Nahum also speaks of lots being cast to determine who gets valuable prisoners (3:10). This dehumanization of victims, treating them like commodities, is one of the charges that Obadiah levels against Edom in this brief but brawny book of doom written against Israel's ancient brother to the south.

"They divide my garments among them, and for my clothing they cast *goral*," the Messiah prays (Ps. 22:18). All four Evangelists record the Roman soldiers doing just that after they performed their gory crucifixion duties. There hung our bleeding God, dehumanized, dying, dead. But the Messiah also knew, from Psalm 16, a song of resurrection (Acts 2:24–32), that the only *goral* that mattered was the one his Father held in his hand (Ps. 16:5), the lot in the beautiful inheritance of resurrection (v. 6).

Holy Father, "you are my Lord; I have no good apart from you" (Ps. 16:2).

Jonah the Downer ירד

JONAH ROSE TO FLEE TO TARSHISH FROM THE PRESENCE
OF THE LORD. HE WENT DOWN TO JOPPA AND FOUND
A SHIP GOING TO TARSHISH. SO HE PAID THE FARE
AND WENT DOWN INTO IT, TO GO WITH THEM TO
TARSHISH, AWAY FROM THE PRESENCE OF THE LORD.

JONAH 1:3

Consider these two phrases: "Things are looking up for me!" and "I'm feeling down today." We associate "up" with good and "down" with bad. Jonah exemplifies this tendency; he's literally a downer. Four times the verb *yarad* ("to go down") is used in his story: he *yarad* to Joppa and *yarad* into the ship (v. 3); he *yarad* into the inner part of the ship (v. 5); and in the big fish, he *yarad* to the depths of the sea (2:3). He went down and God brought him down. Sometimes it's only at our lowest point that we can truly hear words from on high.

Arrogant hearts deafen our ears to God's words. So the Lord disciplines us, humbles us, *yarads* us to open up space in our ears and hearts. We go down and there discover Christ, awaiting us, to speak wisdom and grace in our time of need. He will lift us up again, even as Jonah reemerged from the fish's belly, for he himself blazed the trail out of the depths.

Lord Jesus, "hide not your face from me, lest I be like those who go down to the pit" (Ps. 143:7).

Hurled into Watery Exile טול

[JONAH] SAID TO THEM, "PICK ME UP AND HURL ME INTO THE SEA; THEN THE SEA WILL QUIET DOWN FOR YOU, FOR I KNOW IT IS BECAUSE OF ME THAT THIS GREAT TEMPEST HAS COME UPON YOU."

JONAH 1:12

Jonah's story is about more than just one Israelite. It is a window into a broader world of what God was up to. Long before, the Lord had warned Israel that should they forsake him to serve idols, then he would make Israel jealous by focusing on Gentile nations (Deut. 32:21). That's precisely what he's doing by sending a prophet, not to his own people, but to the Assyrian city of Nineveh. What's more, God threatened to *tul* ("hurl") rebellious individuals (Isa. 22:17) and his nation into exile (Jer. 16:13). That same verb, *tul*, is used when the sailors *tul* ("hurl") Jonah into the sea. And in the Israelite mind, seas (Isa. 17:12–13) and sea monsters (Isa. 30:7) were emblematic of Gentiles and their leaders.

Jonah, therefore, by being hurled into "exile" in the sea, represents all Israel going into a future exile. And his regurgitating reentrance onto dry land pictures Israel's return from the Gentile sea of exile. That's all the more reason why Jesus compared himself to this prophet (Matt. 12:40). He truly is Israel-reduced-to-one who undergoes the ultimate exile in death to bring us all back to life again.

Hurl us not away from you, O Lord, but hold us, by grace, in the palm of your hand.

The Shortest Sermon הפך

[JONAH] CALLED OUT, "YET FORTY DAYS,
AND NINEVEH SHALL BE OVERTHROWN!"

JONAH 3:4

Five Hebrew words—that's how long Jonah's sermon was. But he did get right to the point: "Yet forty days, and Nineveh shall be *hafak*." *Hafak* is the verb frequently used to describe the overthrow of Sodom and Gomorrah (Gen. 19:25; Deut. 29:23; Lam. 4:6). Should Nineveh not repent, the same punishment awaited this Assyrian city. But of course they did turn from their evil way (3:10). Fascinatingly, when they repented, another aspect of *hafak* applied, because while it means "overturn," this verb can also mean "turn, change, transform." The psalmist cries, "You have *hafak* ['turned'] for me my mourning into dancing; you have loosed my sackcloth and girded me with gladness" (30:11). So God did for Nineveh! As the Lord had threatened to *hafak* ("overturn") the city, when they put on sackcloth in repentance, he *hafak* ("turned") their mourning into dancing.

The last thing this xenophobic missionary wanted was for his audience to repent—yet they did, big-time. Even the cows wore sackcloth (3:8)! Jonah's story vividly reminds us that it's the Spirit's job to give repentance and work faith—not the preacher's. No one can repent, no one come to God, no one can believe, "No one can say, 'Jesus is Lord,' except in the Holy Spirit" (1 Cor. 12:3). He turns hearts to him.

All praise to you, Holy Spirit, for calling us by the Gospel to faith in Christ Jesus.

King Jonah of Schadenfreude רע

WHEN GOD SAW WHAT THEY DID, HOW THEY TURNED FROM THEIR EVIL WAY, GOD RELENTED OF THE DISASTER THAT HE HAD SAID HE WOULD DO TO THEM, AND HE DID NOT DO IT. BUT IT DISPLEASED JONAH EXCEEDINGLY, AND HE WAS ANGRY.

JONAH 3:10–4:1

You can't see it in English, but hiding in these two verses are four references to *ra* ("evil"). We might render it this way: "When God saw what they did, how they turned from their evil [*ra*] way, God relented of the evil [*ra*] that he had said he would do to them, and he did not do it. But it eviled [*ra'a*] a great evil [*ra*] to Jonah, and he was angry." When someone derives twisted pleasure over bad things happening to others, Germans call it "schadenfreude." Had God rained fire and brimstone down on Nineveh, then danced atop their ashes, Jonah would have been the king of schadenfreude. As it was, it "eviled a great evil" to him that he served "a gracious God and merciful, slow to anger and abounding in steadfast love [*chesed*], and relenting from disaster" (4:2).

Jonah embodies all those who are scandalized by the audacious mercy of a God who says, "I forgive you," when the world screams, "Punish!" Thank God that, in Christ, he absolves our *ra* and abounds in *chesed*.

"I said, 'I will confess my transgressions to the LORD,' and you forgave the iniquity of my sin" (Ps. 32:5).

O Insignificant Town of Bethlehem צעיר

BUT YOU, O BETHLEHEM EPHRATHAH, WHO ARE
TOO LITTLE TO BE AMONG THE CLANS OF JUDAH,
FROM YOU SHALL COME FORTH FOR ME ONE
WHO IS TO BE RULER IN ISRAEL, WHOSE COMING
FORTH IS FROM OF OLD, FROM ANCIENT DAYS.

MICAH 5:2

Bethlehem's OT reputation is a mixed bag. Two dark stories from Judges involve people from Bethlehem—a Levite (17:7) and a concubine (19:2). The first story ends in rank idolatry and a bloody massacre, the other in gang rape and dismemberment. Two marks against Bethlehem. But the narrative of Ruth and the birth of David also take place there. Two marks for Bethlehem. One fact is certain: Bethlehem had no weight to throw around. It had no military or political muscles to flex. It was a runt. In Micah's words, it was *tza'ir*, the "smallest, youngest, littlest," with the connotation of "insignificant." Populous and important Jerusalem, about six miles away, overshadowed this village full of ordinary people doing ordinary Israelite things.

David was the eighth and youngest son of Jesse. Yet the Lord chose that seemingly insignificant boy to be the greatest king of Israel. How fitting, then, for the God who has a thing for the mundane to choose Bethlehem as the hometown of the Son of David, the "ruler in Israel." He is a Lord who cloaks his glory in the ordinary.

Stir up our hearts, O Lord, to be ready to celebrate the birth of our Savior from Bethlehem.

Household Enemies נבל

THE SON TREATS THE FATHER WITH CONTEMPT, THE
DAUGHTER RISES UP AGAINST HER MOTHER, THE
DAUGHTER-IN-LAW AGAINST HER MOTHER-IN-LAW; A
MAN'S ENEMIES ARE THE MEN OF HIS OWN HOUSE. BUT
AS FOR ME, I WILL LOOK TO THE LORD; I WILL WAIT FOR
THE GOD OF MY SALVATION; MY GOD WILL HEAR ME.

MICAH 7:6-7

"Woe is me!" So Micah begins his lament (7:1). He's not bemoaning a catastrophe but the fact that he can't locate one righteous person: "There is no one upright among mankind" (7:2). One and all—prince, judge, neighbors, friends, even the woman he holds in bed (vv. 3–5)—none of them are trustworthy. "The best of them is like a brier" (v. 4). Even in the family, the son engages in *naval* toward his father—that is, he treats him like a fool, with contempt. Israel too had "scoffed [*naval*] at the Rock" of their salvation (Deut. 32:15). Micah's conclusion? "A man's enemies are the men of his own house."

Jesus quotes Micah when he calls his followers to love him more than everyone, to take up our cross and follow him (Matt. 10:34–39). As did Micah, we put our faith not in people, but "look to the LORD," to his Son, the God of our salvation. Since "the godly has perished from the earth," we look to the God of the whole earth, for he is trustworthy.

It is better to take refuge in you, O Lord, than to trust in man (Ps. 118:8).

God's Battle Cry גָּעַר

[THE LORD'S] WAY IS IN WHIRLWIND AND STORM,
AND THE CLOUDS ARE THE DUST OF HIS FEET.
HE REBUKES THE SEA AND MAKES IT DRY; HE
DRIES UP ALL THE RIVERS; BASHAN AND CARMEL
WITHER; THE BLOOM OF LEBANON WITHERS.

NAHUM 1:3–4

The eyes of prophets view what is always there and never seen. The realm of reality on the other side of our sensory perception. They see as with angelic eyes. Thus Nahum sees rivers dried up, mountains withering, and hills dissolving at the presence of God. The Lord, "avenging and wrathful" (v. 2), is on the warpath against Nineveh. God "rebukes [*ga'ar*] the sea," clearly echoing what happened at the Red Sea (Ps. 106:9). The verb *ga'ar*, however, and its related noun, *g'arah*, often denote not a rebuke but a battle cry. Yahweh, "a man of war" (Exod. 15:3), roars a battle cry so terrible, so nightmarish, that even seas flee backward in fear, leaving nothing but dust behind.

On the last day, "the Lord himself will descend from heaven with a shout [*keleusma*, a Greek word that can also mean 'battle cry']" (1 Thess. 4:16 NASB). Jesus returns as Warrior and King to vanquish every foe, kill and bury death once and for all (1 Cor. 15:26), and bring us across the Red Sea of this world into the promised land of his kingdom.

Keep us awake and watchful, Lord of hosts, always ready to lift up our heads and see our redemption drawing nigh.

Laid Waste שָׁדַד

AND ALL WHO LOOK AT YOU WILL SHRINK FROM YOU
AND SAY, "WASTED IS NINEVEH; WHO WILL GRIEVE FOR
HER?" WHERE SHALL I SEEK COMFORTERS FOR YOU?

NAHUM 3:7

Las Vegas. Rome. New York. Moscow. Each of these modern cities is bigger than their land mass. They stand for something. They are symbols of larger realities. In the Bible, two urban centers in particular became negative symbols: Babylon and Nineveh. They were emblems of evil. The book of Nahum, which is a prophecy of the destruction of Nineveh in 612 BC, should be read this way. It is about more than one city's demise; it's about the ultimate devastation of every anti-God worldly power. "*Shadad* is Nineveh," Nahum says. There is heavy irony here, for Nineveh was infamous for *shadad*, for destroying, despoiling, perpetrating violence. As they had done to others, so it would now be done to them. In a pun on his name, Nahum (*Nachum* ["comfort"]) asks, "Where shall I seek *m'nachamim* ['comforters'] for you?"

Nineveh's historic destruction foreshadowed the world's final destruction. What shall we do as we await that day? Pray for the worldwide Nineveh in which we sojourn. Bear witness of the God who wants none to perish but all to believe. And continue to hope in the Christ, the victorious Warrior who stands with his foot on the neck of sin and death.

Strengthen our hearts, ready our hands, and direct our feet, O Lord, to follow you.

Make It Plain באר

AND THE LORD ANSWERED ME: "WRITE THE VISION; MAKE IT PLAIN ON TABLETS, SO HE MAY RUN WHO READS IT."

HABAKKUK 2:2

Deuteronomy could be called the *Ba'ar* Book. In the introduction, we read that "Moses undertook to *ba'ar* this law" (1:5)—that is, to "explain, elucidate, make very clear." Moses, like a diligent rabbi, was punctiliously unpacking the Torah. Near the end of Deuteronomy, he instructed Israel to write, on stones, all the words of the Torah "very plainly [*ba'ar*]" (Deut. 27:8). No scribbling or eight-point Hebrew font! God uses this same word when addressing Habakkuk, "Write the vision; make it plain [*ba'ar*] on tablets, so he may run who reads it." Make it so legible, so clear, that someone who sprints by can read it on the run. Habakkuk's message of coming Babylonian attacks dare not be footnoted, whispered, or reduced to some esoteric code. It needed to be published for all Israel's eyes to see. Paint it on a billboard. Make it plain as day.

What good is God's Word if it remains unknown, unseen, unpublished? *Ba'ar* that Word. Make it clear. Unveil that merciful Word for all the world to see. As in Habakkuk's time, the Lord speaks that Word so that "the righteous shall live by his faith" (2:4). But where does faith come from? "Faith comes from hearing, and hearing through the word of Christ" (Rom. 10:17).

Jesus, Word of our Father, "speak, for your servant is listening" (1 Sam. 3:10 NIV).

In Wrath, Remember Mercy רגז

O LORD, I HAVE HEARD THE REPORT OF YOU, AND YOUR WORK, O LORD, DO I FEAR. IN THE MIDST OF THE YEARS REVIVE IT; IN THE MIDST OF THE YEARS MAKE IT KNOWN; IN WRATH REMEMBER MERCY.

HABAKKUK 3:2

In his speech to Job, God depicts the warhorse—laughing at fear, snorting, sniffing the air, lusting for battle. His stomping hooves devour the ground with "fierceness and *rogez* ['rage']" (39:24). *Rogez* is a kind of trembling agitation or wild anger. Think of the saying "trembling with rage." Habakkuk uses this word in one of the shortest, most eloquent prayers in Scripture: "In *rogez*, remember mercy." The prophet foresaw and foretold the horror on the horizon. The Chaldeans, the Babylonians, with horses swifter than leopards, fiercer than wolves, were swooping in like eagles to devour Israel (1:8). God too was on his way, pestilence before him, plagues on his heels (3:5). Habakkuk himself says, "My body trembled [*ragaz*—the verbal form of *rogez*]" (3:16). He trembled with fear, for God trembled with wrath.

To whom can you turn when God is angry? To God alone. Habakkuk knew this as well as we do, so he prayed, "In wrath, remember mercy." Remember, O Lord, that you are a God of compassion, slow to anger, long-suffering, who gave your very lifeblood for us. Save. Forgive. Hear us as we pray:

"Remember your mercy, O LORD, and your steadfast love, for they have been from of old" (Ps. 25:6).

Settled on Their Lees שׁמר

"AT THAT TIME I WILL SEARCH JERUSALEM WITH
LAMPS, AND I WILL PUNISH THE MEN WHO ARE
COMPLACENT, THOSE WHO SAY IN THEIR HEARTS, 'THE
LORD WILL NOT DO GOOD, NOR WILL HE DO ILL.'"

ZEPHANIAH 1:12

"Complacent" (ESV), "stagnant in spirit" (NASB), "unworried" (CEV): each of these translations is attempting to make understandable a colorful Hebrew phrase drawn from viticulture: "settled on their lees" (KJV). *Shemer* means "lees" or "dregs of wine." It's the sediment of dead yeast, seeds, and pulp that settles on the bottom during the winemaking process. People who are "settled on their lees" have sunk down into ease and complacency like those lees. The NT parallel would be the church of Laodicea, which was neither cold nor hot but lukewarm (Rev. 3:15-16). They are a variety of "practical atheists": they don't necessarily deny God's existence but live as if he didn't exist or matter. As Zephaniah says, they claim, "The LORD will not do good, nor will he do ill."

How much better, rather than being settled on our lees, to drink deeply and zealously of the wine from Christ's altar—the blood of the grape and the blood of our Savior. To lift up the cup of salvation and call on the name of the Lord (Ps. 116:13). To be intoxicated by his mercy, merry in his grace, settled on his love.

Create in our hearts, merciful Savior, a thirst and yearning to drink deeply from your cup of blessing.

When God Sings רנה

THE LORD YOUR GOD IS IN YOUR MIDST, A MIGHTY
ONE WHO WILL SAVE; HE WILL REJOICE OVER YOU
WITH GLADNESS; HE WILL QUIET YOU BY HIS LOVE;
HE WILL EXULT OVER YOU WITH LOUD SINGING.

ZEPHANIAH 3:17

One of the most unforgettable scenes in C. S. Lewis's *The Magician's Nephew* is when Aslan begins to sing Narnia into existence. This resonates so deeply because, at one time or another, we've all been touched by the creative power of music. Nothing seeps into our souls like song. It moves, inspires, uplifts, stirs something ancient within us. God may not have sung the words of Genesis 1, but he certainly fashioned within the heart of humanity deep recesses that can only be reached by music and singing. So when Zephaniah says that the Lord our God, our Savior, will exult over us with *rinnah*, with "loud singing," with "cries of jubilation," it is hard to imagine a clearer picture of his passionate and creative love. He has "taken away the judgments against" us (v. 15), rejoiced over us with gladness, quieted us by his love, and sung songs that re-create us anew.

Angels sing, "Glory to God in the highest" when the Christ Child is born. Behind that angelic choir, however, is another voice—that of the Father, singing over us and singing over his Son, by whom we are at peace with him.

Sing into our hearts, dear Father, the words of grace that alone can heal and give us peace.

O Come, Desire of Nations חמדה

FOR THUS SAYS THE LORD OF HOSTS: YET ONCE
MORE, IN A LITTLE WHILE, I WILL SHAKE THE
HEAVENS AND THE EARTH AND THE SEA AND THE
DRY LAND. AND I WILL SHAKE ALL NATIONS, SO
THAT THE TREASURES OF ALL NATIONS SHALL COME
IN, AND I WILL FILL THIS HOUSE WITH GLORY, SAYS
THE LORD OF HOSTS. THE SILVER IS MINE, AND THE
GOLD IS MINE, DECLARES THE LORD OF HOSTS.

HAGGAI 2:6-8

Haggai was the proverbial burr under Israel's saddle. He agitated the people until they quit dilly-dallying and finished rebuilding the Lord's temple. Though this temple seemed paltry compared to Solomon's (2:3), Haggai prophesied that God would shake "all nations" so that their *chemdah* would come to beautify the sanctuary. *Chemdah* ("a desirable, precious, delightful thing") has sometimes been understood to be the Messiah—thus the hymn stanza "O come, Desire of nations"—but it likely refers here to the *chemdah* of silver and gold in the following verse.

But God had future, better plans in mind as well. He would bring a much superior "desirable thing" to the temple: the *chemdah* of his Son. When Jesus' parents brought him as a baby to the temple (Luke 2:22), he filled that house with a greater glory than it ever had before (Hag. 2:9), and in it the Father gave his people peace (Luke 2:29).

Blessed are you, Jesus, most desirable gift of the Father, for your holy birth among us.

360

God's Signet Ring חותם

"ON THAT DAY, DECLARES THE LORD OF HOSTS,
I WILL TAKE YOU, O ZERUBBABEL MY SERVANT,
THE SON OF SHEALTIEL, DECLARES THE LORD,
AND MAKE YOU LIKE A SIGNET RING, FOR I HAVE
CHOSEN YOU, DECLARES THE LORD OF HOSTS."

HAGGAI 2:23

A *chotam* is a seal that, when impressed on clay or wax, served as an authentication, authorization, or claim of property. A *chotam* could be a cylinder seal worn like a necklace or a signet ring on the finger. Jacob had a *chotam* that he unwittingly gave to sneaky Tamar (Gen. 38:18). Jezebel wrote letters in Ahab's name and authenticated them with his seal (1 Kings 21:8). Two generations before Zerubbabel, God had told his grandfather, King Jehoiachin, that though he were a *chotam* on God's right hand, he'd rip him off and hand him to the Babylonians (Jer. 22:24–25). Haggai now reverses that prophecy of doom into hope, for through Zerubbabel, the Lord will renew the line of King David. God will make him "like a *chotam*."

Signet-ring-Zerubbabel, one of many descendants of David, served as an archetype of the coming messianic Son of David. "On [Jesus] God the Father has set his seal" (John 6:27). Because of that seal, all authority in heaven and on earth has been given to him (Matt. 28:18) as the King of the world. The manger cradles the sealed Son of God.

Lord Jesus, "set me as a seal upon your heart"; claim me as your own (Song 8:6).

Donkey Throne חמור

REJOICE GREATLY, O DAUGHTER OF ZION! SHOUT
ALOUD, O DAUGHTER OF JERUSALEM! BEHOLD, YOUR
KING IS COMING TO YOU; RIGHTEOUS AND HAVING
SALVATION IS HE, HUMBLE AND MOUNTED ON A
DONKEY, ON A COLT, THE FOAL OF A DONKEY.

ZECHARIAH 9:9

The Messiah is linked to donkeys all the way back in Genesis, when Jacob, in blessing Judah, said a ruler would come from his lineage (49:8–12). Using poetic hyperbole, Jacob says the blessings that arise with him will be so magnificent that he'll bind "his donkey's [*aton*] colt [*ayir*] to the choice vine"—usually a big no-no because the colt would destroy the vine. But there will be so many vines—or the vines will be so strong—that it won't matter. Fast-forward to the end of David's life, and the son of David, Solomon, rides his father's choice *pirdah* ("female mule") into Jerusalem to mark him as the rightful heir to throne (1 Kings 1:33). Zechariah prophesies that Israel's king, the Anointed one, will ride into Zion "mounted on a donkey [*chamor*], on a colt [*ayir*], the foal of a donkey [*aton*]."

The scene on Palm Sunday is thus biblically kaleidoscopic. The colors of Genesis, 1 Kings, and Zechariah mix and mingle together. Here is Judah's heir. Here is the Son of David. Here is Israel's king. He rides into Jerusalem "righteous and having salvation" for us.

Ride into our midst, King Messiah, into our lives, families, and churches, to give us salvation.

The Pierced דקר

"AND I WILL POUR OUT ON THE HOUSE OF DAVID AND THE INHABITANTS OF JERUSALEM A SPIRIT OF GRACE AND PLEAS FOR MERCY, SO THAT, WHEN THEY LOOK ON ME, ON HIM WHOM THEY HAVE PIERCED, THEY SHALL MOURN FOR HIM, AS ONE MOURNS FOR AN ONLY CHILD, AND WEEP BITTERLY OVER HIM, AS ONE WEEPS OVER A FIRSTBORN."

ZECHARIAH 12:10

Two weapons *daqar* ("pierce") someone: sword and spear. Phinehas used his spear to double-*daqar* a couple during their idolatrous intercourse (Num. 25:8). Abimelech's servant used a sword to *daqar* him (Judg. 9:54). When God, in Zechariah, says the Israelites will "look on me, on him whom they have *daqar*," he is referring to wounds by a sword or spear that result in death. They mourn for him as for a firstborn son.

While the Father's firstborn Son hung dead on the cross, "one of the soldiers pierced his side with a spear" (John 19:34). "These things took place that the Scripture might be fulfilled . . . : 'They will look on him whom they have pierced'" (19:36–37). In Revelation, when Christ returns, "every eye will see him, even those who pierced him" (1:7). We grieve because our sin caused those pierced wounds, but we also rejoice because in them is the sole source of our salvation, for "with his wounds we are healed" (Isa. 53:5).

Pour out on us, dear Father, the Spirit of your grace, that we might mourn our sin and rejoice in the healing wounds of our Savior.

Aaronic Unblessing חלל

FOR MY NAME WILL BE GREAT AMONG THE NATIONS,
SAYS THE LORD OF HOSTS. BUT YOU PROFANE IT WHEN
YOU SAY THAT THE LORD'S TABLE IS POLLUTED, AND
ITS FRUIT, THAT IS, ITS FOOD MAY BE DESPISED.

MALACHI 1:11-12

Malachi's rhetorical attack on corrupt priests is razor-sharp rhetorically and biblically ingenious. He takes the language of the Priestly Blessing (Num. 6:23-27) and turns it upside down through a whole series of clever puns. The priests are to put God's name on the people, but they despise it (1:6). Rather than God lifting up his face upon them (1:9), he will smear dung on their faces (2:3). Rather than a blessing, he will send upon them a curse (2:2). Malachi tells them to "entreat" (*chalah*) God's favor, but they have "profaned" (*chalal*) his altar (1:9, 12). The goal of the Priestly Blessing is for the Lord to be gracious (*chanan*), but in vain (*chinnam*) the priests kindle fire on the altar (1:9-10). Malachi's sermon might well be titled "The Aaronic Unblessing."

We are not surprised, therefore, when Malachi says the Messiah will purify and refine the sons of Levi (3:1-4). And so he did. Christ has purified for himself a royal, "holy priesthood, to offer spiritual sacrifices acceptable to God through" himself (1 Pet. 2:5), to "proclaim the excellencies of him who called [us] out of darkness into his marvelous light" of mercy (v. 9).

Jesus, our great and merciful High Priest, lift up your countenance on us and give us peace.

The Rising Sun of Righteousness זרח

BUT FOR YOU WHO FEAR MY NAME, THE SUN OF RIGHTEOUSNESS SHALL RISE WITH HEALING IN ITS WINGS. YOU SHALL GO OUT LEAPING LIKE CALVES FROM THE STALL.

MALACHI 4:2

Today, as we close the door on this year, many of us will look back—perhaps with a tear or sigh—on days or weeks when every hour felt like midnight. A darkness so tangible we can taste its bitter blackness. The fires of past hopes lay ashen and cold on the floor of our wrecked lives. For others, years like this will come. In a world so fragile, frail, and failing, they are almost inevitable. That is why God's words through Malachi, in this final chapter of the Old Testament, are a blazing beacon of light for us, to shine backward and forward on seasons of suffering. The *Shemesh Tz'daqah*, the Sun of Righteousness, will *zarach* ("rise or shine") with healing in his wings.

The sun rose on Jacob, after a night of wrestling with God, when he limped onward with both a new wound and a new name (Gen. 32:31). So also the Christ-Sun *zarach* on us, to heal, restore, and enliven hope. Perhaps we don't feel much like leaping calves yet, but like Jacob, we limp till we leap. Shining on us, in a love that will never set, is the Christ who will never stop unveiling mercy.

All praise, glory, and honor be to the Father, through the Son, and in the Holy Spirit. Amen.